Advance Prais

"Nelson has distilled the practical experience of a successful career as a classroom teacher and psychologist into a set of simple but effective strategies for kids and parents to observe and change youth's growing imbalanced relationships to food, sleep, sex and fear. These imbalances have caused great emotional pain due principally to the growing influence of the corporate world. . . ."

—**Stephen Parker, PsyD, licensed psychologist, adjunct assistant school professor, Saint Mary's University of Minnesota, University of St. Thomas**

"Psychologist James Nelson offers an insightful look at the coalescence of factors over the past half-century that he calls the 'economic culture,' which has produced a progressive, insidious, and very negative impact on the youth in our society. He looks deeply at basic drives and psychological motivations that come together to create a toxic environment for our children and youth."

—**Joel L. Esmay, MD, Fellow American Academy of Family Practitioners (FAAFP), and Medical Consultant to Anoka County, Minnesota**

"As a Probation Officer and parent for over twenty-two years, the wisdom offered in *Running on Empty* should be a must-read for case workers, counselors, parents, and educators who work toward changing the destructive choices of our youth. . . . Nelson offers unique insights as to the causes for youth's struggles, while providing concrete answers that can help us reduce, repair, and prevent the pain plaguing growing numbers of our young."

—**Debora Granja, supervising probation officer in Santa Clara's Juvenile Division of Probation**

"Drawing on decades of experience working with youth in and out of the classroom, James W. Nelson provides compelling insight into the major economic and cultural forces undermining what young people need to thrive. *Running on Empty* . . . is chock-full of useful activities, exercises, and questions—a powerful road map for youth and adults alike to reclaim lives of joy, purpose, and peace."

—Erin Walsh, MA, trainer at the Mind Positive Parenting and Search Institute, University of Minnesota

"James W. Nelson's *Running on Empty* is a rare book that can be labeled 'trans-formative' without risk of exaggeration. . . . A powerful opportunity to reaffirm what is most important in life; I began to read it hoping in could help me be a better teacher. I finished convinced I had the ability and power to not only be a better teacher, but a better husband, father, and citizen as well."

—Nathan R. Miller, author of *Teaching in Circles: My Journeys in Teaching High School*

"*Running on Empty*, written by a master teacher and a talented clinical psychologist, should be required reading for anyone entering the fields of K-12 education, church youth group, social work with youth, etc. This book is written by a practitioner for practitioners."

—David L. Bonthius, principal 25 yrs. and program director of MA in education at St. Mary's University

"In every classroom across America, in any socioeconomic or cultural group of any age or gender, you will find young people who are 'running on empty.' . . . James Nelson's presents REAL stories woven with clarity, sensitivity, and lightness unlike books written about the 'throw-away' youth of today. *Running on Empty* will serve as an indispensable tool for those who support the most vulnerable and neglected youth in our schools and communities. . . ."

—Peggy Berger, MA, instructional coach for five-school districts in the Tri-Valley Induction Project

"I'm recommending this first of a kind self-help book to every educator who works in the trenches and needs a boost of understanding and practical exercises. . . . This book digs deep into the transformation of our youth due to our addictive technological lifestyle. Not only is James Nelson a witty intellectual, he was born to be a storyteller. *Running on Empty* will leave a permanent imprint on your heart."

—Beth Quest, special education coordinator and twenty-year teacher, Mounds View, Minnesota

Running on EMPTY

Transcending the Economic Culture's Seduction of Our Youth

JAMES W. NELSON, L.P. RET.

BEAVER'S
POND
PRESS

Unless otherwise noted, all verses of scripture are taken from the New King James Version. Copyright © 1982 by Thomas Nelson, Inc. Used by permission. All rights reserved.

When noted (NIV), verses are from THE HOLY BIBLE, NEW INTERNATIONAL VERSION®, NIV® Copyright © 1973, 1978, 1984, 2011 by Biblica, Inc.™ Used by permission. All rights reserved worldwide.

ISBN 13: 978-1-59298-475-6

Library of Congress Catalog Number: 2012906072

Printed in the United States of America

First Printing: 2012

16 15 14 13 12   5 4 3 2 1

Cover and interior design by James Monroe Design, LLC.

Beaver's Pond Press, Inc.
7108 Ohms Lane
Edina, MN 55439–2129
(952) 829-8818

www.BeaversPondPress.com

To order, visit www.BeaversPondBooks.com
or call (800) 901-3480. Reseller discounts available.

I dedicate this book to my son Nate who taught me the value of honesty; to my daughter Jessica whose kindness and compassionate heart continue to inspire me; to my wife Candice whose unfailing support and expansive intuition I marvel at daily; and to my spiritual teachers, Swami Veda, Swami Rama, and Jesus Christ who have taught me the purpose of life.

Contents

Foreword vii

Acknowledgments ix

Introduction xi

Chapter 1
The Million Dollar Question 1

Chapter 2
Trends of Our Times 7

Chapter 3
The Fundamental Causes of Emotional Pain 17

Chapter 4
The Hunger Urge Gone Awry 25

Chapter 5
Sex and the Loss of Innocence 43

Chapter 6
Sleep Glorious Sleep 57

Chapter 7
Multiple Personality Disorder:The Self-Preservation
Urge on Steroids 73

Chapter 8
Pavlov's Dogs Have Nothing on Us 101

Chapter 9
"I've Got Some Swamp Land in Florida .121

Chapter 10
Seeking Balance in an Imbalanced World 135

Chapter 11
Unintended Ripples and Expectations of the Economic Culture . . .147

Chapter 12
Disintegrating Values and Relationships in the Economic Culture. .167

Chapter 13
"Hello, I'm in My Room—Is Anyone Out There?" 177

Chapter 14
The Exploitation and Expansion of Fear 195

Chapter 15
The Essential Elements for Change 211

Chapter 16
Redefining Success 227

Chapter 17
The Promise of Purpose 233

Chapter 18
The Mind/Body/Breath Connection 261

Chapter 19
Are You Your Shoe? A Case of Mistaken Identity 281

Chapter 20
Final Thoughts on Our Journey to Joy 303

About the Author 317

Foreword

America's next generation is struggling like never before. Given that any nation's future is wholly dependent on the hearts and minds of its young citizens, America is facing potentially disastrous times ahead. Based on his extensive personal experience as a psychologist and educator, Jim Nelson tackles this critical issue head on in two significant ways. He describes the root causes of our young people's pain, and most importantly, offers practical suggestions that promise to alleviate this suffering. He leaves us with a positive vision that, if followed, will not only derail this unfolding cultural calamity, but will ultimately deepen our understanding of human nature and the forces that lie within. If we choose to head in this direction, the creative potential of our youth will be unlocked and encouraged, rather than buried and abused.

Running on Empty explores and explains the so-called primitive urges—hunger, sex, sleep, and self-preservation—and how they profoundly affect the thoughts, emotions, and actions of our lives. Each of these primal urges is examined in the context of the economic culture's values, messages, and manipulations. This has powerful negative consequences for and long-term cumulative effects on our youth, their families, schools, and ultimately the entire society.

The pervasive presence of the economic culture has become accepted to such a large degree that its damaging effects on the physical, emotional, and spiritual health of our youth is not recognized. In response, this book shows the relationship between the messages of the economic culture and the four primitive urges, with the pain, anger, anxiety, depression, jealousy, fear, grief, and hopelessness that results when they are not in balance. Bullying, suicide, and gang violence are often the products of such painful emotions, and they have become so commonplace in America that we quietly acquiesce and accept them as the norm. This acceptance in and of itself is striking, as it heralds the demise of our very society.

This new paradigm put forth in *Running on Empty* has its source in the ancient wisdom of yoga psychology, namely, that all negative and painful emotional struggles are caused by imbalances in our primitive urges. To the extent that the economic culture is primarily responsible for these imbalances, a major purpose of this book is to initiate an end to this destructive influence by shining a light on this causal relationship. With the clear intent to change this downward spiral, the book offers thoughtful, concrete, and practical exercises that can be implemented by all adults who work with young people. These exercises are easily adaptable to any age group, are implicitly inspirational, and have proven to be transformational in the lives of students and clients alike. In this context, a fifth human urge, the urge for personal growth and transcendence, becomes the focus and fuel for hope and positive change. Revealed through introspection and mindfulness, this urge offers meaning and purpose to our lives and can lead to self-discovery in its deepest sense.

This book is not only timely, but also necessary if we are to eliminate the source of this pain that threatens to put an end to our society as it now exists. Listen carefully to what this book proclaims. It is only by increasing our own awareness that we can serve as a catalyst for beneficial change in our young people and, thereby, the society that surrounds us.

—**Ron Valle**
Ron Valle, PhD, is associate professor,
America School of Professional Psychology, San Francisco; cofounder
of the Awakening Counseling Center;
and coauthor with Mary Mohs of *Opening to Dying and Grieving:
A Sacred Journey* (Yes International Publishers, 2006).

Acknowledgments

My thanks to all the support and encouragement I received from family friends and colleagues in the writing of this book. I particularly thank my lifelong friend Michael Smith who helped in the editing but, most importantly, provided wonderful feedback throughout the year-long process that was insightful, inspirational, and served to deepen our friendship.

Introduction

"Be kind, for everyone you meet is fighting a harder battle."

—PLATO

There is a growing disharmony and malaise in young people in the US and throughout the world. Sadly, true feelings of contentment are often missing from their lives. However, I must immediately clarify that this observation is not about judging or blaming young people. Our youth have little choice but to respond to the dominant cultural messages, which offer a flawed blueprint for a happy life. And although they are not to blame, our youth will have to play a principal role in changing the societal trends at the root of their suffering. The perspectives and suggestions in *Running on Empty* are shared in the hope that, with the help of all involved, young people will discover some essentials in life that will provide them with the deeper contentment that is their rightful inheritance.

Young people struggle to articulate the source of their despair because the societal forces weighing on them are pervasive, and this is all they have known. These forces have shifted many away from a moral and ethical compass that would provide guidance in creating a life with direction and meaning. The constant bombardment of the implicit and explicit messages of our "economic culture" have confused a sense of purpose with economic interests and the power of money—and muffled and even silenced their intuition and conscience, creating pain and misery. Youth are being led away from fulfilling life's purpose, which is the discovery of their true SELF.

To seduce means to lead away or lead astray, and this is exactly what the economic culture is doing to young people. They are being led into false, transient notions of self; they are lost in unfulfilling desires pitched by the economic culture. Many struggle with a debilitating lethargy and almost omnipresent boredom interrupted briefly by intermittent islands of excitation. Some have literally been destroyed by growing cynicism and jaded emotions that suffocate hope and feed depression, which all too often ends in self-injurious behaviors and even suicide. *Running on Empty* articulates a way out of this growing tragedy.

I come from a family of writers; and though I had never written a book, youth struggles had been on my mind for a long time. After retiring, I decided to engage in forty days of silence, to develop clarity about the future I wanted to create. I finished thirty-three days of silence before falling ill, but it was already clear that writing this book was a part of that future.

An elderly man asked God, "How much time do I have left?" He was expecting God's answer to be in terms of years, but instead God said, "Enough time to make a difference." I could be the man in that story. Witnessing youth's increasing struggles, and inspired by their resiliency and the transformative potential of their self-awareness experiments, I want to share important insights that could make a difference—a difference in young people's futures.

Throughout my career I felt encouraged by seeing hundreds of young people who were able to reverse course from the seductive and destructive messages of the larger culture. At the end of several chapters, I have included exercises, and in some cases experiments, that have helped others change imbalanced habits, patterns, and attitudes. The direct experience gained through these personal exercises has successfully increased self-awareness for those involved. These experiences led to greater control over destructive habits and patterns and brought change that resulted in greater happiness and contentment to our youth. The results of their experiments are shared here in their own words, though I have changed a few identifying details to insure privacy. I hope their words will inspire others (young people and those working with young people) to use these ideas to create new self-awareness opportunities.

Though one purpose in writing this book was to highlight changes in our society that have made growing up more painful, less satisfying, and more aimless for many, my overarching purpose is to provide a pathway of hope for young people. Their pain has often served as a catalyst for their participation in self-awareness experiments, and the results gave them the insight and motivation to counter the effects of the dominant culture, revealing a promising potential for a more meaningful life.

Though my experience has been mostly with American youth, the information and observations are applicable to young people in other industrialized countries, and even economically emerging third-world countries. My intent is that every reader can extract something beneficial and practical for themselves, as well as help turn the tide away from the growing malaise that threatens the very spirits of our young people. Hopefully, these conversations will open the door for further dialogue with young people, and with the parents, teachers, and other caregivers who guide them.

Chapter 1
The Million Dollar Question

"Through pride we are ever deceiving ourselves.
But . . . deep down, conscience, a still small voice says to
us, something is out of tune."

—CARL JUNG

"People are getting smarter nowadays; they are letting
lawyers, instead of their conscience, be their guide."

—WILL ROGERS

One night back in the early 1980s, I came across a newspaper article about a provocative survey question. The survey revealed that 11 percent of people asked said they would kill someone for a million dollars if they were guaranteed not to be caught. I was struck by the survey and also by its synchronicity. At the time, I was teaching a unit on abnormal psychology (which I called "Maladjustments in Living," because "abnormal" was a loaded term) in my high school psychology course. The next day we would be examining antisocial personality disorder, or psychopaths (some might call them sociopaths), in the common vernacular. The most distinguishing characteristic of psychopaths is that they lack a conscience. I decided that I would begin the study of

1

antisocial personality disorder by having my students, the majority of whom were honors students, answer the survey question.

To the question, "Would you kill somebody for a million dollars if you were guaranteed not to be caught?" I added, "Why or why not?" Students wrote down their answers privately, and I facilitated a discussion. In the first few years, two to four students a day answered yes to the question. Twenty years later, there were twenty-five to forty students per day! This amounted to approximately a tenfold increase in just twenty years.

Questions and comments like these arose in the ensuing discussions.

"Would I have to see my victim, or could I kill him remotely, because I'd do it for sure if I didn't have to be there."

"I would do it if it was a Hitler-like person." This second response was excluded from the data because there was a moral basis for the yes.

"If I didn't know him, then, yeah, I'd kill him."

Some other students questioned this, saying: "How could you kill someone, knowing it was somebody's child, sister, or dad?"

These students of conscience were often quickly attacked and accused of lying. "It's a million dollars—you're just trying to look good. For a million dollars you know you would do it, too," was a frequent retort.

"I would do it for a lot less than that," became common in recent years—and an actual "bidding war" would break out. Many said they would kill for as little as a few hundred dollars. One student said, and he meant it, "I would do it for two dollars."

I was saddened because having grown to like these students over the course of the semester, it was disturbing to witness their cavalier, callous, and selfish attitude.

Many students had revealed in these discussions, at the very least, an underdeveloped conscience. I recognized, then and now, that this survey and the discussion that ensued, was just one piece of data regarding youth's values. People have pointed out: if those students had to face this choice in reality, it would significantly reduce those who would act on their "yes." This is likely true, but the large statistical change over such a relatively short period of time is disturbing and significant. Disturbing also was a shift in the way the students supported their answers, showing an increased emphasis on economic consider-ations. The fact they were concerned about having to be at the death scene seemed less about the victim's pain and more about how it might affect or inconvenience *them*.

This shift began a deeper contemplation of the many ways students were changing and what was driving this change. For example, early in my teaching career, if I caught a student cheating, the student showed remorse, often apologized, and looked embarrassed. In my last years of teaching, the response was frequently hostile or derisive. They some-times even laughed. "Why are you making such a big deal about that? Everyone cheats." Increasingly, students viewed good grades, however imperfect, not as a reflection of hard work, increased knowledge, growth, determination, and discipline, but as a symbol of status; so, for them, the ends justified the means, and cheating was the means for future status or wealth.

Their motivation for learning and their definition of success were tied increasingly to extrinsic rewards, not intrinsic ones. Education as a means for self-discovery, self-discipline, and character development was missing in all but the rarest of students. Their career goals of making money, acquiring toys, or pursuing hedonistic pleasures—material or status related—were related increasingly to their unexamined notion of purpose. Extrinsic rewards have always been more easily parlayed into immediate gratification and pleasure, but a rapidly increasing percentage of students were viewing the world through an economic prism without questioning the idea of money as a means to happiness. As one student said, "If money is not the most important thing in the world, it sure is not far behind whatever's in first place."

A study cited by Richard Leider in the second rendition of his best-selling book *The Power of Purpose* at first glance seems unrelated to the "million dollar question," but is also emblematic of a profound shift that has created great pain and a penetrating malaise for our youth. The study was of sixty students at an American university, who had survived their suicide attempt. They were surveyed to determine the underlying causes for this self-destructive act. Researchers were surprised to find that the vast majority of students were performing well academically and had good relationships with their parents and peers.

There usually are some identifiable triggers that serve as catalysts for suicide attempts. However, when researchers asked why these students had attempted to kill themselves, eighty-five percent said, essentially, "Why not?" They had concluded that life didn't have any meaning, was often difficult and painful; and so when things got hard, it really didn't matter if they ended their lives.

Both the "million dollar" students and the "suicide attempt" students had one thing in common: life didn't matter that much. I will continue to explain how a growing number of young people have come to this painful conclusion. In a survey, reported in the June 2011 *AARP Magazine*, of all adults, eighteen-to-twenty-four-years-olds had the lowest levels of happiness. Almost three out of four young adults, seventy-four percent, reported being unhappy. This malaise started my inquiry into trends that were deeply troubling, gaining momentum, and eroding young people's happiness and further fraying the fabric of unity in America.

Exercise:

Discussion Questions for Revealing Students' Values

The questions here have elicited valuable information about students' values and their worldview. Each can serve to generate discussion, and help teachers develop a better understanding of student's values and perspectives while enlivening their curriculum. It is often beneficial to have students write a page or two, and then begin the discussion to minimize peer influence.

1. If the earth were to be hit in one week with a huge asteroid that would destroy the planet, how would you spend that week?

2. If you won twenty million dollars in the lottery, what would you do with it?

3. If you could have one compliment paid to you, who would you want to say it and what would you like them to say?

4. If you were on your deathbed, reflecting on your life, what would you hope that people would say about you and your life at your funeral? What would you hope that people would not mention?

5. Who are you? (I asked this question the first day of psychology class, and it will be a focal point later in this book.)

Chapter 2
Trends of Our Times

"Perhaps in time, the so-called Dark Ages will be thought of as including our own."

—George C. Lichtenberg

"Never let mistakes or wrong direction, of which every person falls into many, discourage you. There is precious instruction to be got by finding out where we went wrong."

—Thomas Carlyle

There has been a cultural shift that has blindsided all of us. The most powerful influence on young people, and most adults, is the pervasive intrusion of the aforementioned "economic culture." This culture, supported by media and advertisers, has permeated every aspect of our lives. This has brought tremendous changes, many of them with negative consequences that have not yet been fully understood.

Values and Perspectives of the Economic Culture

Economic considerations have always been a part of our culture; but in the past, there was a healthier separation between one's job and one's educational, political, social, ethical, religious, and spiritual pursuits. The influence of what I will continue throughout this book to refer to as the economic culture has grown dramatically over the last few decades.

Here are a few of the values and assumptions of the economic culture that have become so pervasive in our lives:

1. External objects and activities are the sources of happiness. Therefore, the more objects and activities, the greater happiness you'll experience. The assumption is that fun equals happiness.

2. A person's status and worth are determined by how successfully one performs and achieves within economic culture parameters.

3. The profit-driven "free" market economic culture has a survival-of-the-fittest mentality, an intense competitive-versus-cooperative ethic, and an individualistic-versus-collective value system.

This is a sufficient but incomplete description. I offer this abbreviated version now to present a simplistic sense of what is being implied; a deeper, more detailed explanation of the economic culture unfolds throughout the course of this book.

The power and influence of the economic culture is still growing. The 2010 Supreme Court ruling, giving corporations the status of an individual "person" and equating their use of money to free speech, has far-reaching implications. The corporate "voice," in the form of money, now competes on equal constitutional footing with the people's voice in expounding its rights. This allows no limitation on the "decibel level," the volume of money that unions and corporations ("individuals") can contribute to influence elections. In fact, a person cannot even inquire as to where the "noise" is coming from, because disclosure of the corporate contributor isn't required or it comes so late in the process that it renders the inquiry irrelevant.

The economic culture has penetrated into people's social, political, educational, and religious lives, changing the moral and ethical values of our society. For example, John Stossel of *20/20* hosted a special several years ago on "Greed is Good." When the mainstream media began touting greed's virtues, it signaled, along with other observations, that a significant shift was taking place. Greed is one of Catholicism's seven "mortal" sins. In fact, if you examine all seven of those mortal sins—pride, envy, anger, gluttony (excesses of all kinds), lust, sloth, and greed—you have a nutshell version of the disturbing trends of our times.

Corporate messages of conspicuous consumption of all kinds as a means to happiness now permeate our society. Getting ahead and advancing over others by any means, even if it violates ethical behavior, is filtering into the value system of our youth. Cheating, influence peddling, Ponzi schemes, bribes for elected officials, insider trading, sexual scandal, and hypocrisy, with the selfish and deceptive value system modeled by Gordon Gecko on *Wall Street,* have found their way into our students' values and lives. Cheating in schools is not only epidemic among students, but is now brushed aside with hardly a flicker of conscience, as better grades imply higher status. Students paying thousands of dollars to have surrogates take their college entrance exams are no longer isolated events. Teachers are co-opted and often end up "teaching to the test," essentially "dumbing down" a more subtle or superior curriculum. Some teachers have even participated in modifying students' test scores in order to make themselves and their school appear successful in the eyes of the media and parents, as well as to procure government funding. This sacrifice of curriculum integrity is one more example of disintegrating ethical norms.

Teachers are sometimes co-opted by offers of merit pay and/or threats of job loss. These kinds of incentives and punitive consequences are based on a corporate model for modifying or coercing certain behaviors. They do nothing to enliven intrinsic sources of motivation to inspire teachers' intuitive wisdom or enhance students' passion for learning.

Changes in Youth Behaviors

In the 1950s, students were disciplined or suspended from school for running in the halls, chewing gum, speaking out of turn, spitting, etc. Children being "seen but not heard," for good or bad, captured the spirit of that era. In the twenty-first century, suspension or expulsion is for offenses such as drug use and dealing, sexual harassment, bringing weapons to school, assault, and death threats. The extent of this negative shift in the past half century is constantly seen on the twenty-four-hour news channels.

"Tomorrow, the first graduating class of Coon Rapids High School, in honor of their last day of school before commencement, will have a 'Slop Day.' This was requested by the student council and approved by the administration," the principal announced, as I sat in my last-hour study hall. *Finally my last day!* I thought. *I am so ready to leave high school, and dressing casually is a bonus. I am finally outta here and dressing like a slob will be cool.* I met my girlfriend after class and dropped her off at her home. I started thinking about what to wear on Slop Day, and as I was near a clothing store, I stopped to look at some clothes. I wanted to wear shorts and didn't have any that I liked. I found a pair of "bleeding madras" plaid-patterned shorts. Bleeding madras was the newest rage, so I added a bleeding madras top that matched. I threw in a grey T-shirt, which was also becoming popular, paid for it all, and headed home.

I got up early the next morning, put on socks, sandals, and shorts. I buttoned up my madras top over my gray T-shirt and drove off to school. I walked through the front door where some friends were gathered, and they began laughing hysterically. I thought it was because I had overdone it by buying a new outfit for Slop Day. They were dressed mostly in jeans and casual shirts, but it was more than that: I am color-blind and apparently the matching top and bottom made me look like a Scotch-tape dispenser. They could not stop laughing. I turned three shades of red. I was already insecure about my appearance, so I made a beeline to the nearest bathroom, removed my top, and wore just the gray T-shirt and shorts. The contrast was apparently helpful as my friends stopped laughing and began talking about graduation. I hung my bleeding madras shirt in my locker and headed to my first-hour class, but I never made it. As I started walking

10

down the hallway, the assistant principal grabbed me and escorted me to his office. I was suspended from school because my brand new gray T-shirt was interpreted as an act of rebellion—apparently I pushed the Slop Day dress code too far.

The need to buy a new outfit on Slop Day speaks volumes about the depth of my insecurity. My madras ensemble would no doubt inspire laughter in any era. In light of how far student dress codes have deteriorated, my outfit could now be considered formal wear. This story illustrates just one of many standards that have shifted in the last few decades.

Economic Echoes from Another Era

Perhaps more instructive in understanding the rapid cultural shifts impacting youth than dress codes is examining some ethical principles put forward by Mohandas Gandhi. Gandhi's profound and deeply layered insights emerged out of his struggles with the British, whose empire had fractured Indian culture. The economic benefits from India, built on the backs of the poor who were powerless against the British military and financial might, flowed almost exclusively to the elite. Despite their raw power, Gandhi's moral authority, inspiration, and vision brought down this vast colonial empire. Gandhi's insights speak powerfully to our own times as the penetrating reach and effects of our economic culture are in many ways even more insidious than the one that exploited India. At least the British had the honesty to call it an empire.

Here are Gandhi's simple and profound insights, which he named The Seven Deadly Social Sins:

1. Politics without principle.

2. Commerce without morality.

3. Science without humanity.

4. Knowledge without character.

5. Wealth without work.

6. Pleasure without conscience.

7. Worship without sacrifice.

The Dominating Influence of Corporate Values

Do these "deadly sins" seem relevant to our times? As noted previously, the economic culture now permeates our social lives, our relational lives, our education system, our politics, our science, and our ethical, moral, and spiritual lives. The economic culture is not benign, and it is not value free. Embedded in the corporate economic paradigm are explicit and implicit values that are quickly transforming and eroding centuries-old ideals. The core values implied in Gandhi's list were once unifying principles shared by nearly the entire society.

A fuller awareness of both the positive and negative consequences of the economic culture is evolving. Many people reflect in their individual actions a value system that is at odds with the greed, extreme individualism, hedonism, hyper-competitiveness, and the self-absorption championed by the economic culture. For others, however, the values of the economic culture have consciously or unconsciously infiltrated and impoverished their family lives, as well as their recreational, political, social, and spiritual lives. People are living with inconsistencies between their core ethical and spiritual values, and selfish messages and hidden values of the economic culture. These incompatibilities are often unconscious and remain unresolved, or are quickly rationalized away with minimal contemplation in order to silence their consciences. They are so immersed in the values of the economic culture that greed isn't recognized as greed, or it is seen as beneficial. The most damaged of these people have lost connection to their consciences and the awareness of the sacredness of all life. They exploit human vulnerabilities, including those of children, for their own personal gain.

The message that "greed is good" would have been unthinkable a generation or two ago, but this message has taken hold. The top 400 income earners make almost the same as the forty-six million people in this country who are at or below the poverty level. MSNBC reported in December 2011 that the income of six Walton family members who own Walmart is the same as one-third of America's people—the equivalent of ninety-three million Americans.[1] Meanwhile, one in five children now lives in poverty, and within the African-American community, it is four in ten children.[2] Huge bonuses paid to Wall Street executives are rationalized as necessary to keep the economic engine humming, as unemployed people from Main Street seek in vain for an eight-dollar-an-hour job.

Sadly, the suffering caused by a value system embedded with greed and opulence is particularly acute for our youth, who, having grown up in this cultural paradigm, have no other frame of reference. Some of the pain is an unintended consequence of an economic philosophy of life that is unsustainable, misguided, and destructive. However, there is also an *intentional* psychological manipulation of our youth's desire system by some of the most skilled psychologists on the planet: those working in ad agencies. Ad agencies manipulate humanity's basic urges, turning wants into needs, and creating desires where none previously existed. We will demonstrate the links between this manipulation and the creation of historically unprecedented imbalances that sabotage young people's energy and escalate their emotional pain.

Fortunately, parents and families still have the most direct impact on the health, happiness, and values of children, but the stress and demands on them are also growing. We all share the responsibility to make childhood safe and loving, while instilling values that support mental health and a social conscience. Unfortunately, the values of the economic culture with fast-paced, stress-filled lifestyles are fracturing the nuclear family, and in many cases also fragmenting and dissolving the extended family. Many parents have also been seduced by the messages of the economic culture. Others, despite heroic efforts, struggle to swim against that tsunami, and watch their children being swamped by the deluge.

I do not suggest that we live as pessimists; but disturbing trends need to be identified and analyzed honestly, so we can deal constructively with their causes and then mitigate the suffering they create. The lyrics from "Do It," the 1972 song by Jesse Winchester, illustrate a worthwhile perspective to cultivate as we examine these trends: "If

---

1.   Rachel Maddow show, December 2011.

2.   Forum on Child and Family Statistics, www.child stats.gov, 2011.

we're treading on thin ice, then we might as well dance." So let's dance, because dancing—staying playful and not losing our sense of humor—is the kind of energy we need to foster a solution.

Alarming Trends

Obviously, economic activity is an important part of every culture. If this activity serves real human needs and facilitates a life of purpose, then it plays its appropriate role. However, the goals of the current economic culture often ignore both of these ends. It emphasizes consumption for consumption's sake as a means to happiness, and cares little about wedding production and consumption to purposeful and balanced living. Greed and extreme individualism, now staples of the economic culture, have spawned a disturbing self-absorption and a materialistic, externally focused life.

No trend applies to everyone. Individuals are not statistics. Many young people are consciously participating in worthwhile activities and making their lives about positive, purposeful choices. An impartial observer, however, would confirm that the trends we are addressing signal shifts in a destructive direction. Here is a brief sampling of some of the decreasing and increasing trends that have occurred over the last few decades:

1. There has been a decrease in civility, listening, statesmanship, the art of compromise, patience, "other-centeredness," connection to nature, humility, innocence, empathy, compassion, gratitude, purposeful living, ethical and spiritual understanding, and a dramatic loss of trust in each other.

2. There has been an increase in fear, bullying, sarcasm, violence and hostility, gangs, antisocial behavior, cheating, selfishness, rampant materialism, lack of accountability, feelings of victimization, hyper-competitiveness, self-promotion, lawsuits, greed, hedonism, mental health problems, loneliness, alienation, drug experimentation, and addictions of all kinds, including Internet addictions, sexual exploitation, impulsivity, and self-injurious behaviors such as cutting and suicide.

This is not an exhaustive list, but it provides samples of a downward spiral that has happened quickly and has affected every member of society, with youth being hit the hardest. Certainly many people are doing compassionate and important work on behalf of young people. There are significant islands of selfless service that have resisted the tidal wave of the dominant economic messages of extreme individualism, conspicuous consumption, self-absorption, and the pursuit of happiness in the external world. Some young people have already set their sails against the currents of the economic culture, letting their conscience serve as their compass.

When we have a better understanding of the destructive forces, we all can participate in making the individual and collective changes necessary to build a better future for all involved.

"Do not fear the winds of adversity. Remember: a kite rises against the wind rather than with it."[3] Even though the trends are deeply disconcerting and entrenched, being morose is not the answer.

---

3.   Author unknown.

Chapter 3
The Fundamental Causes of Emotional Pain

"Truth is waiting to be seen,
but our eyes are clouded with longing."

—MEISTER ECKHART

"In all abundance there is lack."

—HIPPOCRATES

Negative emotions often seem to spring up so instantaneously that it feels like we have very little ability to influence their occurrence or their intensity. This leaves us in a powerless position where negative emotions seemingly dictate automatic, impulsive, and defensive behaviors. To understand the origin of emotions, from where they emerge, and whether we unconsciously play a role in their occurrence, and to lay the groundwork for understanding the powerful emotional forces behind the downward trends hurting youth, we will look briefly at developmental psychology.

The Pleasure/Pain Template

All human beings in early childhood develop a template that predisposes them to seek pleasure and avoid pain. Newborns have not developed an ego; they have no separate sense of self. Their identity, therefore, is completely emerged in their experience. If they are hungry and suckling at mother's breast, they are in absolute heaven. All their needs, for touch, nutrition, security, etc., are met without much effort on their part. If mom interrupts breast feeding and lays her baby down to rush to the kitchen to take a boiling pan off the stove, the baby is suddenly in hell. Feeling disconnected, alone, hungry, and powerless to change the situation, the newborn screams in panic. Newborn children's minds identify totally with whatever is happening to them moment to moment.

The ego, the sense of an autonomous self, develops slowly. Even a two-year-old—whose ego is still developing—is often taken over by the pain when he stubs his toe, and is almost inconsolable. Most twenty-year-olds will shrug off the hurt; they are able to do this because their minds aren't totally identified with the pain. This pleasure-pain template, starting at birth to seek pleasure and avoid pain at all costs, is intensely seared into the psyches of the human's desire system. This deeply imprinted desire to run to pleasure and away from pain will ultimately exhaust us, and throw us out of balance. The pleasures we seek are fleeting and we quickly habituate to them, and yet we return to the pleasure-pursuing treadmill, like a gerbil running faster and faster on his wheel, unsure how to safely exit. We also exhaust ourselves running from the pain of our insecurities, hurts, and fears; but the pain we run from usually ends up running us. This pleasure-pain template helps fuel our expectations and attachments; which, when blocked or thwarted, ignite strong emotional reactions that throw us out of balance.

This fact is not lost on pharmaceutical companies, media advertisers, and other members of the economic culture's corporate world. They have a warehouse of options to enhance pleasure, and to stop, avoid, or numb our physical and emotional pain. Emotions, when properly directed, fuel motivation, inspire creativity, and give an "evaluative tone" that helps us decide when something is worthwhile and meaningful. Cultivating positive emotions such as peace, joy, and love is essential for human happiness. But, when emotions are out of balance and misdirected, they obscure our natural joy, often destroying relationships and the lives of individuals.

Primitive Urges

The students were buzzing as I finished taking attendance. I walked to the back of the room. "Shhhh," I said dramatically as I looked up and down the hallway and quietly closed the door. I lowered my voice and spoke in a hushed tone. "I don't want anyone to hear what we're going to talk about. This is a public school, and parts of this could get a little steamy. You may be the only high school psychology class in the nation to explore this topic. Today we are going to talk about your—'four primitive urges.'" I now had their attention, which they sustained as we explored the role of these urges in their emotional life.

In addition to the pleasure-pain template, all animals, including humans, are born with four primitive urges. "Primitive" is not a negative term but connotes that these four urges are basic and fundamental. These universal drives, the need for food, sex, sleep, and self-preservation, motivate us to:

1. Seek nourishment to maintain life.

2. Seek out sexual partners to create new life.

3. Get rest to revitalize and maintain health.

4. Avoid life-threatening situations and defend ourselves against threats.

These four primitive urges are critical because they help us sustain life.[4]

Much of what we do each day is based on the four primitive urges and, because we as human beings have an expansive imagination, we have created an astounding array of ways to satisfy these urges. Some of

---

4. Emotions to Enlightenment by Swami Rama and Swami Ajaya, Himalayan International Institute of Yoga Science and Philosophy, 1976.

the expanded desires that we link to these four primitive urges drive choices that are not in our best interest. We are led astray by surrogate products and desires promoted by the economic culture that takes us away from positively and easily satisfying these basic urges.

A businessman, for example, might work himself to the bone for many years in order to buy a cabin on a lake where he feels he can relax. He travels every weekend, battling traffic for hours, spends a few hours at the lake, and again takes to the highway so he can return to work to help pay for that cabin. He could simply have taken a nap. This would satisfy the primitive urge for rest, but that's too simple.

The economic culture, supported by media messages and advertisement agencies, have a bewildering supply of enticements that all say, "You cannot have A without first buying B." Instead of choosing simple, healthy options to satisfy each of our four primitive urges, they have created elaborate layers of obstacles in the form of products in order to maximize profits. They do this knowing that many of the products they are pushing actually cause destructive imbalances in their consumers' four primitive urges, leading to physical, emotional, and mental suffering. T.S. Eliot, speaking of the confusion and distraction created by the economic culture, wrote:

> These with a thousand small deliberations
> Protracted the profit of their chilled delirium,
> Excite the membrane, when the sense has cooled,
> With pungent sauces, multiply variety
> In a wilderness of mirrors.[5]

When we get lost in the wilderness of mirrors that is the economic culture, seeking one vanity or another leads us to the great loneliness, the loss of our true self. A growing tragedy for youth is that they are being seduced by external vanities; if they could only turn their gaze inward, they would find their way home. This is an old story told in many cultures and religions, where people get so lost in the desires of the senses that they vanquish their spiritual aspirations. It is the story of Adam in the Garden of Eden. However, our temptress is relentlessly

---

5.　Poems by T.S. Eliot. New York: A.A. Knopf, 1920.

working 24/7 in a sophisticated seducement that is supported by technological wizards and the dominant icons of the society.

Most people are unaware that when these four primitive urges are poorly regulated or imbalanced, they arouse negative emotions, including anger, jealousy, anxiety, greed, fear, and depression. Simply put, if you are deprived of food, sleep, or sex, or your existence or self-esteem is threatened, negative emotions arise. The saying that desire is the mother of all emotions is true. *Every* emotional problem stems from imbalances in one of these four primitive urges. Poorly regulated primitive urges also deplete our energy. Increased emotional struggles and decreased energy have made young people's ability to cope with or transcend life's challenges, so they can actually enjoy life, extremely difficult. If we are to increase their happiness, young people must understand precisely how their poor choices surrounding these four primitive urges deplete their energy and increase their emotional suffering.

The childhood developmental process that imprints the inclination to seek pleasure and avoid pain, when combined with imbalances in these primitive urges, brings forward powerful and painful emotions. We all know that emotions often trump rational considerations, and our emotions often determine what we think or obsess about. Strong emotions often lead to impulsive decisions that further compound our emotional pain.

Emotional reactivity and volatility are becoming the hallmark of a growing number of youth. Dr. Usharbudh Arya, a Sanskrit scholar and spiritual mentor, captures this trend: "I notice that for every one inch of problem, I see three yards of emotion. For every one inch of problem, I see three yards of commotion." This is increasingly true. The poor regulation by youth of the primitive urges of food, sleep, sex, and self-preservation is responsible for their growing lethargy, their emotional reactivity, their emotional lability (mood swings), and their more frequent experience of painful emotions. All of this emotional disharmony creates tremendous suffering that limits their experience of joy, peace, and love. How people direct, regulate, and attempt to satisfy these four urges determines the quality of lives they will lead.

In the majority of our young people, more than one of these urges is profoundly out of balance in ways that are historically unprecedented. This imbalance is at the heart of young people's increased anxiety, anger, despair, loneliness, depression, and an overall feeling of living a purposeless existence. Until changes are made to rebalance these fundamental urges, youth will never experience lasting fulfillment or happiness. These four primitive urges, when in balance, bring forward a subtle, expansive, and joyful energy.

The primitive urge of self-preservation is in many ways the most powerful of the four primitive urges, because it is the reason we pursue the others. Related to a basic ignorance of our fundamental nature, it becomes the source for most of our fears, anger, and selfish desires, creating the majority of our stress and suffering. Understanding self-preservation and its vast emotional and psychological implications is a more subtle undertaking, and we will examine it in depth after first exploring food, sex, and sleep. Imbalanced choices, promoted by the economic culture to satisfy these four primitive urges, leave youth running on fumes to navigate life's challenges, with misleading sign posts as guides. Examining each urge separately will allow us to identify specific dramatic changes the economic culture has crafted, and the physical, emotional, mental, and spiritual toll it is inflicting.

Exercise:
Desire and Emotions
Self-Awareness Journal

For one week in a journal, write down your observations of your habits regarding your desires, cravings, emotional reactions, and thoughts related to the four primitive urges. During this practice of self-observation, try to develop a picture of yourself "just as you are" at this time in your life. You are establishing baseline data you can use to evaluate the effectiveness of any future changes you might choose to make. Do this exercise without any judgment. Have the neutrality of a scientist who is interested only in gathering facts and information. Consider the following questions for your journal:

1. What are my desires, cravings, habits, and perspectives regarding food, sleep, sex, consumption (shopping), relationships, and my activity and inactivity?

2. What am I like on a physical, mental, and emotional level, and how do my choices related to the primitive urges affect these states?

3. Overall, how would I describe my lifestyle, and what have I realized as a result of these self-observations?

4. Are there any imbalances or changes worth considering as a result of the observations this journal of self-awareness revealed?

Chapter 4
The Hunger Urge Gone Awry

"Sharing food with someone is an intimate act that should not be indulged in lightly."

—M.F.K. Fisher

"I went into McDonald's yesterday and said, 'I'd like some fries.' The girl at the counter said, 'Would you like some fries with that?'"

—Jay Leno

The urge to eat is a desire common to all species. How you satisfy this urge is critical in terms of its energetic effects. Magellan and his crew, while sailing around the world, ran out of food. They stopped their hunger urge by eating rats. When the rats were gone, they ate their shoes. Shoe leather will stop your hunger pains, but offers no nutrition or energy. Many of the products we find in our grocery aisles, like shoe leather, are actually energy depleting. They take more energy to digest and metabolize than they supply, due to the poor quality of their ingredients or their lack of freshness. There is a "brave new world" of food into which youth have been born. Changes in the production distribution, quality, and quantity of food have contributed to a deep lethargy that has affected our physical, emotional, mental, and social well being. Since WWII, we have all become "test tubes" for food experiments driven by worldwide profit-driven conglomerates, and the results of their experiments are alarming.

Corporate Eating

One example of the "new age" of food is the fast food restaurant, which appeared around 1950, and now blankets the landscape. Fast food takes up approximately one-third of people's food budget, and if microwave foods are included, the percentage increases dramatically. Young people have grown up playing on McDonald's playgrounds, accumulating action figures, and swallowing "Happy Meals." These often create positive memories for children, like Christmas cookies at Grandma's, but also establish rushed eating patterns that carry into adulthood. This hurried eating style is reinforced by short school lunch periods, which compromise efficient digestion.

Despite some improvements in fast food options, qualitatively these foods are usually less fresh and higher in fat, calories, sugar, salt, and other additives than earlier homemade alternatives. High fat, sugar, and salt contents, we know, have major health consequences. Diabetes is highly correlated with obesity and plagues one in ten adults in the world. Its prevalence is rising rapidly in youth and manifesting at earlier ages. Currently just over 61 percent of Americans are overweight or obese, with percentages continuing to increase in the younger age groups.[6] A recent study, reported in the *American Journal of Health Promotion*, examined over 7,500 babies and revealed that one-third of nine-months-old babies are now considered overweight or obese by doctors. If current trends continue, close to half of all adults in America would be obese by 2040. Diabetes, highly correlated with obesity, increases the risk of heart attack, kidney failure, blindness, and some infections. Blood sugar level fluctuations that accompany diabetes can

6.   "Americans are Beating the Battle of the Bulge—they say," Star Tribune, Oct. 8, 2011.

also profoundly affect an individual's energy and mood. Many of mankind's diseases and health issues are generated by poor choices surrounding our hunger urge.

The Family Impact of Fast Food

There are social and emotional consequences to the "fast food revolution" beyond the nutritional downsides. Take-out, quick-service dining has severely reduced the regularity and frequency of family mealtime. Some people have grown up in families where grace was said at each family meal. Regardless of one's view on the religious sentiments expressed, there is a scientific health benefit to quieting down and showing gratitude before meals. This sense of calmness and well-being before meals allows enough time for saliva and other gastric juices to be secreted to aid in the digestion of food. Gandhi said, "Drink your solids; chew your liquids," because our stomach doesn't have teeth. A peaceful mind while eating also helps activate the parasympathetic nervous system, aiding in the digestion of food and facilitating the extraction of the food's nutrients. A calm atmosphere also encourages positive family conversation and cohesiveness.

The chances that quiet appreciation and the benefits that it bestows takes place while racing through the drive-through are remote. The economic culture's emphasis on fast-paced living, embodied in dozens of fast food chains, has changed some of the natural rhythms of family life. There is significant research on the benefits to children and adolescents of family time and family meals. Most of us know this intuitively. Throughout human history and in cultures across the planet, "breaking bread" together was a primary means of connecting to family, friends, and even developing connections with strangers. Meals together are a way to share interests, love, and to show hospitality. Many studies point to the critical importance of growing up in a home where meals are shared together.

Unfortunately, family meals are becoming more the exception than the rule for many in our society. Studies consistently show that shared family dinner time in families has decreased by around 33 percent over the last three decades. For millions of young people each day eating out with friends, going through a drive-through restaurant, or microwaving something and retiring to their bedroom to eat has become commonplace. Busy schedules and individual priorities have made family dinner time increasingly rare. A University of Michigan study found that the single strongest predictor of better achievement scores and fewer behavior problems was having more meal time together. The largest federally funded study of American teenagers revealed a strong correlation between the number of shared family meals and children's psychological adjustment, lower rates of drug and alcohol use, improved academic success, delayed sexual behavior, and lower suicide risk.[7]

There are enormous health concerns due to changes in the quality and quantity of our diet. Fast food restaurants and "gas station shopping malls" offer to "supersize" this and that. Aisles and aisles of "fun food" in food stores that are devoid of nutrition have undermined our energy and health. This new culture of eating not only has a profound impact on individuals, but it is also threatening family cohesiveness with painful repercussions for the entire society. These changes are relatively new and are unprecedented in the traditional dietary requirements of humans. We are guinea pigs in the corporate world's grand dining experiment.

High-Risk Low-Energy Foods

In addition to the processing and empty calories of fast foods, there are literally thousands of additives in our foods that never existed until recently in human diets. These additives extend the product's shelf life, or make the food "attractive," with nitrates, color dyes, and other agents. Carnauba wax, for example, is put in some candies to give the surface sheen. It is an extremely hard wax, so hard, in fact, that it is used on bowling alleys. Carnauba wax is just one of hundreds of examples of concocted substances that were never a part of our evolutionary food history. It is almost impossible to digest, but the body expends energy trying.

Chemical fertilizers, herbicides, pesticides, and hormones (particularly damaging to youth) end up in our foods and in the blood stream

---

7.   The archives of Pediatrics and Adolescent Medicine, August 2004.

and fat cells of our bodies. Often when overweight people decide to diet, these toxins, which are stored in the fat cells, are released into the bloodstream, causing illness. This obviously has a damaging effect on people's resolve to lose weight. Most food additives have had limited testing and research on how their chemical compounds combine. How in combination do these ubiquitous chemicals affect synapse firing, neurotransmitters, the endocrine system, and other aspects of the developing brains of our children is another unknown in the agribusiness grand experiment.

An article in the Minneapolis *Star Tribune* suggests that the impact on the brain of certain foods, ushered in by the trillion-dollar food and beverage industry, is alarmingly significant. "A growing body of medical research at leading universities and government laboratories suggests that processed foods and sugary drinks aren't simply unhealthy. They can hijack the brain in ways that resemble addictions to cocaine, nicotine, and other drugs. 'The data is so overwhelming the field has to accept it,' said Nora Volkow, director of the National Institute on Drug Abuse. 'We are finding tremendous overlap between drugs in the brain and food in the brain.' Studies have found sugary drinks and fatty foods can produce addictive behavior in animals. Brain scans of obese people and compulsive eaters, meanwhile, reveal disturbances in brain reward circuits similar to those experienced by drug abusers."[8]

Despite a rapidly growing body of evidence on the addictive properties of certain foods, food company executives and their lobbyists, like the cigarette companies years earlier, insist that nothing has been proved. Science continues to suggest otherwise. This same *Star Tribune* article reports that in 2011 alone, twenty-eight scientific studies and research papers on food addiction were published, demonstrating the strong addictive properties of a variety of foods. Sugar, corn syrup, and other sweetening agents now found ubiquitously in many foods perhaps do more than just sweeten; they may produce cravings similar to hardcore drug addiction.

Another study, reported by CNN in January 2012, cited new research that the hypothalamus, a part of the brain that regulates the hunger/thirst urge, is scarred in laboratory animals fed high-fat foods.

---

8.   "Some Food as Addictive as Cocaine," Star Tribune, November 5, 2011.

This damage occurred in just three days, and was irreversible if the high-fat diet continued for several weeks.[9] The significance of this study, if it is replicated in humans, is that the scarring of the hypothalamus led to overeating because the hunger signal itself was damaged. Earlier research, cited in David A. Kessler's best-selling book *The End of Overeating*, showed that animals, regardless of whether they were hungry or not, worked hard to reach foods with high fat, sugar, or salt content. The addictive qualities of these ingredients are well known and intentionally manipulated by the food industry to develop addictive attachments to their products. No wonder diets leading to permanent weight loss are so rare.

In addition, depleted topsoil, blown away by deforestation and agribusiness methods of growing food, deprives food of essential nutrients for good health. The average amount of topsoil on America's family farms in 1900 was eighty inches. In 2011, there was an average of just eight inches.[10] The loss of seventy-two inches of humus-rich topsoil, which provides essential nutrients to sustain a vibrant life, impacts everyone's health; and the negative nutritional and health consequences for developing children are amplified further.

Fast food has also entered the home through frozen entrees zapped in microwave ovens. Adolescents and young adults, if they are not eating the fast-food-chain offerings, often microwave much of their food. Numerous studies have shown microwaving, through its intense temperatures, changes the molecular structure of food, destroying most of its nutrients and depleting the energy one can derive from it. This is rarely reported but broadly known. A medical study of children nine to fourteen found that the more often children had regular traditional meals with their families, with minimal use of microwaves, the healthier their dietary patterns were. They ate more fresh fruits and vegetables, less saturated fats, fewer fried foods and soda, and consumed more vitamins and micronutrients.[11]

---

9. Journal of Clinical Investigation, Dr. Michael Schwartz, as reported on CNN on Jan. 7, 2012.

10. Dr. David Alkalay at Yoga Conference, University of St. Thomas, St. Paul, MN, July 2011.

11. The National Center on Addiction and Substance Abuse at Columbia University, Miriam Weinsten.

The majority of people eat fewer fresh foods now than throughout most of human history. Which has more energy or vitality: a carrot just picked from the ground, or one picked then stored in a can for nine months? You can literally taste the energetic difference of the fresh-picked carrot expressing itself on your tastebuds.

In China, they call vital energy *chi*. In yoga it is called *prana*. Much of our food is energetically challenged. It lacks *chi* or *prana*; it lacks energy. For example, approximately half the nutritional value of a carrot is lost twenty-four hours after it is picked.

Canned fruits and vegetables have minimal nutritional value. Frozen foods are better, and fresh foods are obviously the best. However, once a food's umbilical cord to the earth has been severed, the nutrition depletion clock starts ticking on even so-called fresh foods. The point of maximum nutrition for fruits and vegetables is generally when they are ripe, but they are generally picked weeks before to compensate for shipping time, depriving customers of much of their energizing nutrients. For the first twelve years of school, most children are served very little in their lunches that is nutritionally and energetically fresh. The qualitative downward shift in our food, particularly for children and adolescents, given the rapid growth of the body and brain during this period, is worthy of our concern.

The Emotional, Energetic, and Educational Impact of Food Changes

This is a small sampling of food changes that are new in human history. Changes brought on by agribusiness, where food is often shipped across the globe and preserved for months, have an energetic cost on more than one level. The effect of energy-depleted, chemically contaminated food on young people generally shows itself in agitation or sluggishness. The astounding fact is that a young person showing signs of depression, anxiety, mood swings, irritability, and other physical complaints is rarely asked by his therapist about the quality of his diet. Over the course of my teaching and therapeutic career, I saw a quantum increase in the numbers of disinterested, unmotivated, deeply lethargic, and depressed children and adolescents. A significant factor in this growing litany of youth's struggles is the dietary changes ushered in by the food industry that have sacrificed their energy and vitality to increased profits.

As we examine the other three primitive urges, there has also been an energetic cost due to imbalances in each of those, due mostly to the economic culture's influence. The cumulative effect of this "energy outage," due to imbalanced primitive urges, is that many young people are truly "running on empty." The energetic fumes they are operating on are insufficient to meet the challenges of life, fueling their depression, anxiety, and struggles with concentration and motivation.

Lethargy Personified

At the start of a new semester, I was quietly taking attendance when I heard a "thud" from the back of the room. Ted had once again passed out. His head was face down on his desk. I went over to him: "Wake up, Ted. You can't sleep in my class." Ted slowly lifted his head. There was a red welt on his forehead. "Ted, this has to stop. This is the fourth time in less than two weeks that you've been out cold in the first ten minutes of class."

"Sorry, but I'm bored, and when I am bored, I get sleepy," Ted said with a yawn.

"But Ted, we haven't even started class. I could have lit my armpits on fire and you would have missed it. Stop after class. We need to figure out what's going on."

After class, Ted and I visited. He assured me he wasn't on drugs or medication of any kind. I told him about narcolepsy, a sleep disorder where a person can suddenly fall asleep. "Could that be it?"

He said, "No, I stay up really late sometimes, but not the last few nights."

I then asked him what he had for lunch, because lunchtime immediately preceded my class. He said, "Oh, I eat pretty much the same thing every day: two orders of fries and a shake."

I occasionally had lunch duty, and observed the a la carte choices. Ted was exhibit A for the energetic costs of the a la carte menu that provided empty calories. Ted helped heighten my awareness that many other students returning to class after lunch were also exhibiting a comatose-like state.

This chronic lethargy became increasingly problematic in my classes after lunch, following the school's change to an a la carte menu. I jokingly offered my students neck braces to prevent whiplash and forehead bruises, as their necks started a helicopter-like circling motion, ending in a sudden jerk, before "crashing" to their desks. Of course, students on the "Ted diet" blamed my boring lectures for their befogged mental state, which I concede might have been a contributing factor. These same students attempted to deny any role fifty grams of fat, a dozen teaspoons of sugar, and almost 2,000 empty calories might have played in inducing their zombie-like condition. Their resistance caused me to develop some experiential options to settle the question whether the food or my lecture was to blame.

Advertisers have obtained their goal of increasing profits by offering a myriad of "food choices" independent of their energy or nutritional value. These products often come with cute or "playful" names to hook young consumers: Ho Ho's, Ding Dongs, Bugles, Twinkies, Nerds, Snicker-Doodles, etc., which belie their harmful effects. I intentionally called these products rather than food, because the very definition of a food is something that provides a healthful nutrient.

Hunger Schmunger

Even more disturbing is that advertisers have helped make food choices independent of the basic hunger urge itself. Consumers, and young people in particular, base their food choices more and more on appearance, conditioned tastes, and manufactured desires. These desires, for specific "favorite" foods, are created by psychologically sophisticated ad campaigns and food chemists. Now, when these foods are put in front of us, at a party for instance, hungry or not, we usually eat them. And we eat regardless of their effect on our energy or the nutritional value.

When we do something that we know is bad for us, and we don't stop, it's called an addiction. All of us have more addictions than we admit, many developed by ad people who prefer to call them positive associations or "branding." The psychological processes whereby people become emotionally hooked to such products through exploitation of our four primitive urges will be detailed in Chapter 8.

Overeating, Energy, and Emotions

Overeating, losing track of our hunger urge as a consequence of desire, affects our well-being in a variety of ways. It depletes energy as the body gives its full attention to breaking down the excess food, thus depriving the mind of energy necessary to concentrate. Overeating also creates feelings similar to depression by overtaxing the liver, which is responsible for regulating a consistent release of blood sugar into the blood stream. The liver synthesizes sugar glucose from the carbohydrates and starches we eat. Glucose is the most important carbohydrate in the body's metabolism. It's essentially pure energy and is used to feed every cell in our body.[12] Basically all food we eat is converted to sugar. When we add an additional 120 to 150 pounds of extra sugar per year to our diet, as citizens of developed countries do, it creates imbalances and disease. One consequence correlated with these extra pounds of simple sugars is a higher rate of cancer.

There are emotional effects as well. People report that they are more irritable when they overeat, and their outlook becomes more pessimistic and negative due to low energy and the sluggishness it creates. The reverse is also true; our moods influence the food choices we make. Depressed people often choose poorer quality foods. Dan White, who killed Harvey Milk in San Francisco years ago, became infamous, in part, for his so called "Twinkie defense." He received only a six-year sentence, and people have mistakenly concluded that his lighter sentence was due to the jury concluding that his Twinkie addiction caused him to kill. In fact, what his attorney argued was that his addiction was a symptom of a growing depression that compromised his thinking and behavior. Depressed people who select nonnutritious foods will have less energy to change destructive habit patterns, like

---

12. Dr. Schultz in Detox Special Report Part II, 6.

getting lost in anger or self-destructive thoughts. There is a synergistic relationship wherein poor food choices increase the likelihood of developing depression, and depression further exacerbates poorer food choices. Most of my depressed clients, when motivated to make and sustain dietary changes by adding fresh, quality foods in proper portions, reported a reduction in their depressive symptoms.

In addition, food has often been paired with nurturing. We try to use food in an effort to fill some emotional hole related to our fourth primitive urge of self-preservation or self-worth. This effort is never successful, but it has consequences. Dr. Arya, a teacher of mine, says this more succinctly: "People fill themselves because they don't feel fulfilled." Whenever one of our primitive urges is out of balance, because they are deeply interdependent, one imbalance ripples into the others. Relatively quickly we can find ourselves in an energetic funk, in mental/emotional pain, or physically sick with no understanding as to why. Suffice it to say, emotions are intimately woven into our food choices, and this reality is expertly exploited by advertisers on behalf of the food industry.

Schools, Food, and Corporate Bribes

My school district made an additional $200,000 a year after changing to an a la carte menu. The fact that was touted in its newsletter suggested something about its priorities: that financial profit took priority over the health of the students. A study released in 2011 showed that one out of five adolescents now has high blood pressure due to sodium (i.e., salt), obesity (i.e., fats and sugar), and lack of exercise.[13] The brightly lit pop machines in the commons area, and some eye-catching advertising on the walls of the school, suggested that the food "choices" were more conditioned than free.

Several teachers at faculty meetings argued against introducing vending machines containing chips, candy bars, cookies, and gum. The principal vigorously defended his decision, stating that these were young

---

13. Epidemiology, online journal, November 1, 2009 reporting on a six-year study concluded in 2008 where 20,000 teenagers were tracked and it revealed that one in five adolescents had high blood pressure.

adults who had to learn to make their own "choices," even if their choices were bad. One problem with his logic was that students' choices were severely limited by the vending machines having no healthy options. I protested, knowing the harmful effects that vending machines would have on students' health and learning, and also because they compromised the line between the profit-driven economic culture and the independence of educational institutions. My perspective lost, to the more compelling $35,000 a year offered by these corporations to place their machines in our schools. How great the profits were, I do not know; but I suspect their larger goal was to condition tastes and to create future demand over the course of a lifetime. We need to recognize that McDonald's doesn't put playground equipment in their restaurants because of its love of children.

In 2011, Congress, alarmed at the obesity, diabetes, and high blood pressure epidemic in children, vowed to make major changes in the quality of school lunches. It insisted that school lunches contain less fat and more fiber, fresh fruits, and vegetables. The deteriorating health of our youth, it said, was a tragedy, and it was a top priority to reverse this trend. On November 16 the same year, Congress passed legislation that was supposed to accomplish this goal. This was just weeks after the beverage and restaurant industries spent five million dollars successfully lobbying to weaken the *voluntary* food-marketing guidelines for children. The legislators voted to classify French fries as a high-fiber food, and pizza sauce as a vegetable. This was a complete capitulation to the potato and pizza industry lobbyists, who on behalf of corporate sponsors continue to make huge profits off the deteriorating health of our children.

Thirty-two million children participate in federally funded school lunches. This means all taxpayers are helping to finance the poor-quality foods in school lunches that create the obesity, diabetes, and high blood pressure problems that are all highly correlated with premature death. One doctor, remarking on the discouraging trend in children's blood pressure, said, "Unless this upward trend in high blood pressure is reversed, we could be facing an explosion of new cardiovascular disease cases in young adults."[14] By age four, one in five children is

---

14.   Ibid.

already plagued by obesity and without real changes in children's school lunches, those children will struggle to reverse their plight. So when high-fat pizza and high-sodium pizza sauce qualifies as a vegetable, you are witnessing the insidious reach, power, and priorities of the economic culture.

Over the years, it was sad for me to witness the growing lethargy of so many young people. One of the mortal sins of Catholicism, conceptualized approximately 1,500 years ago, is more robust now than at any time in human history: sloth. The lack of zest for living that many youth exhibit has far-reaching consequences. The surge in the consumption of "energy" drinks by youth reflects their attempt to counter their deepening malaise. Their marketing names are revealing: Zombie Blood, Full Throttle, Killer Buzz. Stimulating the sympathetic nervous system, these recently developed concoctions give a short and occasionally dangerous energy burst. Like coffee and soda, whose consumption among youth has also grown significantly, these energy drinks can heighten anxiety and ultimately further deplete long-term energy. Adolescents are now the leading consumers of soda, and soda provides only empty (nonnutritional) calories at a critical time in a child's development. Soda contributes significantly to increases in cavities, diabetes, obesity, and other serious health issues that impact energy, emotions, and joy.

Food, Self-Awareness, and Transformative Change

There is, however, a hopeful tale to tell. I learned from students that it is possible, and relatively quick, to reverse these trends. Hundreds of students made significant progress by participating in experiments where they observed the effects of their dietary changes. Initially I primed the pump of participation by offering them extra credit, but extrinsic reinforcement was often replaced by intrinsic interest. Students were asked to become informed consumers by studying the ingredients on packages. They were asked to eat food that had reduced fat and sugar, to add more fresh fruits and vegetables to their diets, and to not overeat.

The experiment was for twenty-one days. Each day, they journaled the effects of their dietary experiments. They were to indicate changes in such things as their energy, alertness, attitude, sleep, irritability, and mood throughout the day and evening. As their bodies and minds began to align with their new regimen, their journals became fascinating to read. Many students, particularly the heavy sugar eaters, initially reported withdrawal-like symptoms. A few reported having dreams of giant candy bars. After some initial struggles, almost every student commented on having increased energy and greater emotional control. Many lost weight, and there were frequent reports of having a better night's rest. Some expressed surprise at their increased concentration and better overall performance in school. Most gratifying, for their psychology teacher, was that the vast majority said they felt happier. Summarizing their three-week experiment, almost every student in their last journal entry said that they intended to maintain their new diets permanently.

Food Fight

An interesting little insurrection broke out after I introduced the twenty-one-day Dietary Change Option. For many students, to be separated from their junk foods for twenty-one days seemed like an eternity, and there was no way to entice them into the experiment.

One student proclaimed, "They get thirty-five points of extra credit for three weeks of eating good stuff. What if I volunteer to eat nothing but junk food? Can I get extra credit for that?"

Laughter broke out.

I considered the possibilities of this proposal. "Yes, I **will** give you extra credit for eating **only** junk food for two days," I said with a wry smile.

"Really? This will be great!" chimed in another student, capturing his junk food peers' enthusiasm.

Suddenly, rebellion broke out, but this time from the students who had just committed to twenty-one days of sacrifice. I quickly quelled the insurrection by informing the "junkies" that they would get only ten extra credit points as their experiment lasted only two days, and it would also require written permission from their parents, always mindful to limit my legal exposure! They still were happy with the terms and felt that receiving ten points for eating their favorite foods was a gift. Their playful "walk in the park," however, turned out to be a slog through Molasses Swamp.

Psychologically, if a person exaggerates some habit pattern, it often leads to recoil in the opposite direction, eventually leading to a better balance. This is exactly what happened. After stuffing their faces with junk food for two full days, they too became committed to changing their diet. Their desire for change was motivated by how absolutely terrible they felt.

Students were required to make entries in their journals every two to three hours over the course of the two days. There entries were fun and revealing. Some, through overindulgence, lost interest in the foods they formerly craved. All complained of fatigue. Their bodies ached and their sleep was restless. Some spoke of "hair-trigger" irritability, or how their minds had become mush. Somewhere, in every "junkie's" food journal, there was a plea for nutritious food.

One student proclaimed, "My kingdom for a carrot."

Another student's plea was born of apparent desperation: "How about an apple, for God's sake!"

It is helpful to enlist adolescents in change through experiential learning and be supportive of the feedback their choices bring forward. Coercion or lecturing often brings resistance with adolescents, which further solidifies their imbalanced habits. Taking responsibility for their choices, and observing the direct feedback from those choices, was empowering and transformative for them. Even Ted, the student with the bruised forehead, gave the experiment a try, and after it was completed, I never again saw his "helicopter neck swirl" or had to wake him.

The depleted and uneven energy of the "junkies," due to their poor regulation of the primitive urge of hunger, actually provided motivation for them to pursue a different course. At some level, they knew that an imbalance in this urge had caused their suffering. If we have low energy, life's challenges can overwhelm us and trigger negative emotional responses. These experiments heightened their self-awareness and showed them that their increased emotional reactivity, decreased concentration, and fluctuating moods were influenced by dietary choices. There's a saying in yoga psychology: "Awareness cures."

There is a longing deep within all of us for growth and balance.

This longing motivated students to engage in this experiment and other transformative self-awareness experiments. The experiment at the end of this chapter can increase awareness of imbalances relative to the hunger urge.

Awareness of the negative consequences of agribusiness' food agenda is growing, and it is fueling an enormous shift toward buying fresh, locally grown, and organic foods, which provides hope for a better future. We have discussed how the desires created by the psychological manipulation of the basic urge of hunger have real consequences. Energy is the currency of life and, when it is depleted (as we experience when were sick), it is difficult to maintain positive attitudes or emotions, and we struggle to handle the challenges of life.

Experiment:
Refining Choices Around Your Hunger Urge

There are only a few sources for our energy, and food is one of the most significant. Making gradual refinements in balancing our primitive urge of hunger (which includes thirst) can help us live with more zest and joy as well as sustain long-term greater health. This can be adapted for classroom, counseling, and even family settings to increase self-awareness. There are two parts to this experiment:

1. Keep a food journal for one week, noting what you eat, and how mindfully you eat. Liquefy your food before swallowing—our stomachs don't have teeth. This extra chewing boosts energy, improves health, and increases the enjoyment of food while supporting weight loss. Be mindful of the after-effects following eating and drinking. How are your energy and your mood affected by what you have just consumed?

2. After Experiment #1, choose something in your diet that you would like to improve, and then for three weeks commit to making it happen. You could cut down sugar by 10 percent, reduce your food intake by 10 percent, chew 10 percent more, or be 10 percent more present while you eat. Whichever of these options you choose, monitor the change in your journal, as this supports long-term change. This type of experiment can be adapted to any of the four primitive urges.

41

Chapter 5
Sex and the Loss of Innocence

"Sex education may be a good idea in the schools, but I don't believe the kids should be given homework."

—BILL COSBY

"Sex, with all its pleasure, at its core is a deep longing for losing the lonely self of ego in the ecstasy of union with the divine."

—JIM NELSON

The connection between the primitive urge of sex and our emotions may not be obvious. Upon reflection, however, one can see that this primitive urge often leads to ensnarled emotional entanglements and even addictive behaviors. From flirting to affairs, from pornographic addictions to sexual molestation of children, from abuses involving ministers of the church to scandals involving ministers of state, the power of this urge has led to emotionally driven decisions that trump all logic. Many people have little ability to regulate their sexual urges and give free rein to their desires, violating their consciences and shattering the lives of countless others in the process. Since the days of Mark Anthony and

Cleopatra, the highest government officials around the globe have lost their positions and their reputations due to their inability to balance the sexual urge with their leadership responsibilities. This powerful urge is now permeating the lives of children, adolescents, and adults in ways that we have never experienced before.

Contemplate for a moment what has changed in the past fifty years in terms of the cultural attitudes toward sex and the frequency of children's exposure to sex. What are the consequences of those changes? Children are now living through a second sexual revolution. The first revolution in the 1960s with all of its excesses was a reaction to cultural suppression, repression, and hypocrisy pertaining to normal sexual desires. This second revolution of the twenty-first century is characterized by the unbridled commercial exploitation of sex to sell products, and a lack of appropriate boundaries around sexual behavior and sexual issues.

Children have much earlier access and exposure to constant sexual stimulation. Think of the thousands of ways young people are saturated with sexual titillation. Magazines, billboards, TV shows with constant sexual innuendo, X-rated cable channels, video games, explicit sexual advertising intentionally targeted at youth, Internet pop-ups, sexting, easy access to pornography—all of these are inundating the minds of children and adolescents. Sexual content is also portrayed as sex for sex's sake, for selfish gratification, devoid of love or respect. Human beings are sexual beings throughout their developmental lives, but the lack of action to curb age-inappropriate sexual exposure for children and adolescents is disturbing.

Sex, the Profit Motive, and the Increasing Pressures on Youth

This constant bombardment of sexual innuendo and sexual imagery is almost entirely driven by legal corporate commerce seeking profits. It is being done with great intentionality and with great skill. Pairing repetitive images relating to the primitive urge of sex with merchandise is a well-researched strategy employed by advertisers to boost sales, regardless of who is exposed to it.

This early exposure to sexual material and messages adds to the stress and confusion of growing up in our culture. Blinded by profits, Hollywood and ad agencies act as if children's constant sexual exposure is benign. On the contrary, the messages are very powerful, and children's desire to be sexually sophisticated before they are emotionally ready takes a heavy toll. A fellow teacher of mine who taught elementary school said that some second-grade girls come to school with lipstick, mascara, nylons, and high heels, wearing their sisters' bras stuffed with Kleenex. The boys are asked at recess by some of these girls to put down their Nintendos and participate in mock marriages. Teen pregnancy (children raising children) and STDs are two potentially overwhelming and frequent outcomes of early exposure to sex. Approximately 40 percent of all American children born today are born outside of marriage. The rate is close to 70 percent in black communities.[15] This is enormously stressful for parents and children, and is a leading predictor of future poor academic performance and poor economic prospects for the child. The long-term social and economic implications of this situation for our entire society are inestimable.

The fact that puberty is starting at earlier ages may also be linked to the economic culture. Puberty takes place two years earlier on average than it did a few decades ago. Children are essentially losing two years of their childhood. Some scientists believe this may be a byproduct of earlier and more frequent external sexual stimulation by the media, which triggers the biological developmental processes in the body-brain-mind complex to start earlier.

This external sexual titillation synergistically combines with female growth hormones that are fed to cows to promote weight gain for greater beef and milk production, and is also used in chickens to increase growth and egg laying. The combination of more frequent external sexual titillation and internal hormonal stimulation speeds up the sexual developmental process, accounting for early onset puberty. There are different variations of the female hormone estrogen that have been added to our food supply over the last fifty years. Because of this additional exposure to estrogen, early onset puberty is essentially occurring

---

15. "Broken Families: The Neglected Explanation for Economic Disparity" by Mitch Pearlstein, Star Tribune in Sunday Commentaries, September 3, 2011.

in females, with breasts and menstruation taking place for many early in elementary school. There is emerging evidence that young boys are also exhibiting breast development.

Diethylstilbestrol was the first estrogen hormone synthesized in 1938. One byproduct of its use was increased mammary growth. It was originally developed from natural growth hormones that triggered growth spurts and puberty in female adolescents. This early breast development and other indications of puberty have alarmed scientists and doctors. More and more children, as early as age five, are showing breast development. Puberty now starts for 15 percent of children by age seven.[16] These hormones are in our food to maximize profits, and are promoted as safe by the food industry. For millions of years these synthetic hormones were not in our food, and scientists are raising serious questions about their safety.

No one asked the cows if they preferred to lactate continually or gain weight rapidly before being slaughtered. Now these hormones might be manifesting in our children as early-onset puberty. Puberty is coming earlier, but there's no corresponding early onset of emotional maturity and thoughtful decision making for our youth. Children are left with the sexual urges of a young adult without the emotional maturity to manage those urges. Not one second grade girl, whose breasts made her the object of stares and sexual innuendo jokes, had a voice in the profit-driven decision to spike hormone levels in her diet. We do know, however, that females who start menstruation earlier have a greater risk for developing cancer.

Sex: Something Gained but Something Lost

Recent changes in sexual norms and boundaries that would have been inconceivable just a generation ago suggest how quickly and tragically things have eroded. There are consequences to the early sexualization of our youth. Ideas like "friends with benefits," where people engage in casual sex with friends, dissolve relational and

---

16.   Research on early onset puberty, Journal of the American Academy of Pediatrics, May 21, 2010.

intimacy boundaries for hedonistic and all too often exploitive purposes. Oral sex for friends in the hallways of middle schools is another example of boundaries blurring between friends and intimate relationships, all in the name of hedonistic "fun." Sexting, sending cell phone sexual messages and photos, which often involves pressure and intimidation, is becoming increasingly commonplace. Students, whose conscience or fear resists the peer pressure of these new sexual expectations, question what kind of world they are living in, or wonder if they are out of step.

Internet-driven dating patterns, where young adults gather in groups to ultimately hook up for no-strings-attached sex, are becoming increasingly common. Sex is an intimate act. If sex is driven only by pleasure, devoid of love or even respect, is it possible that such casual encounters can be undertaken without considerable individual and collective fallout? Will the lives of babies born from these encounters be unaffected by the lack of psychological intimacy and the circumstances that brought about their conception?

Toddlers, Tiaras, and the "Adulteration" of Children

Approximately fifty years ago Marilyn Monroe, who was presumed to have committed suicide, said, "A sex symbol becomes a thing. I just hate to be a thing." Females being portrayed as sexual objects (and, increasingly, males also) has worsened despite the so-called Women's Liberation Movement. The huge tragedy in the constant bombardment of age-inappropriate sexual imagery is children's early loss of innocence. The very young are becoming "little adults." Their natural childhood playfulness and nonsexual exploration of life is taking a back seat to greed. I have traveled to less-developed countries where, despite poverty, inquisitiveness and wonder are still expressed fully in children's simple interactions with nature or playmates. This kind of free play, and the inquisitiveness reflected in children's ubiquitous "why" questions, is essential for their development and creativity. The electronic toys offered by the economic culture often contain questionable sexual imagery; they also offer a homogenized sameness that stirs little innovation in a child because they allow for little intrinsic creativity. The natural wonder of children and their innocence should be preserved for as long as possible; and it is a tragedy that for many it has ended in grade school.

Childhood beauty pageants are just one of the more obvious signs of this "adulteration" of youth. False eyelashes, wigs, fake teeth, spray-on tans, sexually suggestive dresses, and in one case parent-approved Botox injections for a six-year-old were supplied to enhance the contestant's chance of "winning." The economic culture creates and underwrites this entertainment. The title of one of the shows that highlights this world, *Toddlers and Tiaras*, is itself disconcerting. Pedophiles find these shows alluring. This world starts for some children less than one month after birth, so this isn't a choice for them; decisions are being driven by the interests and desires of parents.

A recent videotape of one of these beauty pageant contests showed a five-year-old dressed very provocatively, wearing black mesh stockings, sexually gyrating her hips while singing a song that commented on her booty. She won the contest. Later, it was announced this girl was retiring at age six. She had won many contests and had started "her" pursuit of fame at eighteen months. She was interviewed nationally on a high-rated morning TV talk show and was asked why she was retiring so young. She responded, "I want to spend more time on my future career." The interviewer asked what career she was thinking of pursuing at age six. She paused a long time as though she was trying to remember someone else's answer, and then said, "Being a superstar!"

In another case in 2011, people were outraged when a three-year-old was dressed in a nearly identical version of one of Julia Roberts' *Pretty Woman* hooker outfits. The three-year-old paraded before the judges with choreographed movements "appropriate" for her attire. Apparently not everyone was outraged, because she won the contest with the judges awarding her the highest title across all age groups.

Many parents, trying to escape their economic woes and wanting the best material benefits for their children, assume they will achieve a bigger slice of the American dream by successfully participating in ultra-competitive events that pit children against each other. These parents have accepted the economic culture's paradigm that happiness is achieved through increased status and money. Meanwhile the children's needs get lost in the shuffle for fame and fortune. Children need to deeply connect to parents through unrushed, stress-free, loving interactions. They need playtime to express their natural creativity, free from the performance anxiety caused by feeling that their worth is on the line if they don't win.

Something Gained—Something Lost

The world of childhood pageants is saturated with the messages and values of the economic culture. Producers and advertisers seek profits and ratings through selective editing. Extreme behaviors of parents and children are shown to audiences who watch with voyeuristic horror and repulsion, even as they contribute to corporate profits and ratings.

Anorexia and bulimia, and the self-loathing inherent in those illnesses, also reflect the power of the media's images. These life-threatening illnesses have been manifesting in younger and younger age groups. The constant bombardment by advertisers and the media of thin and unrealistic perfectly Photoshopped models penetrates early and deep into the psyche of children. Proof of the media's powerful influence was revealed in a study done between 1995 and 1998 by Dr. Anne Becker and colleagues from Harvard Medical School. The BBC in May 2002 summarized the results of that study: "Doctors say they found further evidence to suggest television programs encourage eating disorders among teenage girls . . . The introduction of television in two towns in the Pacific Islands of Fiji . . . Found that levels of poor body image and incidents of eating disorders among girls increased since they were first exposed to television . . . Doctors interviewed and tested two sets of Fijian schoolgirls within a few weeks of the introduction of television . . . in 1995 and then again in 1998. In 1995, the number of girls who self-induced vomiting to control weight was zero. Three years later after the introduction of television it was 11 percent. . . . In 1998, 69 percent said they had gone on diets to lose weight, and 74 percent said they were 'too big or too fat.' The study showed that girls with a television set were three times more likely to show symptoms of eating disorders. In interviews, the girls said they admired television characters and tried to copy them."[17]

This famous study illustrates the risks of exposing youth to constant sexual imagery often pairing those images with products to increase sales. The embedded message is that appearance is the barometer of worth. Self-esteem, when tied to something as superficial and uncertain as hoping to gain acceptance through one's appearance, is fragile in the extreme and a source of great anxiety, particularly for females. The stress of deciding whether to become sexually active or to participate in sexting to fit in with your friends can be overwhelming. For many teenagers, sex is not some forbidden pleasure, it is awkward and confusing—if not traumatic. Imagine a teenage boy or girl struggling with a fragile sense of worth, and they are abruptly dumped or humiliated when their sexting photos hit cyberspace.

Young people are often devastated psychologically by the realization that they have been taken advantage of, that the pressures and expectations that they experienced in what they believed was a caring relationship were exploitive. It was never about intimacy, caring, acceptance, or love. It was only about satisfying someone else's pleasure and bolstering their prestige, leaving the victim as a pawn in their game of self-gratification. Hedonism, doing what feels good to you regardless of its impact on others, is part of the implicit value system sold by the economic culture.

The Future Effects of Exploiting Sex

The scars of our children's premature sexualization and exploitation show up years later in their future intimate adult relationships. This often manifests as neediness in relationships or as distrust due to the fear that they will be used again, making the probability of future loving and successful relationships less likely. Ignoring this collateral damage of the media's obsession with sexual messages and imagery to enhance profits leaves youth exposed and vulnerable.

There is also an energetic cost to poorly regulated sexual urges that

---

17. "Television Link to eating disorders," BBC News World Edition, Friday 31 May 2002.

is rarely mentioned. We know that sex, culminating in orgasm, leads to one of the quickest losses of energy of any human activity. Daily exposure to sexual titillation, through hundreds of sexual innuendos and images via the media, has an energetic cost. The whole universe is energy. The effect of the media's constant sexual bombardment leads to the rise and fall of mental excitement (energy) due to this constant sexual "tease." This siphoning of energy contributes to significant mental and physical fatigue.

This slow continual leakage of energy due to media "sexploitation," combined with the energy drainage due to imbalances in the other primitive urges, takes a toll. Sexually attractive models, paired with products to enhance profits, is a staple of advertising. These media messages, suggesting that one's worth and acceptance is gained through sex appeal and sexual activity, is damaging to youth's self-confidence, self-worth, and their future.

Deborah Pike Olsen, writing in the 2011 *Parenting* magazine article "Having the Sex Talk: Is Your Tween Too Sexy Too Soon?" highlights some of the costs of this early sexualization of our youth:

> Studies have shown that girls who are obsessed with their appearance are more likely to start smoking earlier, become depressed, and develop an eating disorder as they get older. When girls reach the teen years, those who value themselves for their sexual attractiveness are more likely to do risky things, such as avoid using condoms during sex since they are not comfortable asserting themselves in sexual situations. These girls are also less likely to focus on academic tasks and physical activities.
>
> Boys, meanwhile, are getting the message that they need to have an attractive girlfriend to be accepted . . . and appear to be sexually active and tough . . . They may become depressed if they don't measure up.[18]

The question is being asked whether ten-year-olds are becoming the "new twenties," as more and more youth lose their childhood and adolescence to premature adulthood. We are sexual creatures, but

---

18.   "Having the Sex Talk: Is Your Tween Too Sexy Too Soon?" by Deborah Pike Olsen, Parenting, November 5, 2011.

awareness of what is age appropriate seems to have been lost in the economic culture's lust for profits. The media's constant sexual emphasis devalues other qualities in our youth, such as determination, compassion, and intelligence. The emphasis and value given to these positive qualities takes a backseat to being sexually attractive.

Transcending the Economic Culture's Expectations—A Case Study

I wanted my students to know that we don't have to follow the economic culture's expectations of beauty or any other suggestions embedded in that culture. Just as women challenged expectations of their roles in the workplace and access to sports opportunities years earlier, they could challenge the economic culture's suggestions about beauty. I challenged any female in my class who regularly wore makeup to go without it for a minimum of one week. There was always great hesitation by the vast majority of female students who wore makeup to take on this challenge. Fear is contractive energy and inhibits the risk-taking required for change. Appropriate humor creates spaciousness and more expansive energy, which facilitates detaching from that fear.

Here is a joke I used to help the girls in my classes not take their looks so seriously:

In surgery for a heart attack, a middle-aged woman has a vision of God by her bedside. "Will I die?" she asks. God says, "No, you have thirty more years to live."

With thirty more years to look forward to, she decides to make the best of it. So since she's in the hospital, she gets breast implants, liposuction, a tummy tuck, a hair transplant, and collagen injections in her lips. She looks great!

The day she's discharged, she exits the hospital with a swagger, crosses the street, and is immediately hit by an ambulance and killed. Up in heaven, she sees God. "You said I had thirty more years to live," she complains.

"That's true," says God.

"So what happened?" she asked.

God shrugs. "I just didn't recognize you."[19]

Laughter, again, is an antidote to fear. Female students seemed more open to considering this no-makeup option after laughing at stories like this. I also reminded them of the extra sleep they would get by having a less extensive beauty regimen each morning. I even surveyed how much longer they could sleep in; and for many it was close to a half-hour. But, like the twenty-one-day Dietary Change Option, many still refused, particularly the young women wearing the most makeup. Sometimes their emphatic emotional refusals suggested real fear born of deep-seated insecurities.

"You mean you don't have as much worth and belief in yourself if you come to school without makeup?" I asked, trying to get them to reconsider. "Guys don't need to put on a mask before we head out to school; we must be inherently more beautiful than females." I continued to playfully challenge their resistance. "Were you less attractive than males when you were in kindergarten and wore no makeup?" I kept gently baiting them until they grudgingly acknowledged that their hesitation to not wearing makeup was conditioned by the messages of the culture. "So, you want Madison Avenue to control you through fears of rejection, and you're willing to comply with the standards of beauty they set?"

These questions inspired several female students to take on the challenge of facing the demons their conditioned fears had brought about that had limited their sense of worth. Often it was the brightest students who understood and resented that this fear had been implanted into their psyche. They were required to journal their experience each day for one week. Here is a portion of Karen's journal entries:

Day 1: I almost changed my mind this morning. I was surprised by how afraid I was to leave the house and head to school without any makeup. I was surprised, too, by how harsh my negative self-talk was. "God, you look horrible,"—statements like that and worse. It showed how much my worth was connected to my appearance. When I arrived at school, I noticed how I didn't want to make eye

---

19. "America's 10 Funniest Jokes" by Andy Simmons, Reader's Digest, June 2009, 108.

contact. I felt naked without my makeup. It was a hard day and I was glad I didn't have to go to work. I went home after school and crashed.

Day 2: I woke up in a good mood, went into the bathroom and then remembered this was going to be a no-makeup day. My mood changed. I knew I was facing another day of self-doubt. Throughout this day, I noticed that this experiment had made me feel much more introverted. I didn't engage people in conversation as much, and my eye contact problem continued. It's interesting because I noticed I am myself once I get home.

Day 3: I am beginning to appreciate that I am able to sleep an extra 20-plus minutes each morning. I walked the hallways of school with a little more bounce in my step today. I noticed I am starting to have more thoughts like—"What the heck, if people don't like the way I look, it's their problem. I am who I am." It's like I'm cheer-leading for myself.

Day 4: I woke up realizing I have to go to work after school, and I am dreading interacting with customers as "Plain Jane." But, on the plus side, I am noticing that my complexion is actually getting better now that I've given up the makeup. So three bonuses from this experiment, my complexion, my longer sleep, and soon—my extra credit!

Day 5: It was no big deal at work last night. I was so busy, I forgot I wasn't wearing makeup. I also realize that I don't have to look at myself, so why should I worry! I didn't share this in my journal earlier because I was embarrassed, but on the first day my boyfriend asked what I was doing. I didn't know what he meant. And then he said he didn't like the way I looked without makeup. I was hurt, and even more hurt when he said, "Maybe we shouldn't walk around together until this experiment is over." I couldn't believe it—he tried to shrug it off and say he was just "goofing around," but I think he was covering his tracks—the JERK!!! Since then I have actually become more committed to seeing this through.

Day 6: Things are getting easier. My complexion is the best it's been in years. I'm back talking to people and making eye contact. I have adopted an attitude that if people thought I was cute as a kid before makeup, I couldn't have lost all my cuteness. I actually feel more confident these last couple of days. I am not always running to the mirror, worried that something's not right. I'm right!

Day 7: This started out scary, and I didn't know if I would continue all week. It's almost embarrassing to say that because, why should makeup make such a difference in my confidence? The truth is it never really did, because I was still looking in the mirror all the time. The last couple of days, I'm back to my normal personality and don't care that I'm not wearing makeup. I think in the future I might wear a little especially on special occasions, but it will be my choice and, either way, I will be fine. One last thing, it's amazing, but I find myself more confident around my boyfriend because of this experiment. I am who I am, and he likes it or he doesn't. He's not the only fish in the sea, you know!

All of us are influenced by the messages of the economic culture. The constant imagery of thin and flawless models repeated constantly can create enormous self-doubt, insecurities, emotional pain, and confusion for young people. We can encourage young women like Karen to question and confront those messages through self-awareness experiments. The psychological techniques advertisers knowingly employ to exploit youth's vulnerabilities will be exposed in Chapter 8 after examining the Primitive Urges of Sleep and Self-preservation.

Chapter 6
Sleep Glorious Sleep

"Sleep, rest of things, O pleasing Deity; Peace of the soul, which cares does crucify, Weary bodies refresh and mollify."

—OVID

"Without enough sleep we all become tall two-year-olds."

—JOJO JENSEN, IN DIRT FARMER WISDOM

After decades of research, reports from parents, and direct student feedback, it is clear to me that youth's ability to get a good night's sleep has declined significantly. Well over half of my students reported difficulties in falling asleep, staying asleep, or feeling refreshed upon waking. Many struggled with all three.

Contemplate the normal sleep patterns of people seventy-five years ago compared to the patterns of many young people today. For millennium, people went to bed shortly after dark and arose at dawn or before. Our ancestors adhered to these natural biological cycles called circadian rhythms. Research has shown that regulated exposure to sunlight is a significant factor in helping people with sleep disorders. Sleep researchers and engineers have developed full-spectrum lamps whose lights slowly intensify at dawn to simulate nature's process. This is an attempt to rebalance people's circadian rhythms and to treat growing numbers of people with light deprivation issues that trigger the depression known as seasonal affective disorder (SAD).

Expanding Sleep Issues

Seven percent of Americans use over-the-counter sleep aids and 3 percent use prescription strength sleep medications, which indicates that tens of millions of Americans are experiencing serious sleep issues.[20] Nonprescription drug use to combat sleep problems is also very common, as many youth and adults smoke marijuana to quiet their minds before bedtime. Some prefer alcohol. What few of these people realize is that even though these drugs help them fall asleep, the restorative functions of sleep are compromised because of the drugs' impact on REM sleep and especially on delta sleep. People who rely on these drugs often find that their mornings are challenging, often coma-like, and that their depressive symptoms often intensify. Compensations for morning sluggishness, such as coffee or power drinks, create additional complications. The epidemic of sleep issues is reflected in the fact that the United States now has at least eighty-three recognized sleep disorders. For example, 5 percent of Americans suffer from sleep apnea, a potentially fatal sleep disturbance where breathing stops repeatedly during the night, a potential precursor to heart attacks and strokes.[21] Two million children now suffer from sleep apnea and American's growing sleep struggles are reflected in the fact that there were 374 accredited U.S. sleep centers in 1997, 1,000 in 2006, and 2,365 in 2012.[22]

The importance of sleep has been well researched. In one early sleep study rats died after five days of inadequate sleep. We know men

20. "Get a Good Night's Sleep for Happier Days" by Cathy Frisinger, Star Tribune, March 25, 2008 (reprinted from McClatchy Newspaper article).

21. "Hey U wassup?? Let's zzzzz . . . on tweeting and textings' effects on sleep" by Kristen Tillotson, Star Tribune, December 26, 2011.

22. "Why can't we SLEEP? By Bill Ward, Star Tribune, March 11, 2012.

who sleep less than seven hours have a 26 percent higher death rate.[23] A study reported in the September/October 2011 AARP *Magazine* revealed sleep deprivation actually ages the brain. Neuron regeneration (neurogenesis) is essential for healthy brain function. Sleep is a major contributor to this process, and less sleep means less neuron regeneration. This study interestingly revealed that too much sleep also led to less neuron regeneration.[24] So, because there is a wide variation in sleep needs, the key is to self-assess and find the appropriate balance for maximum invigoration. Two of my fellow teachers required only three hours of sleep a night, and they functioned at a very high level for more than fifty years. Most studies, however, reveal that, unlike adults, children need ten to eleven hours of sleep, and most adolescents need between eight-and-one-half to ten hours per night. Adolescents average less than seven hours of sleep each night, which means that most adolescents are sleep deprived.

Dramatic Unprecedented Changes in Youth's Sleep Patterns

The brain's suprachiasmatic nucleus in the hypothalamus regulates the circadian rhythm. Regular cycles of light and dark are essential to keep this nucleus rhythm in balance.[25] Teenagers are particularly prone to circadian rhythm problems because, for them, every night has become potentially a weekend night. This is unprecedented and is the result of more tempting and addictive electronic gadgets to play with and more discretionary income to purchase them. The variety of entertainment options available at night are hard to say no to, and their sleep suffers. One night an adolescent will go to bed at 4:00 a.m. and sleep until 4:00 the next afternoon. This may be followed by a night of almost no sleep, following a concert or exploration of a new video game. I

---

23. "Snooze or Lose" by Holly St. Lifer, AARP Magazine, You & Your Health, Sept/Oct 2011, 32.

24. "Get a Good Night's Sleep for Happier Days" by Cathy Frisinger, Star Tribune, March 25, 2008 (reprinted from McClatchy Newspaper article).

25. Ibid.

frequently witnessed the results of sleep deprivation and poor sleep regulation in the sunken eyes of my students during my first-hour class. As with imbalances regarding food and sex, disrupted sleep patterns create a host of physical, cognitive, emotional, and social problems for youth, and for those who care for them.

The Consequences of Poor Sleep Regulation and Sleep Deprivation

Studies of people whose work schedules shift frequently show depleted levels of the hormone serotonin, a condition associated with anxiety and depression.[26] Job shift irregularity would be analogous to teenagers' lack of consistency in their sleep times. It is not unlikely that this is also affecting their anxiety and depression levels through serotonin depletion. Most clinicians, when assessing depression, explore sleep problems as one of a checklist of symptoms for assessing depression. It is likely, given that poor regulation of our four primitive urges is the cause of all painful emotions, that sleep disregulation and deprivation play a significant *causal* role in many depressions. E. Joseph Cossman's quote, "The best bridge between depression and hope is a good night sleep," may literally be true.

Sleep is one of our few sources of our energy. When we are sleep deprived, or don't have a consistent sleep schedule, we significantly deplete our overall energy. We become more emotionally reactive, and the emotional "tone" of our minds darkens. Our perceptions become shrouded. We look at life through a darkened prism where enthusiasm, hope, perseverance, acceptance of others' weaknesses, creativity, kindness, and love itself get lost in lethargic gloom. When tired, we paint the world with opaque colors, obscuring our natural joy and playfulness, and often blame others for the darkened dullness that envelops us. The disruption of the primitive urge of sleep is no small thing. We need to understand its causal role in energetically pulling down a shade of pessimistic perceptions over our minds, so that we operate with a view of the

---

26.   "Hey U wassup?? Let's zzzzz . . . on tweeting and textings' effects on sleep" by Kristen Tillotson, Star Tribune, December 26, 2011.

world that invites further depression.

Multiple studies have shown that youth who watch television before bedtime have significantly more sleep issues. This problem is worsening as we now have over one quarter of babies under age two with televisions in their room and almost three quarters of eight- to seventeen-year-olds. It is also known that youth who fall asleep with a TV on decrease the time spent in delta sleep. In the December 26, 2011, *Star Tribune,* cellphone texting is cited as a growing source of sleep disturbance for youth:

> A chronic texter, often a teen, leaves the cellphone on the nightstand to use as an alarm clock. The light and occasional noises of the phone disrupt deep sleep. Sometime during the night, in light sleep or grogginess, the teen instinctively reaches for the phone and starts texting . . . In the morning they don't remember doing it . . . Dr. Conrad Iber, who heads the sleep medicine program at the University of Minnesota, says, "the busier, more stressed out and tired you are, or the more erratic your sleep schedule, the more likely you are to sleep-text. Electronic devices are the enemy of sleep, and of brain function the next day. A third of the population is sleep-deprived, and a larger percentage of teens." Even if you don't sleep-text, another negative side effect of leaving your phone on at night on or near your bed (as four out of five teenagers do) is that you may never fall into deep sleep due to the sudden flashes of light or pinging from any texts you receive. "Tests have shown that if sleep is interrupted by a tone in the middle of the night, it causes daytime sleepiness," Iber said.[27]

Sleep-texting is like techno-sleepwalking; people have no remembrance of it. It also illustrates how technological noises and light interfere with our critical need for deep sleep, also known as delta wave sleep. Drugs, overeating, poorly managed stress, and eating and drinking right before bed also negatively impact deep sleep. These destructive habits along with electronic stimulation keep the brain/body complex more active, inhibiting the full reparative and restorative power of the slower brain wave delta sleep. Interference with quality delta sleep,

---

27. "Get a Good Night's Sleep for Happier Days" by Cathy Frisinger, Star Tribune, March 25, 2008 (reprinted from McClatchy Newspaper article).

critical for waking refreshed, plays a significant role in youth's growing lassitude, boredom, irritability, and depressive and labile moods. Research suggests that these noise and light interruptions may also interfere with the important consolidation of learning and integration of unconscious struggles, which take place during REM Sleep.

Several hormones essential for a balanced life are also impacted by sleep deprivation or irregular sleep patterns. Melatonin aids sleep and is secreted by the pineal gland in the brain during darkness. Many young people sleep during daylight hours, disrupting melatonin production. Overtime, this intensifies insomnia. Two hormones, ghrelin and leptin, which help signal hunger and satiety, are also affected by the quality of one's sleep. Leptin levels fall when sleep is less than the body requires, leading to a hunger urge even after recently eating. Growing evidence links this hormonal deficit to the growing epidemic of child obesity,[28] which brings a host of risks, from psoriasis to increased cholesterol and cardiovascular disease.[29] In fact, the American Family of Pediatrics, in November 2011, recommended that children between the ages of nine and eleven should be screened for high cholesterol. This recommendation was based on the fact that one-third of American children are overweight or obese.[30]

In addition, blood sugar levels fluctuate more in sleep-deprived subjects. In just four nights of being deprived of delta sleep, subjects could not metabolize sugar, and symptoms of type II diabetes emerged.[31] Type II diabetes rates have exploded in our youth over the last few years, and sleep deprivation is now thought to be one of the likely causes. We know fluctuating blood sugar levels affect mood: irritability, a flat, depressed effect, and emotional ups and downs occur more frequently. I have personally witnessed people with hypoglycemia (low blood sugar) exhibit psychotic-like symptoms when their blood sugar levels drop.

One of the most far-reaching effects of poorly regulated sleep and

---

28. "Get a Good Night's Sleep for Happier Days" by Cathy Frisinger, Star Tribune, March 25, 2008 (reprinted from McClatchy Newspaper article).

29. Ibid.

30. American Family of Pediatrics, November 2011.

31. "The Science of Sleep" with Lesley Stahl, 60 minutes, aired March 16, 2008.

sleep deprivation pertains to children's energy, concentration, and motivation. If one's energy is depleted, concentration cannot be maintained, and there is no motivation to achieve. This is a serious problem for increasing numbers of young people. Memory is almost entirely a function of interest and concentration. Not surprisingly, research studies found that memory problems were one of the first effects of poor sleep habits. One can easily see how a sleep-deprived child could exhibit negative behavior and have failing grades and not have the energy or motivation to pull himself out of the situation.

One can only speculate on the long-term effects of poor sleep regulation on creativity, productivity, and success at work, as well as general enjoyment of life. Employers increasingly complain about how difficult it is to get "this generation" to stay focused while on the job, let alone to be at work on time. People are still accountable for their choices, but a growing body of evidence indicates that poor work habits may be due less to flaws in character and more the result of changes in sleep habits conditioned by the economic culture.

Research demonstrated that when fruit flies were sleep deprived they could not even maintain courtship behaviors.[32] Usually sex is something of great interest and motivation for fruit flies and other species, and numerous studies link sleep problems to decreases in human's libido, negatively impacting their intimate relationships. From a biological perspective you can simply say that sleep deprivation or poor sleep regulation equates to stress.

The Interplay of Primitive Urges

The four primitive urges are interconnected; an imbalance in one affects the others. Poor sleep affects your dietary choices; poor diet affects your sleep. Bombarded by a media that sells products through slim, attractive models, it is also likely that youth who are overweight are much more likely to struggle with self-image problems. In other words, imbalanced choices around the primitive urge of sleep can trigger eating problems, resulting in self-worth problems. The ego's

---

32. Ibid.

identification of itself as a body means that, from the ego's culturally conditioned perspective, extra pounds equate to being less worthwhile. This triggers fear in young people that they will not be accepted, particularly by their peers. Then, their shame-based thoughts, replayed consciously or unconsciously many times, may cause depression. Depression further decreases the zest for living and negatively impacts brain chemistry. This in turn creates more sleep struggles, increasing the probability of poorer food choices. A feedback loop is created through the interaction of the four primitive urges, and young people are stuck in a downward spiral that is increasingly difficult to exit, as their emotions, energy, and attitudes run amok.

Poor Sleep Regulation, Emotions, and the Brain

Recent research is revealing other ways the brain is affected by poor, erratic sleep habits. Subjects who were not sleep deprived were shown graphic and very disturbing pictures. They had a moderate response in their amygdala, the part of the brain that processes memory and emotional responses. Sleep-deprived subjects, on the other hand, had a hyperactive response in the amygdala, which corresponds to intense emotional reactivity. They also showed a disconnection between the amygdala and the frontal lobes.[33] The frontal lobes of the brain help us anticipate consequences and are critical in inhibiting intense emotional responses. Many youth seem increasingly unable to manage their emotions. The frontal lobes don't fully develop until our late twenties, making emotional regulation already more challenging for adolescents. Sleep deprivation in youth, triggering an overreaction in the amygdala and the silencing of their frontal lobes, may exacerbate this disadvantage. Interestingly, this same disconnection, the lack of communication between emotional centers and the neocortex of the frontal lobe, is also seen in severe psychiatric disorders.[34]

The body and brain of children go through substantial developmental changes as they age. It is logical that sleep deprivation and

---

33. Ibid.

34. Ibid.

fluctuating sleep schedules, which alter the brain in all ages and in many negative ways, is particularly damaging during maturation. This is having profound effects on youth's physical, emotional, and mental development and function. Parents know mood shifts are one of the hallmarks of adolescence, as a result of the biological changes that accompany this period. The recent negative shifts in sleep habits, ignoring the historical hardwired internal circadian rhythms, increases their emotional control struggles.

Sleep and Accidents

Remember, a classic symptom of poor sleep habits is a decrease in concentration, the inability to sustain attention. Is it any surprise that insurance rates for teenagers are higher, based on the statistical fact that they are much more likely to get into a car accident? These accidents are the leading cause of death for young people. We know sleep deprivation makes everyone more likely to have accidents of all kinds, and young people are perhaps at the greatest risk. Sleep deprivation likely played a role in the Exxon Valdez oil spill, as well as the Three Mile Island and Chernobyl meltdowns.[35] Recently, air traffic controllers who fell asleep putting airline travelers in peril were found to have frequently rotating work schedules. This mirrors the poorly regulated sleep schedules of many youth that increases their risk of accidents. Now hand a cell phone to a sleep-deprived teen driver, mix in a few distracting friends in the backseat, and you have the potential for disaster. You can see why legislation affecting these behaviors has passed, or is pending, in many states.

How to Change Faulty Sleep Habits

We need to not just pass laws, but create a sincere dialogue with our children. We need to share and exchange information on the importance of sleep, and empower youth to develop their own plans to smooth

---

35.   Ibid.

out their dysfunctional sleep patterns. This chapter ends with an experimental option called "Suggestions on How to Get a Good Night's Sleep." Encouraging youth to participate in experiments like this provides them with valuable feedback and increases the likelihood of corrective change. Over 90 percent of my students who engaged in even a few of these "suggestions" for a minimum of one week benefited significantly, many in transformative ways.

Julie was one of those students. Julie was playful, inquisitive, and sometimes displayed an acidic tongue. At times she alluded to frustrations at home. She was also someone I considered having fitted for a neck brace because of her frequent fatigue! She knew I did not allow sleeping in my class and tried hard to honor that rule. Here are excerpts from her one-week journal.

Day 1: I chose four of the ten suggestions on your sleep sheet to start my sleep journal. I will stretch prior to getting into bed. I will lie in crocodile for five to ten minutes to deepen diaphragmatic breathing. I will quit eating two hours before bedtime and not overeat. And I will count my breaths while doing 2:1 breathing, allowing my exhalation to be twice as long as my inhalation. You say this will calm my mind and body and should help me drift gently into sleep. I'm betting on you, Mr. Nelson! I have struggled with insomnia a longtime, and it has gotten worse in high school. I feel like a zombie most mornings and can be a bitch when my sleep is messed up, which is most of the time. I feel bad when I lash out at family or friends. I know my sleep affects my moods and energy, so it will be interesting to see if this stuff helps. Well, off to practice my "Suggestions."

Day 2: Last night I did my four practices. I liked the stretching and it helped remove some stress. I lay in Crocodile for several minutes and, though I found it a little uncomfortable, it did seem to deepen my breathing and relieve a little stress. It still took me about an hour before I dropped off.

Day 3: Did the four practices last night, and I think I am trying too hard to get my exhalation double my inhalation, and that tenses me up. Again, it took about an hour to fall asleep. I was still tired and irritable today, and little things still got on my nerves.

Day 4: Did my four things, getting the hang of the double exhalation breathing. Longer exhalations seem to quiet my mind and relax me. The stretching is becoming enjoyable, and I'm getting use to crocodile. I fell asleep in about a half hour. Yippee.

Day 5: Liking this—I'm on a roll. Fell asleep in, I would guess, less than a half hour. I think not eating before bed is helping me, too. I always ate something before bed. I was definitely more alert the last two mornings—normally I don't wake up until after my nap in English class, 3rd hour! Overall, I had a fun day.

Day 6: Sleeping better and I'm not waking up as much during the night. I am groggy the first few minutes after waking up, but then my energy picks up much quicker than before. I love 2:1 breathing! I sometimes do it sitting in class to take my stress away. I notice I am less stressed overall, and I feel more settled. The last two days I had fewer arguments with my family. Even my brother seems to be less of a jerk, and we had a cool talk about our relationship. You don't realize what a miracle that is, and I know it's because of this sleep experiment.

Day 7: Last night was the last day of the sleep experiment. But it won't be the end for me. Poor sleep was a nightmare for me, hey, kind of a pun there! I can't believe the progress I have made in just one week. Here are some benefits I noticed. I am definitely less irritable. I don't feel as sleepy in class, and I have more energy and I can focus more. I am not a zombie for as long in the morning. This has helped me in my first-hour math class, which I hate. I studied and actually understood the material and got a pretty good grade on a test yesterday. I would also say I honestly feel happier and more relaxed. I handle frustrations better. I am going to keep this going because it's becoming natural.

Julie gave me permission to share her journal. I often read these journals to new students as it served to inspire them to give this and other experiments a try. Direct experience leading to self-knowledge is the best teacher. If you as a parent, or as someone who works closely with youth, can engage them in developing their own experiential program, their initial "buy in," as well as their follow through, will be much greater.

One additional sleep deprivation issue worth mentioning is the now ubiquitous request for a "sleepover" by children. I leave it to parents' discernment as to the appropriate frequency and timing of honoring those requests. We know very little sleep takes place at sleepovers, and the effects of this deprivation can ripple for days. An occasional sleepover isn't likely to have enormous consequences. The major issue is that frequent sleepovers could start the pattern of widely differing bed and wake-up times, even before adolescence. This is already taking place with many elementary-age children and it can set in motion sleep struggles that are hard to break, and are emotionally painful.

To summarize briefly, quality sleep is critical, and fewer young people are getting quality sleep consistently. This is negatively impacting their energy, which compounds imbalances in their other primitive urges, causing increases in depression, irritability, emotional reactivity, and other painful emotions, while compromising learning and concentration. In short, the recent societal changes affecting the primitive urge of sleep have had a profound negative impact on their physical, emotional, and mental health and well-being.

It is critical to acknowledge the changes surrounding the primitive urge of sleep, and attempt to reverse this recent trend through dialogue and encouraging self-awareness experiments. The "every-night-is-a-weekend" perspective of adolescents is not easy to change, but I have been inspired by hundreds of students and clients who, once they understood the costs of unregulated sleep, were motivated to explore and maintain positive changes in their sleep habits.

Next, we will examine what is in many ways the most powerful primitive urge, the urge for self-preservation. Self-preservation is the reason we seek food, sex, and sleep. One can make the case, therefore, that it is the most fundamental of the primitive urges. Imbalances and misunderstandings related to the self-preservation urge account for most suffering. A clear understanding of this urge will suggest pathways out of young people's pain, which can lead to a brighter future.

Experiential Exercise:

Suggestions on How to Get a Good Night's Sleep

1. Do stretching exercises before bed to release muscle tension, e.g., the Sun Salutation exercise shown below. This exercise should be practiced mindfully four or more times.

2. Relax in the Crocodile posture 8–10 minutes just before falling asleep. (Shown below.) The upper chest is off the floor and the forehead rests straight down on the arm or wrist. Let the breath gradually become deep and smooth.

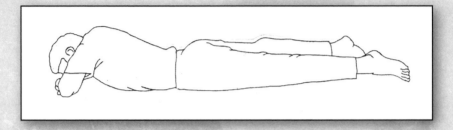

3. Keep regular hours; go to bed and get up at about the same time.

4. Avoid "stimulating" foods—spicy and sugary foods, and caffeinated beverages.

5. Have a cup of warm milk with cinnamon and nutmeg before bedtime to reduce tensions.

6. Eat a light dinner *at least* two or three hours before bedtime.

7. Read something inspirational before bedtime. Thoughts from that reading will carry over and create a positive attitude into the morning's awakening, ensuring that the day will begin on a positive note.

8. Keep to your sleep schedule, regardless of work and life pressures. This will help you be more efficient the following day.

9. Do regular aerobic exercise every day, but not just before going to bed.

10. Cut down on watching computer games, TV, etc., especially in the evening.

A Breathing Exercise for Sleep

When falling asleep is particularly difficult, try the following breathing exercise, gently and with minimal effort.

1. Lie on your back in Savasana as shown below.

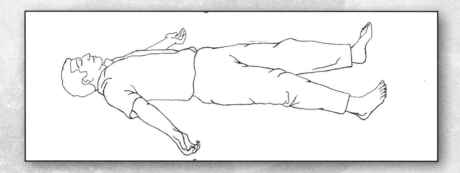

2. Take 8 breaths with your exhalations being twice as long as inhalations.

3. Then roll over to your right side and breathe 16 breaths with the same 2:1 ratio.

4. Then roll to your left side and take 32 breaths, again with the exhalation twice as long as the inhalation.

5. If you are not able to sleep after Step 4, repeat this breathing exercise beginning with Step 1. After a few days, this process will happen without thinking, allowing you to let go and relax at a deeper level. Practicing this breathing practice over time was reported by clients/students to be a key component in improving their sleep.

Most insomnia is due to nervous tension or stress, so it is helpful to keep a sense of humor and not let events weigh too heavily on you. Cultivating mindfulness throughout the day (maintaining a relaxed attention and acceptance of each moment) is the best way to enhance sleep quality. Breath awareness throughout the day can greatly facilitate this mindfulness. This option should be done for a minimum of one to two weeks to encourage change and receive the feedback that will facilitate quality sleep becoming a lifelong habit. Finally, restricting electronic devices in the bedroom with lights and sounds that significantly interfere with deep sleep (delta sleep) is a twenty-first-century phenomena that should be included in the list above.

Chapter 7

Multiple Personality Disorder: The Self-Preservation Urge on Steroids

"To be nobody but myself, in a world which is doing its best
night and day to make me everybody else,
means to fight the hardest battle which any human being can
fight and never stop fighting."

—E.E. CUMMINGS

"All my life, I always wanted to be somebody.
Now I see that I should have been more specific."

—JANE WAGNER

Our most powerful attachments, with their accompanying intense emotional pain, are created through the confusion and imbalances related to the primitive urge of self-preservation. The "four primitive urges," as mentioned earlier, are common to all species in the animal kingdom. The self-preservation desire is the source of the "fight or flight" fear response. In humans, this desire to protect ourselves when threatened through fighting or fleeing gets extended to anything our egos are attached to or have over-identified with. Due to man's creative imagination, the ego's attachments and aversions that develop around the self-preservation urge are subtle, often unconscious, and express themselves in an almost infinite variety of ways. Understanding the emotional pain and confusion the ego's attachments and aversions to objects, people, events, and ideas cause is critical if we are to experience a fulfilling and happy life.

The self-preservation urge is the mother of most of our fear and stress. Every organism wants to *BE*: to live rather than die. Even people who commit suicide do not want to die; they just could not find a way to sufficiently relieve the pain in their lives. An ant spontaneously runs from your finger if you are intent on squishing it. This running occurs instinctively; the desire to flee, or in some circumstances defend, does not have to be taught. In humans, however, the self-preservation fear is represented in a myriad of forms. Most of human's protective energy surrounding the self-preservation urge is used to defend our self-concepts, rather than fighting for our physical survival.

The Proper and Improper Role of the Ego

Humans have an expansive ego. The ego is our notions of who we think we are and who we think we're not. These are usually qualities in our self that we value or reject, because of other's judgments that we have identified with and internalized when we were impressionable children. Positive qualities the self (the ego) identifies with when challenged or threatened often elicit defensiveness. Qualities that we have deemed unacceptable we often repress. When someone accuses us of having those qualities, the ego also responds defensively, often by denying them as the ego fears being associated with those qualities.

These painful and unacceptable notions of self, when repressed, end up unconsciously driving many of our dysfunctional and destructive behaviors. Holding these insecurities, hurts, and fears outside of our awareness also requires a lot of energy, which dampens our joy and enthusiasm. Repression leads us to frequently and unconsciously project these rejected qualities outward, and we end up judging others who exhibit similar qualities. All of this is an outgrowth of the self-preservation urge that in human beings could be called the ego-preservation urge.

The ego is also the aspect of mind that creates a separate sense of self. Our ego allows us to function, act, and carry out our duties in the world. This is its essential role. But, this idea of ourselves as a separate being, "I'm Jim and you are Jane," can also isolate us. If we over-identify with the ego aspect of our personality, it becomes the source of our loneliness and fear. The over-identification of ourselves as only an ego—a personality made up of body, emotions, and mind—obscures the reality that we are, at our core, spiritual beings. That which we call "spirit," "soul," or "consciousness" is infused in all life. Consciousness or spirit enlivens our ego, yet it is beyond our ego and its identifications. The spirit is exempt from the fears and loneliness of the ego—that separate sense of self.

The ego tends to extend itself into everything. The self-preservation urge has been extended by the ego to include the desire for status, power, the accumulation of possessions, and the experiences to which the ego has grown attached. We do not just want to *BE*, the ego wants to be *SOMEBODY*. One of my spiritual mentors compares the ego to a foreman at a factory who forgets his role and starts believing that he is "the boss." He has forgotten that his role is to carry out the boss's directives; he is not the owner. Similarly, our ego's actions need to be guided by our conscience and intuition—our spiritual inclinations. Gandhi said, "I am a lover of my own liberty and so I would do nothing to restrict yours. I simply want to please my own conscience, which is God." Intuition or conscience is the mind receiving the light and direct guidance from God, Consciousness, Spirit, Soul—whatever words we give to that infinite intelligence and wisdom. Intuition, or conscience, represents our deepest inclinations, our better judgment, or our purest feelings. Sometimes we experience this awareness as a "gut feeling."

Television, movies, videos, advertisements, gangs, and other peer group affiliations create images of what being *SOMEBODY* means. The ego is easily influenced by the economic culture's suggestions as to how to attain status, and it makes choices aligned with those suggestions. The constant repetition and promotion of certain self-images leads the ego to strive to attain these "desire-able" notions of self. The ego ends up over-identifying and attaching to hundreds of these often contradictory and limited senses of self.

This over-attachment to the impermanent "little selves" of our personality creates fear in the ego that obscures the "still quiet voice within"—our conscience and intuition. This ego identification blocks the wisdom and joy that is our very nature. The media, for example, creates images of what it means to be a man or a woman. The ego latches onto these limited ideas of acceptable gender qualities, like a man should be strong or a woman should be supportive, etc. These characteristics that we associate with appropriate gender roles and behaviors become little identities. When we fail to live up to these roles or standards, we may feel guilty, embarrassed, ashamed, or inadequate. If, for example, we consider ourselves a very good tennis player and we play poorly and double fault the match away on the last point, our identity as an excellent tennis player is threatened. We respond emotionally and might throw our racket or obsess about our horrible play on our drive home, making ourselves miserable. If someone else criticizes or threatens these "calcified" notions of self, the ego reacts emotionally and feels compelled to defend the false identity.

Many youth, given the dysfunction of their family or due to a childhood trauma, already have a fractured sense of self. Deep-seated insecurities and wounds imprinted in the psyche of their personality create vulnerabilities, insecurities, and defenses. They have many qualities they rejected in themselves because of the hostility or judgment they received as children when they manifested certain personality characteristics or behaviors. These fractured and often unconscious aspects of their ego make working and helping youth struggling with these hurts very challenging.

A Clinical Example of the Ego's Overextension

A thirteen-year-old male client was dragged by his mother into therapy. I decided to first meet with the mother to get some background, and also because her son's eyes were already throwing daggers in the waiting room. I wanted him to have a few moments away from his mother before we met. His mom sat down in my office and began spewing words with machine-gun speed, articulating a stream of behaviors that were getting her son, Ron, into increasingly serious problems. Ron was constantly being thrown into detention for fighting, swearing at teachers, and insubordination of all kinds. The school was threatening expulsion. As she exited my office, her last words were, "Fix him!"

Ron, with his flaming red hair, entered my office with about thirty-five minutes left in the session. He grunted, then turned his chair at an angle to avoid eye contact, slumping like a puffy slipcover, indistinguishable from the contours of the chair. He sat, arms folded, with a penetrating scowl.

I proceeded to ask him questions for the next twenty minutes and received more grunts and short terse answers: "I don't know" and "Maybe" were his favorites. I was used to thirteen-year-old males being non-communicative, but twenty minutes felt like an hour and we were getting nowhere. Then, thank God, for an intuitive flash. Leaving the session early would be the one great motivator for Ron. I told him that he had not been very open with his responses, which elicited a faint knowing smile. I offered to let him go early if he would answer one question honestly.

His posture straightened. "What question?" he asked.

I said he needed to answer the question immediately, with the first thing that came into his mind. He said he would and made me guarantee him, again, if he did, he could leave. "I'm a man of my word, and if you answer honestly, you can leave immediately," I assured him.

I blurted my question loudly with my index finger pointing right at him to discourage hesitation and perhaps scare him into the truth. "Who are you?" I yelled.

He immediately fired back with relish and pride in his voice—"I'm a Bad Ass!"

I had to bite my lip to keep from laughing, but he was serious and began talking nonstop about his "bad ass" behaviors. He started drinking at age eight. He had recently punctured a teacher's tires, and he had a brother who was in prison at age twenty—etc., etc. After going on for several minutes, he caught himself and exclaimed, "Hey, I get to leave!"

He left, but it was the start of a therapeutic relationship.

Ron's short "bad ass" answer spoke volumes. His ego had crystallized around a rigid negative and hostile self-image. He was, however, a *SOMEBODY* by virtue of the degree of his "bad assness." If Ron's whole sense of self can be condensed into two words, then his acting out behaviors at school made perfect sense. My goal as his therapist was to loosen his ego identification so he could notice and nurture some "good ass" qualities and behaviors. Otherwise, he would forever be a prisoner of his own calcified notions of self.

In therapy, over time, I helped Ron remember and recognize that he had another side. It revealed itself in the kindness and love he showed his aging dog. It was expressed with his grandfather with whom he bonded early in life through fishing, camping, and hiking. With his grandfather, Ron was a different boy, respectful and happier. He put his protective armor down, remembering the internalized "good boy" qualities his grandfather's deep acceptance and presence had instilled in him.

Ron, and the rest of us, has hundreds of ego identities. We bring forward a different personality whenever our roles change. For example, at a graduation gathering, we relate differently when talking to our grandmother as opposed to our daughter, or with a sister rather than our boss. Different identity roles change our personality. If these roles are flexible, and we're not too rigidly attached to a specific identity, we and life flow naturally. But, we inhibit growth and change and restrict the awareness of our true self if we become over identified with our transient selves. People's vulnerabilities and insecurities, crystallized fear-based notions of self, are easily exploited by the dominant economic culture and skillful ad agencies. Implicit and explicit corporate values and "image" concerns are deeply conditioned into our youth, whose fragile egos want to impress.

The Media's Manipulation of Ego

Humans extend their sense of self into anything and everything through the language of ego: "my," "mine," "me," and "I." Examples like "My" car, "My" carpeting, or "My" gang—"I'm a Crip" or "I'm a Blood"—gang affiliations that confer status and belonging thereby deepening one's ego identifications. This overextension of one's identity through the language of the ego creates attachments to things that really aren't "us." It's truly a case of mistaken identity. We forget our true self, our spiritual self. Our ego gets attached to things and considers them *ours*, forgetting that nothing is truly ours; we are all renters by virtue of the fact that we all die.

The ego's usurping of our real self has enormous painful emotional consequences. The word "my" and its correlates are the source of most of our misery. "I have a flat tire."

"Oh really, I don't see it. You look perfectly inflated."

The point is: *You* don't have a flat tire; your car has a flat tire. I've seen people kicking their tire when it suddenly punctures or goes flat. This is a tangible example of the ego's overextension and the emotional pain, which goes with this false identification. "My" tire, this inanimate object, has to be kicked and punished for going flat because "my" tire inconvenienced "me."

We cause ourselves so much suffering through this mistaken identity. We have an ego, a separate sense of self, which should take its direction from our true self. The problem is not the ego. The problem is when it thinks it owns the personality (the factory) and grows attached to all the things it believes will embellish it, or the ego becomes averse to anything that it feels would diminish it. In short, when the ego is in charge without direction from the higher self, we get lost, and our attachments and aversions multiply—and we suffer.

Let us look at one more everyday example of the ego's role in causing our emotional pain, through overextending the self-preservation urge. You see an advertisement with an unusually happy salesperson and even happier customer who just purchased a high-quality carpet for 40 percent off. Your existing carpet is still very serviceable but has a few minor wear spots. You "decide" to take advantage of the sale, spend a small fortune, and purchase the carpeting, despite overextending yourself financially. A friend stops by after the carpeting is installed and expresses some distaste for the color choice. "You" are deeply hurt.

We again have somehow attached our sense of self and worth into the carpeting and a thousand other things, and "we" experience hurt. This is the emotional pain or stress inflicted on us by the ego's false identifications. The ego overextends the "self" in self-preservation to include objects, persons, events, and one's beliefs and ideas. Advertisers on behalf of the economic culture play on the numerous strings of ego by constantly tying them to our worth through associating them with products and consumption.

The ego really does feel like it is being attacked when the color choice is questioned. Due to the ego's attachment to the carpet, the friend's comment triggers a fight or flight response. Fleeing, by withdrawing into the hurt, feeling sad and victimized; or avoiding the person who caused the "wound." Alternatively, you might fight by criticizing that person's taste in carpeting to a mutual friend (an ally). You throw guilt, or manifest some other form of hostility, passive-aggressive behavior, or defensiveness. This is the fragile and fearful nature of the ego when it overextends its role, and identifies itself as the capital "I," or the boss. It now has to be infallible and can't make a bad color choice; so the ego feels the need to defend all of its decisions. It loses touch with the true self. The ego's mistaken identity eventually registers in us as some form of pain or stress in the mind.

Attachments and Negative Emotions

Language like "My wife" explains how a person who is emotionally abusive to his own wife still finds it necessary to engage with great ferocity toward someone who criticizes her. Gang names, symbols, and territories are part of this same ego extension. The October 21, 2011, *Washington Post* reported that there has been an alarming 40 percent increase in gang membership between 2008 and 2010, with an estimated 1.4 million youth involved in 33,000 gangs nationwide.[36] Being a gang member is another way for the ego to be SOMEBODY. Youth are often killed when people encroach in someone else's territory or one of their symbols is "dissed." In the news we often hear of people assaulted or murdered over the smallest provocation.

The degree of one's provocation and the intense emotions triggered are not determined by the externals. The intensity of the emotions and reactions are determined by the *degree of attachment or aversion* the "victim" has to a false and limited sense of self. A critical comment about a person's letter jacket, school, car, or appearance can put you in grave danger, depending on the other person's degree of attachment. So, self-preservation, with its egoistic extensions, is the source of our fear. And, fear of a diminished ego is the source of anger and violence.

---

36.   Washington Post, Oct. 21, 2011, as reported on CNN.

Think for a moment. How much of our stress is due to concerns that if we don't do something, or if we don't do it well enough, someone will make a negative assessment of us? This is the pervasive fear of the ego.

Self-preservation and Negative Emotions— A Case Study

Chad, a tall, thin, gangly, and slightly shy seventeen-year-old, like many young people, was searching for a sense of belonging and worth. The culturally suggested "objects" that might satisfy this desire differ depending on the culture. Chad could try to create a heightened sense of value through a particular car, good grades, or a girlfriend. He had done little dating and there was a growing desire in him to take an attractive girl to prom, a combination of his sexual and self-preservation urges. Chad's desire intensified as the time before prom was growing short. He had a growing interest in Linda, whom he had in several classes, and he knew she was not dating anyone at the moment. Chad spent each night rehearsing and mulling over dozens of scenarios as to how to approach Linda. He miraculously was paired up with Linda for a lab session by his biology teacher; and though it wasn't one of his rehearsed scenarios, he courageously asked her to prom.

Linda's initial smile and playfulness were encouraging. Chad's expectations and attachment grew until she said, "I will let you know in a couple of days." Chad's anxiety, born of this uncertainty, spiked. The next morning Chad saw Linda laughing with a couple of guys before school, and his fears that his goal was slipping away heightened his concern. This triggered preexisting insecurities about his looks. He was too skinny. He needed a haircut. His ears were bigger than he remembered. Chad's thoughts only escalated his anxiety, and he couldn't sleep. He was concerned that he wouldn't achieve his goal and that he would lose what was once looking promising. He begins to experience several painful emotions.

A person can desire an object, a person, an event; or can cling to an idea held dear. When that desired item is threatened, that person experiences negative and painful emotions.

Which negative emotion a person, or in this case Chad, will experience depends on:

Fear of not achieving "object" = anxiety. "What if" thoughts focused on negative outcomes in the future begin to dominate Chad's mind. Due to his ego's concern about failure, his fears become obsessive and Chad plays out catastrophizing scenarios over and over in his mind. "If she says no I will be left alone at home on prom night. What an embarrassment." Chad can't sleep and professes, "I'm stressed to the max."

When "object" is not achieved = anger or hurt. Linda rejects his prom offer and his preexisting insecurities lead his ego to accept the notion that it is "rejectable." Chad punches a wall and breaks his hand.

Loss of "object" = grief or sadness. Linda says "yes." Chad is elated but learns on the day of prom that she has strep throat and can't go. He retires to his room, sulks, and plays sad, dark music, which further deepens his grief and despair.

When others achieve your goal = jealousy or envy. Linda goes to prom with one of the "losers" she was talking with before school: *God, he's lucky. It must be the new car he drives,* Chad thinks. This rationale, offered up by Chad's ego, is a cover-up for Chad's preexisting feelings that he is not enough, that he doesn't have what it takes to land a girl like Linda.

The desire for a date or girlfriend isn't the problem. It is Chad's growing expectations and attachments intensified by preexisting insecurities and fears. Human beings with the help of their ego create stories about their deficiencies, which often become self-fulfilling prophesies. It is important to find a truer self-confidence that isn't ego based, if we are to avoid the negative emotions that result from the ego's misidentifications around the self-preservation urge.

Self-Preservation, Abandonment, Self-Injurious Behaviors, and Suicide

The fear of abandonment and bonding issues appear more prevalent in young people. We now have more families where both parents are working and more single parent homes. This shift, combined with treadmill-like schedules, results in babies only weeks or months old spending significant time without a primary bonding figure. It is also more difficult for a growing number of exhausted and stressed-out parents to muster a deeply attentive focus with their children.

Kind, focused, and sustained attention for children is how they experience love that provides the security necessary for healthy development. Many children get less quality and quantity of sustained attention from their parent or parents, particularly early in life. Many youth, as a result of stressed family environments, carry a deep-seated feeling that they are more of a burden than a joy. Some carry significant feelings of abandonment. This is not always conscious, but deeply felt, and often revealed only in a crisis. Children's feelings of being a burden to exhausted overwhelmed parents, coupled with bonding disconnections, are likely factors in the dramatic increases in the diagnosis of borderline personality disorder, or people suffering from borderline "traits." These symptoms or traits include unstable and intense personal relationships, strong feelings of abandonment, unstable self-image, impulsivity, inappropriate intense anger, suicidal behavior or self-mutilation, and affective instability (sudden mood changes). More youth are exhibiting these traits.

Normally, trauma, family conflict, physical or sexual abuse, or emotional neglect are the historical factors involved in the development of a borderline personality. In all of these situations, the developing ego's security is threatened at an early age. Early bonding problems, leading to unconscious feelings of disconnection and abandonment, may be contributing to increases in youth's borderline symptoms. Intensified stresses on families often create less presence and joy in parenting. This is likely experienced by children, subtly over a long period of time, as insufficient emotional support, leading to internalized feelings of being a burden. These feelings of being a burden or not mattering, along with bonding issues, contribute to youth's risk of developing borderline traits. This is often dramatically expressed in self-loathing borderline behaviors like cutting, self-mutilation, and suicide attempts.

We know some of the fastest rate increases in suicide attempts are in our youngest age groups. Twelve- to fourteen-year-old children's rates for suicide attempts have increased by 89 percent in the last couple of decades.[37] A study, in 2008, indicated more than half of college students surveyed had already seriously considered suicide at some point in their lives.[38] To counteract these horrendous trends, we have usually sought a pharmaceutical solution. The use of antidepressants has gone up 400 percent in the past two decades.[39] The steepest increase was among young children. This has occurred despite the fact that antidepressants, with the exception of Prozac, were never approved for children under eighteen. Despite a flood of pharmaceutical interventions, depression and suicide rates have continued to climb. The United States, with 4 percent of the world's population, consumes 52 percent of its medications.[40]

A Harvard doctor who researched antidepressants for thirty-six years concluded[41]: for mild to moderate depression, antidepressants perform at the same level as placebos in ameliorating depression. Taking a pill for depression helped in some cases, but that improvement was unrelated to the chemicals contained in the pill. Improvement was dependent on the belief or expectation that the pill would help, and this expectation was more likely if patients had a positive connection to their doctor. Britain also launched a review of antidepressant efficacy, and came to the same conclusion as the Harvard research. Antidepressants in Britain are now only prescribed for those suffering from severe depression. The doctor and the British Medical Review both found widespread and systematic deception on the part of drug companies to intentionally conceal studies that revealed no difference between placebo and antidepressants.

Antidepressants are an $11 billion industry. There are serious side effects to these expensive and powerful medications that got lost in the profit-motivated deception. These include habituation requiring higher doses (leading to even higher profits), increased risk of suicide,

37. "Screening for Suicide in the Pediatric Emergency and Acute Care Setting," by M.B. Wintersteen, G.S. Diamond, and J.A. Fein, Current Opinion in Pediatrics, 19(4), 2007, 398–404.

38. The Dr. Phil show, aired in 2008.

39. Twin Cities Channel 9 News, Fox affiliate, aired Oct. 4, 2011.

40. Ibid.

41. 60 Minutes, February 19, 2012.

intensification of depressive symptoms when use is terminated, and the chemical alteration of a developing child's brain.

People with borderline personality disorder often suffer from severe depression and, therefore, antidepressants may be helpful. We all carry some abandonment feelings, which is the core symptom of borderline personality disorder. Everything is on a continuum, but the increasing frequency of the borderline diagnosis in youth and at earlier ages is alarming. Borderlines' abandonment fears and perceptions lead to chaotic relationships, which often rupture. They struggle with a consistent sense of self-worth. Borderlines often exhibit intense anger that damages relationships, or they turn on themselves by cutting or engaging in other forms of self-injurious behavior. This is often triggered when they perceive a potential abandonment or a possible rupture of a significant relationship.

Steven Levenken, author of the book *Cutting,* said, "I never met a cutter who liked herself." Dr. Bessel van der Kolk, a psychiatrist from Boston University, discovered something very revealing about cutters. He discovered cutters could keep their arms in ice water for much longer periods of time than non-cutters. They did not feel the pain.[42] Research reveals cutters carry an inner sense of numbness or deadness. Self-injurious behaviors of all kinds are not usually an expression of suicidal intention, but are more related to the desire to feel *something.* It may be that some of youth's emotional flatness, occasionally punctuated by extreme high-risk behaviors, is an outgrowth of the same historic factors that drive some self-injurious behaviors; that is the desire to feel alive.

Self-injury can also be a desperate attempt to gain control of overwhelming anxiety when things feel out of control, or a person fears a relationship is rupturing. Cutters are often perfectionistic, and despite outward appearances, are filled with self-loathing. Borderlines, whether they cut or not, struggle with chronic depression, and are at risk for suicide. Cutting and other self-injurious behaviors are increasing in youth. This behavior reflects a self-loathing, feelings of numbness, things being out of control, and a belief that they don't matter that much. Sometimes youth's seemingly conceited and arrogant actions

---

42. "Helping self-mutilators find their pain" by Judy Foreman, Star Tribune, Health Section, May 11, 2003.

belie the truth: Their arrogance or ostentatious behavior is their ego's feelings of inferiority masquerading as superiority. There really is no such thing as a superiority complex. Often, however, borderlines express little of this bravado, just lifelessness and a penetrating, to use their own words, "emptiness."

Bulimia and anorexia are also showing up in greater numbers in youth. These illnesses share with people suffering from borderline personality disorder that same sense of emptiness, lack of control, and self-loathing. Are there causal links between the dominating influence of the hectic and image-conscious economic culture, and the internal struggles of borderlines, bulimics, anorexics, and escalating young people's suicide rates? Could the pace of life embedded in that culture contribute to stress, family fractures, and bonding failures that leave youth alone struggling with self-esteem scars, feelings of emptiness, and a subtle but penetrating sense of disconnection or emotional abandonment?

Is living in an economic culture, which creates tremendous imbalances in all four primitive urges, sapping the energy of youth, which makes coping with the challenges of life more difficult and overwhelming? Causal links are hard to prove. What we know is that depression and suicide rates for youth have increased dramatically, along with other self-destructive behaviors, including drug addiction, cutting, and dangerous thrill-seeking behaviors. We also know that the economic culture has become a dominating force in our family, social, relational, and political lives. The economic culture's values, explicit and implicit, are usurping the religious, ethical, and spiritual values of our society, while creating a frenetic pace that is robbing many children of the parental presence essential for feelings of love and security.

It is now almost impossible to effectively regulate all four primitive urges, whose imbalances are the source of all stress and painful emotions. Poorly regulated primitive urges sabotage youth's energy and contentment, making their successful navigation of an increasingly complex world more difficult. What is increasingly clear is that chasing the frenetic dreams and desires promoted by the economic culture will not lead to happiness.

It is worth re-emphasizing that the stronger our aversions, attachments, and expectations are linked to our four primitive urges, the stronger the emotional reaction when they are threatened. This is why people with borderline personality disorder struggle with regulating the intensity of their emotional reactions. The underlying fear of abandonment triggers primal fears of survival or self-preservation that bring forward what seem like unreasonable emotionality. The link between the intensity of one's emotions and the degree of one's attachment was *burned* into my mind through a dramatic lesson learned from youth. This time my teachers were my own children.

Another Lesson on Detachment

I went outside on the porch to grab a log for the fireplace. I was shocked to see "my" Volkswagen Jetta on fire in my driveway. It was parked close to the house, and I foolishly entered the burning vehicle in an attempt to put it in neutral and roll it down the driveway before the flames engulfed the house. Just at that moment, my wife Candice came out and screamed at me to get out of the car. She startled me as I had never heard her yell like that, and I quickly exited the car. We called the fire department, warmly bundled our two elementary school-aged children, and rushed them out of the house. The fire was consuming more of the garage and had started to incinerate the porch. My mind was racing. I felt intense anxiety and some anger as it seemed to take forever for "my" fire department to arrive. I say mine because I was on the city council at the time.

I was suddenly struck by the calmness of my children. In fact, they seemed delighted when most of the neighbors ran over, and they seemed almost giddy when a third fire engine pulled into our driveway. They actually laughed when our car exploded, and gazed with almost scientific interest as the car began a slow melt into the driveway. I, on the other hand, had been watching anxiously as firemen's axes destroyed the walls adjoining the garage of "my" house. I had helped design this house, and "my" house was being attacked with flailing axes.

Finally, I began to laugh as my children's demeanor helped me to detach. My attachment had caused me to enter a burning car, minutes before it exploded. My children's calm and playful manner reminded me I had no control over the event, but my emotions were mine to choose. My unconscious attachment to the "me" who designed "my" house had caused my painful emotions, not the event itself. I let go and, like my children, just watched the show. I adopted my children's perspective that we were at a neighborhood bonfire, a block party.

A year later, my wife called me at school, crying. Our new car, which had replaced the melted Jetta, had also spontaneously combusted. The fire department was there; things were under control, but the fire had burned almost identical parts of the garage, porch, and house, while melting another car. You cannot make that up. Two silver cars catching fire, without an obvious cause, led my insurance company to cancel our policy. They must have thought someone in the family was a pyromaniac. This time, however, the detachment lesson I had learned from my children had been internalized. I realized immediately I could not change this odd reality, and though I did not invite anyone over for a marshmallow roast, I remained calm and emotionally neutral.

An interesting sequel to the mystery of the car fires took place years later. A day before I was to return from India to the United States, friends had encouraged me to see a Vedic astrologer who they had found quite amazing. I had never been into astrology, as it runs against my scientific leanings. However, I decided to go when a friend said, "Jim, you really have to see him. It is like he lived with me during some of my most difficult years. He was so accurate." I figured for a few rupees, eleven US dollars, I had little to lose.

The astrologer surprised me by stating immediately that my son did not live in the same state as me, and many of my relatives were educators and writers. He continued, saying that I had an opportunity to run for a high public office and turned it down. He described my bathroom tile, said my wife had stomach issues. All of this was accurate. He was uncanny, and I had not even said anything yet, other than to give him my birth date, and time and place of birth.

He said I should write. There was much more, but what startled me the most was when, in the midst of a sentence he stopped and stated firmly and with emphasis, "You need to quit driving silver cars! They invite bad karma." I sat in silence and never shared the burning cars stories. I also did not tell him that right before coming to India, because of my good credit rating, I signed on the title for my son's new silver Jetta. He had made the purchase; but at that point, until we had time to transfer the title, it was technically my car. The day after the new silver Jetta purchase, I forgot that the new car was parked in my driveway, and I backed out of my garage and smashed the entire passenger side of his new car!

This burning car incident reveals once again that it is the degree of one's ego attachments or aversions to something that determines the intensity of one's emotional reactions. When our conditioned attachments, many promoted by the economic culture, are threatened, and we fear we might not achieve them or could lose what we have achieved, we will experience stress of one kind or another.

It was very helpful to explain to young people the relationship between the four primitive urges and a person's energy and emotions. They were often able to see how the choices they made, driven by their desires and attachments surrounding one of these urges, had led to their subsequent emotional reactivity and pain. Young people, like everyone else, have attachments around their self-worth that create destructive habits. We cannot change anything we are not conscious of, and habits are things we do unconsciously. We can, however, help youth increase their awareness so that they can consciously examine their attachments and the stories they create around them. This awareness can help alter habit patterns that otherwise would keep them stuck in cycles of recurring pain.

One experiment that helped increase students' and clients' awareness was to have them notice each time they became defensive. Defensiveness reveals an area of insecurity and the false identification of the ego, an attachment to a limited notion of ourselves. Could they internalize that whatever they felt compelled to defend, really could not add or subtract from their inherent worth, the value of their soul? Many learned to accept rejected parts of themselves, and "embrace their shadow," to use the terminology of psychologist Carl Jung. Some were able to see that their defensiveness was driven by fears that were echoes of childhood scars.

Awareness and Self-Acceptance

I walked into the classroom wearing a sign around my neck that read, "I get controlling when I'm uncomfortable with my feelings." Students in the back squinted to read it, and all seemed interested and amused. "Remember I won't ask you to try something I myself have not experimented with or tried." We had been discussing personality theorists, the last being the famous psychologist Carl Rogers, who encourages giving oneself "unconditional positive regard." I reminded the students of yesterday's discussion of the transformative power of self-acceptance.

"Are there any brave souls who would be willing to join me in walking the hallways with 2,500 students and staff gawking at you, broadcasting a weakness of yours?" I asked.

Questions streamed forth: "How long do we have to wear the stupid sign?"

"Do I have to wear it to work?"

"How much extra credit do I get for making a complete fool of myself?"

"You have to wear it one full week, including at least one place other than school. Work generally isn't a good place to wear it, as it would be disruptive. You will get fifteen points of extra credit by keeping a daily journal and summarizing your experience."

"I don't know what to put on my sign" was a frequent comment.

"Write on it some aspect of your personality that you have judged to be a weakness or flaw; a characteristic you don't like. If nothing comes to mind, just ask your parents. They are likely to have an idea or two for you," I suggested with a smile.

"No one should do this if you will feel strong shame, though all of us are likely to feel a little awkward at first. The idea is these 'weaknesses' don't take away from us being worthwhile; we can't lose our basic worth. We will start tomorrow, but check with me about what you're planning to put on your sign. Remember it has to be readable from a distance."

Approximately one-fourth of each class came with signs the next day. Many of the signs were artistically decorated, while others were thrown together quickly. Occasionally a brave student's sign would be hung over their head, displaying their message on both sides of their torso. It looked like they'd been hired to walk up and down a sidewalk promoting a local restaurant: "Eat at Joe's."

The signs said things like:

"I judge people constantly."

"I have a sarcastic sense of humor."

"I am easily irritated."

"I'm often defensive."

"I hide my feelings."

"I don't like myself when I get angry."

Students were encouraged throughout the week to accept themselves just as they were. They were to reflect on their self-assessed weaknesses and imbalances and the consequences of these habit patterns. I kept reminding them that these signs reflect only habits that may cause us problems, but they cannot cancel our inherent worth. I reminded them that it is only the ego that fears experiencing the loss of its worth, and that the ego is just a cluster of habit patterns. These signs were often transformative as they brought a constant self-awareness of a habit or limited sense of self that students recognized had created some kind of disharmony for them.

Friends and other students often attempted to trigger the weakness broadcast on the sign as they walked the hallways of school. By the end of the week, this actually had an "inoculation effect"—it made many students less emotionally reactive. They became more neutral or detached, and more accepting of their weakness. Their buttons could not as easily be pushed or triggered by outside circumstances. This acceptance allowed for some integration and an actual reduction in the expression of their "flawed" behavior. In just a single week, their increased awareness and self-acceptance almost always softened or diluted the habit pattern, while pointing the way for continued progress. This increased control and reduction of a longstanding habit that they were motivated to change proved very satisfying for them.

It often required courage to be so transparent, wearing signs broadcasting weaknesses in the hallways with their peers, at a time where peer relationships are youth's lifeblood. Adolescence is a time, across the globe and in all cultures, when youth prefer the company of those their own age. In the October 2011 edition of *National Geographic*, an article entitled, "The New Science of the Teenage Brain," makes a convincing case that much of the desire for teenage peer connection is part of human's evolutionary developmental process. Adolescence, in every culture, is the time of greatest risk-taking behaviors that can expose youth to grave danger. This desire for peer connection and risk taking, researchers demonstrated, is part of the brain's maturation and

an evolutionary process that prepares adolescents for future independent adulthood.[43]

The research surprisingly revealed that adolescents solve problems
and assess risk in the same way and as successfully as adults do. This is
true with one exception. If adolescents are assessing risk-taking decisions in front of their peers, the likelihood that they will take a risk
doubles. The natural adolescent development that predisposes them to
seek peer connection and acceptance makes risk-taking behavior in
peer environments more likely. Combine this with the fact that an
increasingly hectic and fractured family life has magnified the likelihood that many of this generation's youth will be raised more by their
peers than by their parents. This only exacerbates youth's maturational
and peer-driven tendency toward risky behavior.

Youth's willingness to wear a sign, given the possibility of varying
degrees of peer rejection or harassment, was an act of courage. Their
journals also revealed that this experiment for some students touched
underlying painful childhood hurts of rejection and powerlessness.
Facing and healing these hurts will require a sustained courage, beyond
one week of wearing a sign. August Wilson points to the value of
emboldening this courage: "Confront the dark parts of yourself . . .
Your willingness to wrestle with your demons will cause your angels to
sing." Carl Jung knew how hard this self-exploration was: "No one can
become conscious of the shadow without considerable moral effort . . . It
involves recognizing the dark aspects of personality as present and real."

Yet, the question of how real these dark aspects of our personality
are is a good one. The word personality comes from the Greek word
persona, meaning a mask. Who is behind the mask and conflicted
aspects of our personality? We will address this question more specifi-
cally in Chapter 19, but Ralph Marston hints at an answer:

> Often it will occur that one part of you desires something that another
> more enlightened part of you knows is not right for you. When this happens,
> it is helpful to remember that neither of those conflicting urges defines you.
> The mere fact that you're able to see the conflict within yourself means

---

43.   "Beautiful Brains" by David Dobbs, National Geographic—The New Science of
      the Teenage Brain. October 2011.

that you are able to rise above that conflict. The fact that you're able to perceive what you're thinking and feeling means that the real you is beyond those thoughts and feelings. When you are longingly tempted to overindulge, or to become angry or resentful or hurtful, and yet know it is not right for you, remember that you can take a step back. Step back to a place where you can look objectively and lovingly at the conflict within you.

Being in such a vantage point, you can let yourself fully experience the desire without allowing that desire to take control of you. You can let that desire out in the open where it harmlessly burns itself out, and then be done with it and free to follow the course you know is right. Inner conflict can be difficult to resolve when you're stuck in the middle of it. So step back to the real you that exists apart from the conflict, where you can settle it peacefully and effectively.[44]

Students, through the increased awareness the signs provided, were able to step back and observe rather than automatically and reflexively respond out of habit. They caught a glimpse of a witnessing presence in them that transcended their habit patterns.

The stronger our attachments, the more intense our emotional reactions will be when those attachments are in jeopardy. These strong emotional reactions indicate attachment to the things of this world or the strength of our identifications with or aversions to limited notions of self. "I'm smart/dumb, athletic/clumsy, jock/freak, ugly/cute, too tall/ too short, etc." All of these "little transient selves," the notions and self-images that we carry around inside our minds, bring forth negative emotions when they are challenged.

Awareness, or neutral observation, brings a nonjudgmental spotlight on our attachments and aversions, and the story the ego creates around them. "No one gets away with putting 'me' down." This kind of statement is worth examining as to the specific personality characteristics we have identified with that trigger the ego's strong emotional reactions. Even after we have responded emotionally to something, it is still worth examining the button that got pushed and ask whether it is truly "me." It is likely just an aspect of our personality that we have

---

44. Ralph Marston, from his "Daily Motivator" quote, January 6, 2003, http://greatday.com.

over-identified with that manifests once in a while, but has no permanence.

Changing deep-seated habit patterns of ego identification is hard work, and it takes time. It is worth doing this hard work, as it allows us to gain more control over our emotions and not live as a victim of circumstance. "The house is burning" is a nonemotionally laden fact, until it becomes "my" house. Analyzing our emotional triggers with a detached perspective increases the likelihood of happier, more harmonious relationships, and we more easily access the joy beyond our self-restrictive identities.

Transcending Limiting Self-Preservation Identities

He leaned into Room 108 as the bell rang, just as he had almost every day of the semester. "I'm here and right on time," Jerry would announce with a barely perceptible smile. Jerry was built like a brick fortress, six-foot, two inches tall and 240 pounds with perfectly square shoulders that you could build a skyscraper on. He had short muscular arms that widened like Sumo wrestlers at his biceps. Jerry wore bib overalls every day, lived on a farm, and was a quiet, observant young man of few words. He was bright but skeptical of ten-dollar words. He always spoke the truth as he saw it. We were just completing a semester of modern world history. Jerry particularly liked the units on Nazi Germany and WWII.

Today was the day students would register for next semester's classes. I was teaching a philosophy class, paired with an English creative writing course. I highlighted some classes and teachers Jerry might enjoy, as he had already told me: "I don't think philosophy fits me and I'm not into writing."

So, when the new semester started, and I heard "I'm here and right on time," as the bell rang, I was more than a little surprised. I was particularly concerned if Jerry would survive the creative writing course. Jerry had revealed a "just the facts, man," writing style. Four weeks into the quarter, I conferenced with Jerry to inform him that he was flunking both classes. Jerry needed the credits, but seemed content to sit in the back row and give me the "I dare you to teach me" look.

The only day Jerry showed any interest was during the third week when several martial arts black belt instructors were illustrating the power of a concentrated mind. Much of the junior class was in the auditorium, enamored with the boards and bricks breaking, as well as the effortless "flipping" of their fellow karate experts. The head of the karate studio, at the end of the demonstration, asked if there were any questions. Jerry raised his hand and exclaimed, "I think it's all a bunch of crap; you couldn't flip me if you wanted to."

I could see a flash of ego on the face of the black belt instructor as he said, "Come down here, young man."

Jerry walked to the stage with the deafening cheers and encouragement of a few hundred students. Mark, the black belt owner of the studio, said, "It's all about leverage, young man. I don't want to hurt you, so my assistants will lay down some extra mats. When I say, put out your hand, prepare yourself for the flip." Jerry uttered something I was glad I couldn't hear. "Ready? Extend your arm."

Jerry extended his arm, the instructor went through numerous gyrations, but Jerry didn't budge. Mark turned red, the crowd went wild, and Jerry was a celebrity; but he was still flunking.

As I conferenced with Jerry, I told him we were going outside today, which seemed to prick his interest. I told him if he participated today, I wouldn't harass him for the rest of the quarter, even if he chose to flunk.

"What are we doing outside?" he asked. "Everyone has to find one thing to absorb their mind in for twenty minutes. It could be an acorn, a blade of grass, a tree, or the clouds passing overhead," I said until Jerry interrupted. "Then what?" he asked with a dreary skepticism.

"I will signal the class to come inside from the football bleachers, and then you are to write a poem about your experience."

His response I remember like it was yesterday, "I ain't poetic."

"How do you know that?" I countered. "You haven't written or turned in an assignment yet."

He ignored my comment and replied, "So, if I give it a shot, you'll get off my back?"

"Yes, I will get off of your back, but, only if you really invest yourself for fifteen to twenty minutes in the activity."

Jerry and thirty other students dispersed in the field and trees that abutted the football field. Twenty minutes later, I signaled the class to return. They came in and immediately started writing. Most looked deeply engaged, except Jerry, who didn't return. I felt some anger as I felt I had been played for a fool. Jerry was probably sipping a pop at the nearby convenience store. I was playing out in my mind what punishment I should dole out, and then I looked to my right down the hallway. There was Jerry wandering toward class, starring at a dandelion, with a glazed look on his face. I decided not to break his trance-like state. He sat down without a word and wrote feverishly until the period ended. The bell rang and he enthusiastically offered his paper at the end of class, asking me to please read it. I told him I was late to my next class clear across the building. I assured him I would read it tonight, and give him feedback tomorrow.

For the first time **ever**, Jerry came early to class. "Did you read it? What did you think?" he asked excitedly. I saved Jerry's poem for years until it was recycled along with most of the student journals. I still remember the title and a portion of the opening lines. "Ode to a Dandelion" by Jerry S . . . "The crimson sun broke the horizon, gently caressing the gold-leafed petals . . ." The whole thing was exquisite poetry, and I told him so.

He smiled and said, "I guess I am poetic."

Jerry changed that day. He was more willing to try new things, and he passed. He had suspended his self-limiting notions of self. He had allowed a deeper, heretofore buried intuitive intelligence express itself in all its grandeur. He had transcended his contracted unconsciously crafted image and discovered that he was more expansive than he thought. He was poetic! Steven Pressfield captures the significance of Jerry's transformation: "Our job in this lifetime is not to shape ourselves into some ideal we imagine we ought to be, but to find out who we already are and become it."

The ego by its very nature limits our full potential. When our attachments are threatened or we cannot acquire the desires of the ego's cravings, we experience fear. Fear is contractive energy and, therefore, it is limiting. If you analyze the kind of stress created by the ego's attachments, you will come to the conclusion that almost all stress is fear. Eckhart Tolle, in his bestselling book *The Power of Now*, says this in a clear and compelling way:

Fear seems to have many causes. Fear of loss, fear of failure, fear of being hurt, and so on; but ultimately all fear is the ego's fear of death, of annihilation. To the ego, death is always just around the corner. In this mind-identified state, fear of death affects every aspect of your life. For example, even such a seemingly trivial and "normal" thing as the compulsive need to be right in an argument and make the other person wrong—defending the mental position with which you have identified—is due to the fear of death period. If you identify with a mental position, then if you are wrong, your mind based sense of self is seriously threatened with annihilation. So you as the ego cannot afford to be wrong. To be wrong is to die period. Wars have been fought over this, and countless relationships have broken down.[45]

As long as we have identified ourselves as our mind, the ego will run our lives. The ego, our ideas of who we are and aren't, because of its impermanence (it is not our true self), is vulnerable to fear and insecurity. *Every* negative or fear-producing thought resulting from our ego's extension of the self-preservation urge depletes our energy. A person can have thousands of these stress-producing thoughts daily. Each fear thought is like a tiny hole punctured into a tire. It starts as a slow leak that is irritating, but with each additional puncture the growing energetic leak leaves us emotionally "flat" making it difficult to engage life, and we find ourselves in a rut and deeply depressed.

These little selves of our ego are threatened anytime we judge ourselves as inadequate, or we do something inconsistent with some idealized sense of self. Our self-images and identifications can also be challenged or threatened by others. This seems to be triggering more hostility, anger, and sometimes horrific violent behavior from young people, born of their ego's fear and "need" to be respected. Fear is the cause of violence and hostility. The ego is always scanning for danger; for some potential threat to its self-created identities. The insecurities that spawn the ego's fears and generate violence and anger are often unconscious, because the ego is unwilling to face the pain that accompanies those insecurities. Increased hostility among youth is reflected in their growing number of arrests. An article in the December 19, 2011, Minneapolis *Star Tribune*, entitled "An Epidemic of Arrests in US," points out that by age twenty-three, 30 percent of youth have already

---

45.　The Power of Now, Eckhart Tolle, Namaste Publishing Inc., 1997, 36.

had a significant brush with the law.[46] This is more than a 25 percent increase since 1965, and it's worth noting that these figures are dramatically higher than almost any other country.[47]

Violence that can lead to arrest often occurs in situations where youth say they were disrespected or "dissed." What has happened to make a perceived lack of respect such a common trigger for youth's rage? The dynamics that we discussed earlier where more youth are exhibiting borderline traits might also apply here. Increased violence and emotional volatility may also be an outgrowth of youth carrying unconscious feelings of being more of a burden than a joy. These violent youth, like people suffering from borderline personality disorder, seem hypersensitive to any form of rejection. This may also be due to subtle bonding failures imprinted in the psyche of children early in life. Bonding issues, combined with stressed and fractured families with preoccupied parents, can lead to deficits in meeting children's emotional needs. These childhood deficits create a largely unconscious lack of self-worth and self-respect, which manifests in intense emotional reactivity when they perceive someone has disrespected them. This can take the form of road rage when someone cuts them off, or them "going off" on someone whose voice carries a tone of criticism or judgment.

This violent behavior expressed by growing numbers of youth is damaging our entire society and is significantly influenced by the frenetic pace, messages, and the values of the economic culture. There are additional effects of that culture we need to examine before a clear path to greater harmony and contentment can fully emerge. In the next chapter we will expose how our four primitive urges are manipulated by advertisers to get us to buy products we don't need and often can't afford, suggesting a degree of happiness destined to disappoint. Ad agencies employ powerful psychological techniques to serve the economic culture, creating desires that produce painful consequences in the emotional lives of youth.

---

46. "An Epidemic of Arrests in US" by Erica Goode from the New York Times, Star Tribune, Dec. 19, 2011.

47. Ibid.

Exercise:

Three Strategies That Support Youth's Emotional Awareness and Growth

Start by encouraging awareness of the feelings that underlie their anger, anxiety, or depression. Have them name the fear or hurt—"I am scared I am going to lose you,"—as opposed to expressing controlling behavior, or always masking feelings by labeling it anger, which is really an expression of fear and hurt. "I feel hurt and disrespected when you relate to me that way," as opposed to acting out or closing down from feelings altogether. "I feel sad and alone, and that's why I drink or get high. I need help in working with these feelings," etc. Getting someone to journal and share the specific feelings underlying the anger and depressed mood can be very useful.

1. Encourage young people to face their hurts and qualities they dislike about themselves with acceptance and compassion. Ask them to imagine a hurting "child" within that needs comforting and encouragement. Visualize that child. Offer words or bring forward visual images that communicate understanding, love, and support.

2. Bring a fear or hurt into your mind intentionally. Imagine you had a volume control so the feeling is there, but you adjust it so it does not overwhelm you. Imagine a warm blanket of compassionate light enveloping that fear or hurt, bringing comfort and healing. Maintain deep, relaxed breathing. Breath is tied to our emotions, quiets the autonomic nervous system, relieves anxiety, and maintains a link to the present moment. We don't get lost in the pain, we mindfully witness it, and allow for its energy to rebalance itself.

3. Youth who are inclined toward meditation should be encouraged to initially read articles or books that they self-select on meditation. Encourage them to do an experiment for a month where they meditate daily for at least ten minutes. They can usually receive guidance as to how to meditate from the articles or books they read. If not, the suggested meditation practice at the end of Chapter 19 is an excellent beginning practice. Meditation gradually connects them to an aspect of themselves that is whole and unwounded, which helps them disidentify from their negative self-images. Father Flanigan, who started Boys Town, reminds us, "There are no bad kids, just kids with bad habits."

Caregivers need to be compassionate and relatively emotionally neutral. Maintaining unconditional acceptance of youth is itself a salve that helps heal youth's self-rejecting wounds.

Chapter 8
Pavlov's Dogs
Have Nothing on Us

"Asked about the power of advertising in research surveys, most agree that it works, but not on them."

—ERIC CLARK

"Many a small thing has been made large by the right kind of advertising."

—MARK TWAIN

We have demonstrated how imbalanced choices around the primitive urges of food, sex, and sleep are reflected in us and in our youth's energy and emotions. What percentage of all advertisements involve in some way one of these four basic urges? The answer would be 100 percent if it were not for the few public service ads, which often run in the middle of the night as a requirement of the FCC. Advertisers understand that our primitive urges are linked to emotions and they use that knowledge to powerfully influence our choices. Each of us is now exposed to approximately 3,000 advertisements a day, which amounts to a year of our life, and is more than a person sixty years ago would have been exposed to in their entire lifetime.[48] Many people's lives, and particularly their discretionary time, now revolve around shopping and watching television.

Inside the "Locker Room" of Advertising— A Personal History

My last undergraduate course was a Psychology of Advertising class. Throughout the quarter, I raised questions that seemed to occasionally irritate my instructor. I was concerned these questions might come back to haunt me as his tests were all essay questions, and grading them would allow him more subjectivity. The questions I raised were largely about the ethics of turning humans unknowingly into two-legged versions of Pavlov's dogs. I was worried when the instructor asked me to remain after class once I had finished the final exam. I completed the final and waited for other students to leave. I was stunned when instead of him expressing his frustrations about my irritating questions, he offered me a job in his advertising firm.

More than once, I have lost my way in the enticements of the corporate world. So my first question wasn't about the nature of the job or working conditions. "What would it pay?" immediately catapulted from my mouth.

"Within two years, $50,000 would be a reasonable expectation," he replied.

I needed a job, and $50,000 was the equivalent of $200,000 in 2012 dollars, but I couldn't accept the offer. Something deep within me at that moment of enticement whispered, "No," and I honored that voice of conscience.

The advertising class had revealed the power of pairing primitive urges with products to manipulate wants into needs. For most consumers, this is largely an unconscious process designed by advertisers to develop strong positive emotional associations with their products. At age twenty-one, I already had deep concerns about the environmental degradation caused by conspicuous consumption; and this, along with

---

48. Story of Stuff, Free Press, A Division of Simon & Schuster, Inc., 2010. Also refer to YouTube video by Annie Leonard.

my ethical concerns regarding the manipulative techniques of advertising, made no the right answer.

Distorting the Hunger Urge—Advertisements and Emotional Imbalance

What are the links between our hunger urge and the positive emotional associations to products created by advertisements? In my twenties, when the imprint of how advertisers manipulate consumer demand was still fresh in my mind, I watched commercials carefully and with a jaded eye. Many food commercials grabbed my attention. Their slogans have stayed in my mind years later, a testimony to their effectiveness. "Aren't you hungry for Burger King now?" A slogan and brand name paired with pictures of the perfect hamburger, frosty shake, and sizzling French fries reached through the television and grabbed hold of my mind. "Sure it's 10:30 at night, but I guess I could grab my keys and pick up something to eat."

I rarely got in my car, but I often caught myself not long after these food commercials in a semiconscious robotic walk to the refrigerator, grazing for something to eat. A desire had been created, and I "needed" something to satisfy this urge, hungry or not. One day, while watching a Dairy Queen commercial on television, I caught myself tilting my head sideways. I smiled to myself, realizing that I had been unconsciously attempting to catch the potential spill of a Blizzard that had been turned upside down in order to emphasize its thickness. The ad wizards had again cast their magic spell.

The positive associations to food products created through advertisements stay long after the ads are over. The association of their products with one or more of the primitive urges creates subtle emotional attachments to these products. These attachments happen automatically and unconsciously because our four primitive urges are the fountains of our emotions. Advertisers aren't really interested in enlisting the viewers' intellect because they know emotions trump reason when it comes to forming strong attachments. In advertisements, including food advertisements, everyone is attractive, happy, and energetic, due presumably to the product advertised. In reality, the

103

food they are promoting may be energy depleting, but the positive visual images associated with the product create desires and attachments. Advertisers are in the business of creating emotional attachments to maximize profit, regardless of any negative long-term consequences.

The strength of advertisers' conditioned attachments is evidenced by the fact that we often eat foods whether or not we are hungry, even knowing that there are many health consequences to overeating. Beyond the comatose feelings that cloud our perceptions, overeating stresses the liver, pancreas, and heart, creating imbalances in the autonomic nervous system. Over time, this takes a terrible toll on our energy and overall health. The awareness that we aren't hungry is muffled or ignored due to a powerful desire system implanted into our minds by advertisers. Despite the happy and energetic pictures, youth are left to deal with the numerous unhappy consequences of imbalances caused by manipulating their hunger/thirst urge. Consequences like obesity, diabetes, and fluctuating energy can cause emotional regulation problems and a crippling lethargy, and potentially an earlier death.

Anxiety also plays a role in the obesity epidemic affecting more of our youth, because it affects our hunger urge. Anxiety is a "what if" fear thought, which brings our mind into the future in anticipation of some potential negative consequence. These thoughts cause a moderate, but constant, level of stress that causes us to eat without awareness. For example, we put jam on a piece of toast as we gaze out the window, looking for a friend who is late picking us up. We are concerned that something bad might have happened to our friend, and we get lost in thoughts with negative scenarios. Sometime later we look down and are surprised to see only crumbs left on the plate. We have no memory of eating the toast, but the crumbs remain as evidence.

This is proof that we do not taste with our tongue; we taste with our minds. The mind jumped to future fantasies about the reasons for the friend being late and missed enjoying the toast in *this* moment. "My mind was absent, I did not see; my mind was absent, I did not hear; my mind was absent, I did not taste," is an ancient expression of the mind's critical role in sense perception. Stress-producing what-if thoughts deny us the satisfaction of deeply enjoying our food, which contributes to overeating. When our mind is preoccupied we think, *I didn't enjoy or savor that last piece of toast, so I will have another.*

There is another way our stressful what-if thoughts (we imagined our friend injured in a ditch, crying out for help) can contribute to obesity. These thoughts can cause us to reach for food for comfort. We are not just seeking psychological comfort, but are unconsciously trying to slow down our anxiety-revved sympathetic nervous system through overeating. Overeating engages the parasympathetic nervous system and calms us down. This neurotic eating is a crude way of seeking balance, and unfortunately contributes to us eating when we're not hungry, which is a key contributor to the obesity epidemic. We do a lot of this unconscious nervous eating. Just watch someone at a suspenseful movie with a suitcase-sized popcorn tub and observe whether they appear to be savoring every kernel.

It is said that depression grows in the rich soil of fatigue. A person struggling with depression often responds to advertisers' artificially created desires for poor-quality foods that deepen their fatigue, further feeding their depression. The thirty extra pounds they gain during the year from overeating, as their body craves missing essential nutrients, only worsens their condition. Their self-loathing thoughts increase as a result of their weight gain. This deflates their sense of worth (ego preservation), and takes an additional toll on their mood. We know that every stressful and negative thought saps energy, which annihilates our hope and impedes our will to change.

Sex and Advertising

There is literally almost no product that has not been paired with sexual imagery. Food, beer, cigars, clothes, toys, videos, chain saws, cars and trucks, and guns are but a small sampling. But my personal favorite is men's and women's colognes. I would have a tough time naming current colognes for women, but they are probably similar to when I did pay attention. My Sin and Aviance are a couple still in my memory bank. The musical jingle for Aviance trumpeted, "You're going to have an Aviance night." If you saw the actual ad, you would have no doubt as to what an "Aviance night" meant. The advertisements for Obsession, a cologne for men and women, if you trusted the magazine ad pictures, pretty much guaranteed you a week-long orgy.

There are many sensual names for women's colognes, and Chanel No. 5 didn't seem that sexy. The name may not be suggestive, but the voice and images in the advertisement surely were.

Scene I: A woman sitting in her swimsuit at the very edge of one side of the pool, legs somewhat apart.

Scene II: A man in a Speedo stands at the other end of a long Hollywood-looking pool directly across from her, and he dives in. He swims the length of the pool under water. You lose track of him due to the camera angle, until suddenly he pops up right between her legs. You might have just as well said, "Here comes Herman the Sperm." At the moment he pops up between her legs, a woman's raspy and sensual voice exclaims, "Experience the difference—Chanel No. 5!"

The Power of Ads—Best Selling Does Not Equal Best Quality

Now if you think this is all just imagery and doesn't impact youth's sexual attitudes or their emotional attachments and purchasing decisions, I have two examples for your consideration.

Close-Up toothpaste became the number-one best-selling toothpaste just weeks after the release of its first commercial. I'm sure it was Close-Up's superior ingredients. I still remember this commercial, perhaps because I was a young man at the time, and I was part of the target demographic. The ad took place in a classroom of high school or college students. An attractive young man and woman, both with terrific teeth, by the way, caught each other's eye. A few sexy glances were exchanged, and a pair of perfectly shaped lipstick marks ended up on his cheek. These images were paired with several mentions of the Close-Up name. I remember thinking at the time, *How stupid!*

We often have that reaction to many inane commercials. But, this isn't about the intellect or the product's ingredients. These commercials are all about our four primitive urges, the fountains of our emotional energy that are paired over and over again with their products to elicit a positive emotional attachment. These attachments happen automatically just as they did in Ivan Pavlov's experiments with dogs. Dogs naturally salivate when they see or smell food. Ivan Pavlov did an experiment where he rang a bell just before giving his dogs food. Soon the dogs salivated to the bells because they were paired with the food. Salivating to bells is not natural dog behavior. We too are conditioned to "salivate"—to have a visceral and positive emotional association to specific products. Advertisers call it branding, but it is sometimes more akin to brainwashing. Add a little music to the sexual imagery to enhance the emotional and visceral response, and you have a best-selling toothpaste in a few weeks.

Music is also linked to our emotions and you will notice a lot of music in commercials. Many of us can remember where we were and who we were with when a particular song comes on the radio. I remember my daughter, less than a year old, walking down the hallway away from the television set when evocative music from an advertisement started playing. My daughter literally whipsawed her head to look at the commercial, smiled, and began rhythmically moving—dancing, if you will. She loved the song or the jingle in the commercial, and in time she would sing along. This was a powerful demonstration of how skillful advertisers can grab hold of the psyche and emotions even of a one-year-old. There are thousands of television ads directed at children to create desires so they will lobby surrogates, known as parents, who will purchase products on their behalf. Despite no significant difference in the ingredients of toothpastes, repeated sexual imagery paired with the Close-Up brand got enough people to salivate it into a best-seller.

I am not proud to admit that I am exhibit number two, highlighting advertisers' powerful influence. I hope that by sharing my own vulnerabilities when I was a teenager I can reveal how advertisements prey on personal insecurities. Remember, we can't help having our four primitive urges, because they are fundamental to our very existence.

I weighed only forty-six pounds in fourth grade, and "bulked up" to ninety-seven pounds by the time I entered tenth grade. My parents, perhaps aware that I was called "shrimp boat" by some of my peers, did their best to assuage my growing insecurity about my body and the toll it was taking on my sense of worth. My parents bought me a glue-like liquid called Weight On in fourth or fifth grade. Perhaps its glue-like consistency was designed to plug every orifice in one's body so nothing could escape, and you had no choice but to gain weight. Regardless, after several months of

Weight On, I still hadn't gained a pound.

I wanted to join a football league at the beginning of sixth grade, but you had to weigh a minimum of sixty pounds to participate, and I only weighed fifty-six pounds. My loving mother "force fed" me bananas, bread, potatoes, and other carbohydrates in massive quantities for the week leading up to the tryout. Despite her best efforts, I went from fifty-six pounds to a whopping fifty-eight pounds. So, with time running out, she carefully sewed two or three pounds of weights concealed in the two back pockets of my football pants.

I arrived at the football field feeling confident, but bloated and sluggish, and I saw no scale. I asked a coach where the scale was and when the weigh-in would take place. He smiled and said, "Oh, we gave up that requirement two years ago." I was horrified that the lead in my pants would somehow be exposed and even more concerned when he blew his whistle and announced, "We are going to do time trials to test your running speed."

Let's just say that "lead-butt Nelson" didn't make it at wide receiver that day.

In seventh grade on Christmas Eve after all of the presents had been opened, my dad announced that he had an extra present just for me. My three envious brothers followed me downstairs where my father revealed a weight set. I was so appreciative of my dad's concern and kindness, and thrilled that I now had a means to add some muscle to my frame. My dad, thankfully, and I am sure intentionally, put only five pounds of weight on each side of the barbell. I went to "jerk" it over my head and, to my shame and embarrassment and the smirks of my brothers, I couldn't do it. I spent the first several weeks working out when my brothers were absent, lifting just the twenty-two-pound bar.

This history reveals the growing insecurity surrounding my physique and my appearance, which was compounded by the growing acne that blanketed my narrow face as I entered high school. I had an unfortunate proclivity for having my largest pimple or "zit" breaking out at the tip of my already large nose. My "friends" called me Rudolph at Christmastime. In the spring just before prom, Rudolph returned early. Luckily, I had just discovered my mom's Cover Girl in her makeup drawer. This gave me a false sense of confidence, as I skillfully covered my acne. Two years later, carpooling to the University of Minnesota with high school friends turned college buddies, I was horrified when one said, "Glad you gave up the Cover Girl; it looked ridiculous." I felt a huge wave of embarrassment, having assumed that I had successfully fooled everyone.

Insecurities and Advertising

This personal history of insecurities is similar to the self-esteem fears with which many adolescents struggle. The cultural notions of masculinity and femininity weigh heavily on millions of youth who do not meet the standards portrayed in the media. These media images reinforce unrealistic, superficial, and impermanent notions of self that delay and obfuscate a deeper experience of their true self—the spiritual self.

My internalized shame about my body compared to the cultural prototypes was unconsciously driving many of my "choices." Perhaps you will not be too surprised at the three colognes that, at age seventeen, sat on top of my dresser. My three favorite and unconsciously chosen colognes were: High Karate (these advertisements highlighted power and athleticism), English Leather (with the slogan, "My man wears English Leather or he wears nothing at all"), and my absolute favorite, Brut, which requires no further explanation.

If you would have asked me at the time, I would have said that I freely and conscientiously chose these colognes and supported my assertion with some articulated nonsense about their fragrance. In reality, the ego-preservation fears or self-esteem concerns had been linked to sexual images and cultural messages suggesting the urgency of having sex appeal. The messages and imagery in these advertisements for colognes spoke to my largely unconscious underlying insecurities and desires, playing on the primitive urges of sex and self-preservation. How deep these childhood insecurities can run is also revealed by my tendency even now to overeat due to the eating patterns established during this period.

Cologne names for men are carefully chosen by advertisers and are always "manly"—Iron, Axe, Musk, and others reinforce a certain masculine image. Musk sounds like you're rotting from the inside out, but it sounds macho. I'm waiting for our corporate consumer culture which has image-making as a central focus to offer a new cologne for men, something like Mule Sweat. "Mule Sweat for the man's man." This is obviously farfetched, but recently I saw an ad for a new cologne for men named Bacon. They add a little squiggly line over the "o" to slightly alter its pronunciation, "bay cone." It's apparently sexier with this more "French" articulation.

Using sex to boost sales for even the most inane products works and makes sense, to advertisers. The constant bombardment and sexual titillation of the senses, however, is inappropriate for much of the audience that will be exposed to advertisers' seductive imagery. The FCC imposes restrictions on what children can view in children's programs and advertising; but this provides little real protection, as a high percentage of children view adult programs that have minimal restrictions. This barrage of sexually suggestive messages and imagery implicitly suggests that our primary identity as a human being is as a sexual being, and this should be our primary concern and pursuit. Sex expressed lovingly is a wonderful thing, but it is worth noting that sex is the only primitive urge that we can, if circumstances require, live without. So sex is not as primary to our identity as advertisers suggest. To the extent that a constant sexual focus distracts us from the discovery of our spiritual self, it will serve to create emotional pain and disappointment.

Research shows that we are more vulnerable to purchase products the less engaged we are during the commercial. The images and suggestions apparently slip more easily into the unconscious the more mindlessly we stare at the commercial. Understanding the importance of increased awareness for learning and change, students were encouraged to watch commercials more consciously. They were asked to observe the association between a product and the specific primitive urge that was being manipulated. The more conscious they were of the process of pairing a product with one of the four primitive urges, the less susceptible they would be to the commercial's suggestions. They would be better positioned to make a choice about purchasing something they needed, versus salivating to an artificial want built on insecurities and image concerns. Consuming products in an attempt to compensate for our fears, hurts, and insecurities does nothing to alleviate or heal them, despite advertisers' seductive claims. We launch a desperate and unsuccessful effort to gain or project worth through consuming products, but this leaves us anxious and aware at some level that the relief they offer is fleeting.

Ads Devoid of Conscience

The preeminence of the profit motive in creating artificial desires was profoundly illustrated during a recent trip to India. I had come down with a bacterial illness, lost a lot of weight, and was eventually brought to a hospital. I was watching Indian television while waiting for the doctor. An advertisement for an air freshener-like product was being promoted. It had flowers and fruits on its label, and it plugged into a wall socket. Young children and a mother enthusiastically danced and paraded back and forth, taking a deep whiff of this air freshener with its new "raspberry aroma." The end of the ad revealed that what I had thought was an air freshener was in fact a multiscented aromatic pesticide that would be released continuously into the family's home to kill bugs.

Advertising and Sleep

Finally, let's examine sleep aids and the advertisements that promote them, as they are part of a multibillion-dollar industry. Pharmaceuticals and bed and mattress manufactures have spent millions developing and promoting solutions for our sleep problems. Their commercials make compelling claims; using their products will help you fall asleep quicker, sleep sounder, and awaken feeling rested and refreshed. Certainly there are circumstances that definitely merit considering their use. People struggling with increasing sore or deteriorating knees, hips, and backs often report that certain types of mattresses alleviate some of their discomfort.

I had insomnia that started in elementary school and continued through high school. It would often take me well over an hour to fall asleep. Sleep medications have colorful ads that are enticing to millions suffering from sleep problems. I was skeptical of the promises and the potential side effects, and never considered a sleep medication. The insomnia I suffered at that time, however, is likely what allows me to still remember in great detail sleep advertisements from that era.

Cue the music: "Take Sominex tonight and sleep, pure and restful sleep, sleep, sleep . . ." A nice little jingle to help remember their product. Pure sleep sure sounded good, along with the scientific studies backing their product. "Studies show that most people who take Sominex fall asleep 27 percent faster." This was convincingly illustrated by a line on a graph.

Scene: "Having trouble sleeping?" The person pictured looks like she hadn't slept for five years and she was featured with rat's nest or Einstein-like hair.

Scene 2: The woman, having discovered Sominex the night before, arises and greets the sunrise with a huge smile, arms stretching to the sky, fully energized. And, miracle of miracles, someone snuck into her room in the middle of the night and did her hair. This robust and zestful imagery is the way we would all like to awaken, and Sominex was obviously the key.

I recognize there are extreme cases where insomnia is out of control and drugs may briefly be necessary. Long-term use of sleep medication, however, increases the likelihood of falls in the elderly, causes moodiness, and actually often increases insomnia due to habituation. This habituation produces a rebound effect where one's insomnia is equal to or even greater than the original level after the drug is terminated. This illustrates that the actual causes of the insomnia have not really been addressed. Sleep medications may suppress symptoms, but the underlying causes remain untouched. The reality is that the causes for almost all sleep problems begin in the mind. How we handle the challenges of life and the choices we make around our four primitive urges are the real sources of sleep disturbance. If we have irregular sleep times; wind our minds up with fear, worry, and anger; don't exercise; and eat poorly and late at night, we are all likely to experience sleep problems.

There are many potential significant side effects directly linked to sleep medications, as evidenced by the steady stream of seemingly endless warnings at the end of their commercials. My eighty-eight-year-old mother, after being prescribed a new sleep medication promoted as having fewer side effects, was found at 3:00 a.m. blocks from her house after falling down. She was lying in the middle of the street, hallucinating, and her visual hallucinations continued for two days. Doctors at the hospital determined she was prescribed a sleep medication that was counter-indicated for her age and health conditions.

There are effective and available options for insomnia beyond drugs, but you won't see an ad for them because they cost nothing. They do require more self-discipline and sometimes a few lifestyle changes that aren't available in a pill. They require good regulation of the sleep urge and consistent practice to help facilitate positive change. They have no side effects and, as mentioned in Chapter 6, they have helped hundreds of students, clients, and friends alike. Advertisements for sleep medications are seductive because we all want a quality night's sleep, and a third of adults and even a higher percentage of adolescents struggle to attain that restorative sleep.[49]

Imagine we are struggling with falling and staying asleep and most mornings we awaken with little energy. Our primitive urge for rest or sleep is now heightened. We see an advertisement pairing sleep medication with images of great sleep. These images start the process of us forming an emotional attachment to their drug. We decide to discuss this with our doctor and she prescribes the pill the advertisement suggested. We initially sleep somewhat better, and our attachment to the sleep medication grows. Over time the medication doesn't seem to be working as well, and we again visit our doctor to get her suggestions.

Emotions erupt when the doctor is unwilling to refill the prescription. She's concerned we may be habituating, or fears we may be developing an addiction. Suddenly we're flooded with negative emotions. Which emotion we express depends on our relationship with the doctor and the nuances of our personality. It may be anger, despair, anxiety, or all three. Our minds have already begun to anticipate that the nightmare of insomnia is again going to take over our lives. It is not withdrawal from the medications that accounts for our emotions, because that process hasn't begun. Attachment to a product that

---

49. "Hey U wassup?? Let's zzzzz . . . on tweeting and textings' effects on sleep" by Kristen Tillotson, Star Tribune December 26, 2011.

initially helped and is now being denied brings anger and triggers what-if thoughts about our insomnia worsening, spawning our anticipatory fear. Pairing products with primitive urges tied to our emotions is the bedrock psychological process that advertisers use to condition an attachment. This increases profits. It also increases the likelihood of emotional reactivity when those objects are threatened, or you are unable to acquire them.

Attachment and Intense Negative Emotions— A Personal History

The first time I remember making a dim connection between attachments and emotional pain was when I was seven. It was Christmastime and my two older brothers asked me if I could chip in a quarter to buy our younger brother, Jack, a gift. I said yes, and we decided to buy him a fishing lure, and we settled on a Dare Devil. We knew this would be a big deal for my brother as he was about to turn five years old in January. We had a cabin, and it was our family's rite of passage to receive a rod and reel around age five. Coming from a family of four boys who loved to fish, it was like an initiation. So our Dare Devil was both a precursor for, and a complement to, the upcoming momentous fifth birthday for Jack.

We bought the Dare Devil, and later that day began carefully wrapping it in nice Christmas paper. Suddenly, the plans changed. My two older brothers had hatched a new idea. They wanted to substitute a Snickers candy bar for the Dare Devil lure. I knew something sinister was afoot, but I wasn't sure what. I knew Jack would have preferred the Dare Devil, but he really liked Snickers, too; so I didn't make much of this change.

The sinister aspect of this plot was later revealed, as every day my brothers planted and watered seeds of expectation with my unsuspecting brother, Jack. They would have Jack shake his small present from Santa. They then said things like, "I think I heard metal sounds, almost like hooks or something. You don't suppose it could be a lure? No, probably not. Nobody has ever gotten a lure before their fifth birthday, and you're only four!" Later, I noticed my brother, when he thought no one was watching, shake his little gift and smile.

Christmas Eve came and when Jack's turn came to open his first present, he rushed to the tree and grabbed the little rectangular box. He had larger box options, but you could see his excitement as he ripped off the paper and opened the box. My parents looked confused and concerned, and I too was surprised when Jack burst into uncontrollable sobbing and then suddenly bolted to his room, slamming the door. The intensity of his pain was confusing, as I thought he would have still really liked the Snickers.

It is obvious now that it wasn't the Snickers that caused my brother's powerful and painful emotions. The seeds of attachment and expectation, which were planted and watered daily, had grown to huge proportions and then were crushed suddenly and unexpectedly.

Advertising and Self-Preservation

Lexus commercials skillfully link worth to consumption, playing on our self-preservation urge. "Lexus for discriminating buyers . . . with Quatra . . . (something or other) breaking system," an erudite voice comments while gripping visual images emanate from the television. Filmed on a stormy night, lightning strikes and a tree falls; but Lexus's unique braking system stops the car just before imminent death. This commercial is actually "doubling up" on our self-preservation urge. We are SOMEBODY because we drive a Lexus and the Lexus saved our life! Our ego, always concerned about self-preservation, often in the form of status, had better consider a Lexus even if it puts us further into debt. Perhaps we could fudge a bit on our income taxes so we could afford one. It is no accident, no pun intended, that Jaguar and Cadillac also often have an elitist tone in the voiceovers in their commercials.

Advertisements for GPS systems, roadside assistance, security systems, and many other products play on our self-preservation urge. Advertisers skillfully use exaggerated fear imagery to enliven our attachment to their products. Political ads are notorious for exploiting the self-preservation urge. Some self-preservation commercials actually suggest we will be abandoned if we don't buy their products. You will sometimes see this in underarm deodorant ads, where people walk off elevators that we just stepped onto because we forgot to apply their brand of underarm deodorant. A similar ad shows people recoiling in horror because we haven't discovered a certain brand of mouthwash and suffer from the humiliation of "morning mouth." All of these seemingly innocent ads hit the unconscious hard, as abandonment is a deep-seated fear. Humans have the longest dependency period of any species, and real abandonment is terrifying because one's very existence is threatened. The unconscious doesn't discriminate between real situations and these visual images and messages, and it responds to the advertiser's suggestions with fear. This abandonment motif embedded in commercials instills an unconscious powerful emotional attachment to the advertiser's product, regardless of its quality or our need for it.

This process of growing attached to the economic culture's ever-expanding list of desirable objects, supposedly offered to satisfy our food, sex, sleep, and self-preservation urges, affects all of us. Advertisers associate their products and notions of worth to these built-in urges, forming attachments that later become the sources of our stress and negative emotions. They do this far more skillfully then my older brothers' crude attempts at manipulating my brother Jack's desires. In fact, there has been a coalescence of cultural factors that have made youth more vulnerable to the corporate culture's manipulation of youth's desires. Janet B. Schor, in her groundbreaking book *Born to Buy*, comments on this "perfect storm":

> By the 1990s, the stage was set for a thorough revolution in youth marketing. Kids had unprecedented spending power. They had unprecedented influence over their parents' spending power. They were watching unprecedented levels of television. And they were on their own far more than the previous generation had been. Now the trick was to get them to buy the products on offer.
>
> The companies responded by upping their ad budgets substantially. . . . Companies hired psychologists, child development specialists, anthropologists, and sociologists to help craft more compelling messages. They developed far more capacity for testing and research and they began delivering their messages in new ways. . . . A number of research outfits now devote enormous time and energy to figure out how to get kids to get their parents to buy stuff.[50]

---

50. Born to Buy by Juliet Schor, Scribner Publications, 2004.

Much of marketing aimed at children are products that used to be directed at older adolescents. There is now a heavy emphasis on the "cool factor," including sophisticated marketing to preschoolers enlisting their ego-preservation urge, their sense of worth, to hook them into buying products. Because children are naturally egocentric and are concrete thinkers, this wedding of worth to personhood easily latches on to the young child's psyche. All that is left is to frequently change the notions of cool, and you have a lifelong anxious consumer. Schor cites a famous study by Cheryl Idell of advertisers' effectiveness in creating a "nag factor" in children, to successfully lobby parents to buy products on their behalf. Schor summarizes Idell's findings:

> Seventy percent of parents are receptive to their children's product requests. A third of them she called indulgers, that is, impulse buyers who don't mind their children requests for nonessentials. Fifteen percent are "kid pals." Childlike themselves, they allow children significant impact on brand selection. Another twenty percent are "conflicted" who dislike kid advertising and don't like their children's requests for nonessentials, but find them hard to resist. That leaves only thirteen percent unaffected by nagging, a "bare necessities" group Idell describes as conservatives whose purchases are well considered.[51]

This commercialization of childhood can lead to spoiled children who are oversexed, more conflicted with their parents, obsessed with status, and unable to distinguish their sense of self from the products they acquire.

Attachments as Addictions

A great deal of our time and energy is spent trying to satisfy the desires that spring out of our four primitive urges. It is in seeking to gain these objects of our desire, or trying to hold onto them once we have grown attached, that we can become anxious and stressed. Our desires, when too intense, can throw us out of emotional balance. It is akin to

---

51. Ibid.

an addict who has become dependent on a drug and then explodes emotionally when he is denied access to it. This is just an extreme example of what leads to unpleasant emotions in all of us.[52] We, too, have become intoxicated with events, people, and the objects of the world—wrapped in images of happiness beautifully packaged, and presented by the pervasive power of the economic culture.

The disappointment when these alluring products turn out to be just trinkets and "fool's gold" causes us to respond in ways not dissimilar to the drug addict. We assumed the high would last longer, and we seek to recapture it by purchasing more. Initially we have many "lures" to choose from, and we get hooked again. All of these enticements end up falling short of our expectations; and, like the addict, we, too, begin to habituate.

A deep malaise begins to settle in as this process has been repeated a thousand times. Like people without water in the desert, we continue to seek even more desperately the next mirage ahead. Many thoughtful young people who I met in therapy or in the classroom come to a point of quiet desperation and ask themselves, "Is this all there is?" This is a necessary place to arrive at, but not a good place to call home. It is a way station for reflection, and a prerequisite for transformative change. It is harder to keep pursuing what we know won't satisfy us, the economic culture paradigm of happiness. We can sink deeper into our existential despair, or chart a new course.

---

52. Emotions to Enlightenment by Swami Rama and Swami Ajaya, Himalayan International Institute of Yoga Science and Philosophy, 1976.

Experiment:
Becoming Conscious of Advertisements

When watching an ad, step back and witness what suggestions are embedded in the ad. In what ways do they try to create positive associations toward their product? How are they enlisting your emotions to strengthen that association through music or other means? What primitive urge is being played on in order to strengthen the association and our emotional connection? What aren't they highlighting that might be a down side of purchasing the product they're promoting: cost, environmental, or other "side effects"? Is the product a need or a want? Some products are beneficial and necessary. Some are fun. Could you be happy without them?

Chapter 9
"I've Got Some Swamp Land in Florida..."

"They, blinded by greed, do not see evil in the destruction of the family, or sin in being treacherous to friends."

—Bhagavad Gita

"The world is too much with us; late and soon getting and spending, we lay waste to our powers."

—William Wordsworth

The economic culture is selling a notion of happiness that is fleeting and destined to fail, while pushing products consumed by millions that have little real value. Many of these products trivialize life as they are not linked to purpose or meaning. The pursuit of and interaction with these objects as a main focus of people's lives keeps everyone occupied, busy, stressed, sometimes broke, but rarely content.

World-renowned anthropologist Margaret Mead bemoaned fifty years ago the new stresses placed on the family: "Nobody has ever asked the nuclear family to live all by itself . . . with no relatives, no support; we've put it in an impossible situation." Pressures on the family have only increased since that was written. Economic changes and demands cause geographical separation that obliterates the support of extended families, leaving parents alone to navigate a changing and more difficult world. Mother Teresa also poignantly captures the family and societal consequences of the economic culture: "Everybody today seems to be in such a terrible rush, anxious for greater developments and greater riches and so on, so that children have little time for their parents. Parents have very little time for each other, and in the home begins the disruption of the peace of the world."

Most of what we purchase is the result of conditioned desires and wants, rather than needs. These nonessential products end up in landfills or stacked in our garages or closets for years, leaving the cleanup for relatives who outlive us. We now generate 4.5 pounds of garbage per person per day, which is three times more than just thirty-five years ago.[53] This is only a fraction of the actual waste generated because for every can of garbage we fill, seventy cans were generated in their production and distribution. Much of this enormous waste problem is attributable to industries' planned obsolescence, wherein products are designed to last for a limited period of time. There is also a conditioned "perceived obsolescence," wherein we are seduced by advertising into believing we need the latest fashion or tech toy. All of this conspicuous consumption increases international tensions, deteriorates water and air quality, and threatens entire ecological systems for future generations. Perhaps we could rationalize this waste and destruction if it created a lasting happiness. However, as individual consumption escalated from the 1950s to current epic proportions, the National Happiness Index declined steadily throughout that same period. Young people are now lost in a fast-paced world and a consumer culture that exhausts, isolates, alienates, obscures purpose, and decreases overall happiness.

How did the economic culture become so pervasive, and so effective at promoting unexamined values that eclipse traditional values? Traditional values, such as the importance of moderation, other-centeredness, thriftiness, stewardship, service, simplicity, refining one's character, and respect and civility toward others, are losing ground to

---

53. Story of Stuff, Free Press, A Division of Simon & Schuster, Inc., 2010. Also refer to YouTube video by Annie Leonard.

the hedonistic values of the economic culture. Respect for the sacredness and interconnectedness of all life, and the need to protect our natural environment, are all but absent in our current economic paradigm.

Contentment dies when these values are usurped by an economic culture that promotes events, activities, and accumulation of things as the pathway to happiness. People are left with various levels of disappointment and despair. Many of us, including parents of struggling youth, realize something is awry. We, too, are often overwhelmed or too busy to contemplate how the seeds of despair are being sown.

Escalating Parental and Family Stress in the Economic Culture

It is harder to be a parent because the negative trends are relatively recent and intensifying. Limit-setting for children was easier when the whole culture supported those limits. Children more readily accepted limit-setting when the extended family and even neighbors could participate in setting boundaries. When the whole community is saying no, the idea that your selfishness is right, and they are wrong, hardly enters a child's consciousness.

It is harder now to create cohesiveness and a community with a shared set of values. The average American moves sixteen times in their lifetime, often for economic reasons. This relatively new geographical mobility compromises the support provided by the extended family, makes close relationships with neighbors more difficult to create, and isolates and places more demands on the nuclear family. Even the nuclear family isn't so nuclear, as increasing demands of the economic culture overwhelm it, leading to divorce and single parents with increasing numbers of children born outside of marriage and many others raised in fragmented or blended families. Even in two-parent homes, there is heightened stress as both parents work, making family-friendly schedules difficult to create and coordinate. This leaves most parents stressed and overextended, particularly given the torrent of activities many youth are enlisted in, which makes children's basic need for positive sustained attention very challenging to satisfy.

In the last few years, research shows more parents are consciously trying to allocate more time to their children despite busy work schedules. This is a great trend, which needs to continue. These parents admit, however, that in order to create this extra time, they have to engage in multitasking while with their children. When parents who have made this commitment are surveyed, they share that they feel rushed and stressed while trying to meet this sincere commitment. This likely compromises the degree of relaxed presence, connection, and deep listening they can bring to these moments with their children. This may be why in a national YMCA study, teenagers rated not having enough time together with their parents as their number-one concern.[54]

Media Values, Family Cohesiveness and Empathy

Numerous other forces are rupturing the cohesiveness of the family. Children withdraw to their own rooms and chart their separate entertainment schedules for the evening or weekend. Many have their own televisions, computers, video games, and other electronic diversions in their room. There many seek out "reality" shows. Reality shows often have a formula where they film emotionally immature, emotionally imbalanced, and emotionally fragile people, acting out or engaging in extreme excesses of one kind or another. Every year there is a need to push limits further, showing more extreme behaviors in order to keep their easily bored voyeuristic audience engaged. The net result is a gradual normalization of aberrant behaviors, which causes a gradual but continual downward shift in youth's values. This "craziness" seems normal to many youth because it is what they have grown up with. This shift in the norms of civility erodes traditional values and negatively influences choices and behaviors. It creates more friction within the family and threatens the cohesiveness of the larger society, as children aggressively push limits. This causes additional imbalances in youth's four primitive urges, increasing their emotional suffering and leaving many young people confused as to the cause for their growing dissatisfaction.

---

54. Talking with Teens: The YMCA Parent and Teen Survey, Global Strategy Group Inc. Final Report, April 2000.

In the past, gathering around the only family television set, whatever its limitations, at least provided some family connection. The family shared a common experience, perhaps laughing or even crying together. Though it was still an electronic medium, it provided some level of family interaction, relationship, and shared experience. Research shows, however, that excessive television and media viewing increases youth's anxiety and fear, leads to poorer diets, poorer academic performance, desensitizes them to violence, and negatively impacts exercise and health. Dr. David Walsh makes the case in his book, *Selling Out America's Children*, that children, ages three to ten, who watch excessive hours of media with sex, violence, and humor are also impacting their brains.

He argues that the limbic system of the brain, when stimulated by sex, violence, and humor, restricts the development of neuronal pathways in the prefrontal cortex of the brain.[55] The limbic system is strongly linked to our emotions. The cerebral cortex is responsible for conceptual ability, abstract ability, empathy, and assessing potential consequences of our actions, helping to regulate our negative emotions. Excessive media exposure, whose themes are often sexual, violent, and riddled with sarcastic humor (hostile humor), means more children will have a restricted ability to empathize. They will be less likely to be concerned with how their behavior affects others. In short, they have effectively been "programmed" to have an underdeveloped conscience.

Research has demonstrated that humans are hard-wired for empathy. However, in our Twitter and texting world, we briefly engage our attention and move on. New research suggests this can contribute to "continuous partial attention," which leads to "social numbing."

> From a social perspective, what's limited isn't attention, but *consideration*, not just hearing but listening, not just seeing a message but understanding its meaning. It may be worth considering how we structure our digital world if the point wasn't just to "pay attention" but to give consideration."[56]

---

55. Raising Non-violent Children in a violent world by Dr. Michael Obsatz, Augsburg Fortress Publisher, 14.

56. "Social Networking and the Brain: Continuous Partial Empathy?" by Jamais Cascio, Fast Company, April 14, 2009, regarding the research by Antonio Damasio and Immordino-Yang.

Science affirms that for empathy and compassion to be fully expressed, it requires time and our full attention. When our prefrontal lobes are bombarded by a constant barrage of stimuli it triggers our self-preservation urge and the fight or flight response. Our higher brain centers shut down and give way to the emotional and more primitive centers of the brain. A 2005 *Harvard Business Review* article put it well:

> [W]hen you are confronted with the sixth decision after the fifth interruption in the midst of a search for the ninth missing piece of information on the day that the third deal has collapsed and the twelfth impossible request has blipped unbidden across your computer screen, your brain begins to panic, reacting just as if that sixth decision were a blood thirsty, man-eating tiger.[57]

This split and interrupted attention, so characteristic of our current culture, not only leads to stress and exhaustion but it also blocks the orbital prefrontal cortex, thus limiting our empathy, which is at the core of human morality.

Media and the Marginalization of Parents

In many homes, children have access to media with very little parental supervision. The expanded consumerism of the economic culture promotes an individualism that has as its shadow, isolation. Each member of the family often has their own electronic preference and can get lost in their individual interests, decreasing family cohesiveness. Infinite options tempt them, broadcast on hundreds of cable or satellite shows or over the Internet. More youth are exposed to damaging messages and imagery than at any time in human history. Family bonding time and expressions of love and focused attention are sacrificed on the altar of each individual's preferred sensory bombardment.

Deeper family connections are also now less likely because many of the new cultural media messages regarding parents are anything but

---

57. "Goodbye to a trivial pursuit" by Peter M. Leschak, Star Tribune, March 4, 2012.

Father Knows Best. Parents are frequently portrayed as stupid, inane, out of touch, and largely irrelevant. Television programs' disdain for parents and adults in general is not softened by the fact that many of these messages come in animated form. In fact, younger age groups are even more drawn to them because of the cartoon characters. This sets in motion potential adversarial attitudes toward adults at younger and younger ages. The attraction to animated characters is part of Disney's success. The top-five popular movies at any given time usually include at least one or two that are animated. Do not assume, however, that the value system historically found in Disney movies pervades their television counterparts. Both are usually creative, but the television versions are riddled with sarcasm, the humor of shame, and are largely dismissive of adults.

Also, don't assume that the value system on these TV animations is not internalized by the young viewers. These shows relentlessly encourage youth to push limits and to do their "own thing," regardless of cultural or parental norms. Given the culture's child-centered focus and this berating of parents, ignoring parental guidance and directives is a logical option for youth. Therefore, setting limits when the larger culture doesn't support, and even challenges the very notion, is difficult. Parents and children end up in a battle of wills even over small things, and much more frequently. My heart goes out to parents trying to set normal and reasonable limits for young people. They are battling an economic culture that powerfully and profitably questions their competence with humor and derision, undermining their authority.

Boredom and the Economic Culture

There is another byproduct of the economic culture creating challenges for parents and particularly teachers. How many times have you heard from young people: "I'M BORED"? You hear it a lot in a school setting. Teachers cannot compete with the fast-passed laugh-a-minute, requires-no-effort sitcoms, or the "drama" of reality shows. This is just one aspect of the boredom epidemic that expresses itself in antagonism toward self-discipline, study, and the academic expectations of schools. Teachers are frequently blamed for underperforming students. But something else contributes to young people's boredom, and it relates to the embedded effects of the economic culture, expressed through the media.

One of the most disconcerting downward trends I've witnessed over forty years as a teacher and a psychologist was the growing lack of passion on the part of young people for learning, for deeply engaging life and the questions it poses.

A spiritual sage was once asked, "What are you looking for before taking on a disciple?"

He answered, "Two things: unselfishness and not being lazy." He then added: "But laziness is the most important, because people can't change anything if they are lazy."

The degree of sloth and boredom I have witnessed in growing numbers was at times staggering, and also tremendously sad. The boredom may in part reflect the contrast of the rapid-fire media, starting with *Sesame Street*; with the necessarily slower-paced nature of meaningful learning in school. A small study released in 2011, on the effects of rapid-paced programs for children, is disconcerting, and will require further research. Four-year-olds who watched just nine minutes of *SpongeBob* performed half as well on four tasks compared to four-year-olds who spent time drawing or who watched *Caillou*, a slower-paced show. The four tasks included their ability to follow rules and delay gratification. The leading author of the study, Angeline Lillard, commented, "Programs that are fast paced and feature unrealistic events may over stimulate the brain, making it harder to trigger executive function, a process used to complete tasks . . . Parents need to consider how frenetic a show is, as well as its content, when deciding what their young children watch."[58]

Researchers speculated that these children's brains were tired from excessive stimulation, so it was difficult for them to focus on the required tasks. Preschoolers watch almost thirty-two hours per week of television or DVDs, and sometimes this takes place at their daycare providers'.[59]

Fast-paced stimulation that increases fatigue may be a contributing

58.   "SpongeBob may soak up too much attention" by Nicole Ostrow from Bloomberg News, Star Tribune, Health and Science section, Sept. 15, 2011.

59.   Ibid.

factor to skyrocketing increases in boredom. However, to really understand the breadth of young people's boredom, we need to understand boredom's fundamental cause. The root cause is a lack of concentration. Few things in the world are inherently boring. This statement assumes, however, that you are able to absorb your mind fully into your experience. Very young children find interest in almost every item, action, or event they experience. For all of us, the most meaningful and enjoyable times of our lives are when our minds are fully engaged.

Why do young people struggle more than ever to focus their minds? Concentration requires energy. Their diet, as already mentioned, often consists of energy-depleted foods. Poor quality food and inadequate sleep regulation insures that concentrating will be difficult. Playing hyperkinetic video games for hours, or watching news programs with three scrolls simultaneously moving across the screen, scatters energy and does little to develop a laser-sharp mind. These things exacerbate the mind's inherent restlessness. The multitasking that youth argues that they are capable of doing, in reality, just reinforces a split concentration. Multitasking is usually just the mind jumping quickly back and forth between tasks. The natural tendency of the mind is to move. The tech world of texting (teenagers average 3,500 texts per month) and tweeting even when driving, along with increased exposure to rapid-action videos and the busyness of youth's schedules, reinforces the mind's tendency to constantly shift focus.

A mind distracted by constant external allurements and bombarded senses makes it more difficult to sustain the concentration necessary to accomplish their goals. Too often they quit before finishing and grow discouraged if their initial efforts don't succeed. Thomas Edison's famous quote: "I have not failed. I have just found 10,000 ways that didn't work," would not likely be uttered today, because we wouldn't sustain our efforts for ten attempts let alone 10,000. It is hard for youth to feel successful and have a positive sense of self if they aren't accomplishing their goals.

It is true that video and computer games require some concentration, because their intensity focuses the mind briefly; but the overstimulation will gradually exhaust the mind. Youth's transfixed hypnotic-like minds, lost in some video fantasy, won't create an energy or concentration that is transferable to other environments. In fact, it makes concentration more difficult to sustain in environments that are without that intense stimulation.

Paradoxically, the very things young people are addictively doing to escape their boredom actually create more of it. There are a plethora of personal high-powered games and gadgets with incredibly realistic graphics for youth. Despite this and the media-driven hoopla showing people camping out to get the latest tech release, there is a growing epidemic of boredom among youth. The frenetic nature of these games and videos dissipates the mind's energy, leading to problems with concentration that are at the root of their boredom.

The Economic Culture's Dysfunctional Mind Training

The embedded consequence of the stimulus bombardment of the economic culture is an unconscious training, reinforcement, and exacerbation of the mind's inherent restlessness. To end their boredom, in order that youth might experience more lasting pleasure and contentment, requires a relaxed and focused mind. This training is made more difficult given the constant bombardment of the senses that has become the norm. Research cited by Electra Draper, in the Minneapolis *Star Tribune*, September 5, 2011, documents the brain's need for down time: "Angelika Dimoka, director of the Center for Neural Decision Making at Temple University, studies how the brain processes information. Her research has found that, as the flow of information increases, activity increases in the region of the brain responsible for decisions and control of emotions—but only to a point . . . Flood the brain with too much information, and activity in this region suddenly drops off. This center for smart thinking not only doesn't increase its performance, it checks out."[60]

Some of the boredom, energetic collapse, flat affects, and emotional regulation issues witnessed in youth may be due to the cumulative effect of the constant stimulus bombardment resulting in an actual "energy outage" in youth's brains. Their happiness in the form of fun or

---

60.   "Think you need a day of rest? You're right" by Electra Draper from the Denver Post, Star Tribune Sept. 5, 2011.

consuming products, suggested by ad agencies on behalf of the economic culture, is short-lived and is largely anticipatory excitement. It is much like watching excited children unwrapping Christmas presents, which they quickly push aside, because there is another pretty wrapped box to rip into. Advertisers create an "itch" in the mind that grows until we scratch it, through consumption. The economic culture offers little training for the mind except in the direction of dysfunctional hyperactivity leading to exhaustion. This inhibits the relaxed concentration necessary for greater happiness and the end of one's boredom.

Some "techno bored" and "expectation dashed" youth have been unknowingly primed by the unfulfilled and hollow promises of notions of happiness suggested by the economic culture. The disappointment with external sources of success and fulfillment have led many youth to seek something more authentic. For these youth the question begins to emerge: "How can I decrease my stress and train my mind to relax and focus?" We address this question of how to train the mind to catalyze youth's potential in Chapters 18, 19, and 20. Through that training they can become masters of their own minds and the author of their own lives.

One thing is for sure, waiting on X-Box 2,222, or another rendition of a video game, won't reduce youth's growing boredom. Boredom, and the energetically depleted and scattered mind behind it, eliminate the possibility of youth realizing their potential. There is a story told by Dr. Arya, a professor and spiritual mentor, when I was in my twenties that is relevant here:

> A young man living in ancient times became very excited. The king was passing through his small town for the first time. The man got up early to be at the edge of the street to insure a good look. He could see the king coming, riding on a gigantic elephant in a carriage that sat on top. Suddenly, as the king and elephant got very close, the carriage began to slip and the king tumbled out, his head about to strike the brick surfaced road. The young man dashed to save the king, catching him just before his head hit the ground. The king, knowing he could have been killed or seriously injured, said to the young man, "I will give you anything you ask. I have jewels, castles, universities and philosophers to tutor your education—whatever you want is yours." The boy, mesmerized while looking directly into the face of the king said, "I would like a haircut just like yours."

Our youth are also settling for the haircut. Their gifts and talents are being squandered by the alluring and the mesmerizing trinkets offered by the economic culture. Youth have a mind that, when focused like a laser, has much greater power and control, and would allow them to accomplish wonderful things. Sadly, more and more youth are performing way below their potential and underutilizing their gifts and talents.

They live with little zest and without purposeful enthusiasm. The world, more than ever, needs their talents fully expressed, but they have been seduced by the economic culture. Young people's minds have been scattered and depleted, like a low watt, flickering fluorescent bulb bouncing off of walls. The repetitive drumbeat of the economic culture has convinced them that more toys and more events would end their boredom and assure their happiness. They are frantically trying to string as many exciting activities together, hoping to capture their restless minds, and scratch the itch that feeds their boredom. However, unless you can consciously direct your mind into each moment, there will always be time between events, and boredom will return.

The promise of the economic culture and the media is: if you can have enough and do enough, you will be happy. Yet, some of the highest suicide rates are in wealthy suburbs. Observing the eyes, faces, and comments of most millionaires who get TV air time doesn't reveal a deep contentment. the *Tao te' Ch'ing* says, "To be content with what one has is to be rich." There's more truth in that statement than the promises and "swampland" being peddled by Madison Avenue. To experience that contentment, the mind has to quit chasing the future and quietly and fully immerse itself into *NOW*. The experiment at the end of this chapter has been successfully used to decrease boredom and enrich lives through increased mindfulness.

Experiment:
Ending Boredom through Mindfulness

Try listening without labeling. Imagine yourself as a newborn without any culturally conditioned verbal labels for your experiences. Spend fifteen minutes or more listening to the sounds that come into your experience. Stay with each sound, hearing it as if for the first time—stay relaxed and quietly focused. Keep coming back to now when the mind wants to go to the future or the past. Hear a flushed toilet, birds, or a vacuum cleaner without the filters of mind—without the labels. Just listen effortlessly and enjoy as if you are a total amnesiac.

When you have finished, notice what was different when you resisted the mind's conditioned tendency to label everything—rather than allowing things to just *BE*. Do this fifteen minutes a day for one week. It will start training the mind to find interest through presence. Christ said, "I will make all things new," and going beyond the limitations of the labeling mind is a step in that direction. You can experiment with other senses, like sight or touch, by repeating the same process—full absorption without labels. The mind, once it labels something, often dismisses it and moves onto the next "something." Train your mind to stay immersed in the moment. Use your senses as portals into a meditative experience. Mindfulness is meditation in action; it enriches life, while ending boredom and stress.

Chapter 10

Seeking Balance in an Imbalanced World

"Everything requires for its existence its own opposite, or else it fades into nothingness."

—CARL JUNG

"The other side of the fear of death is lust . . . the greater the lust the greater the fear of death."

—SWAMI VEDA BHARATI

People know we show our respect, value, and love for them through our deep listening and attention. That is the true meaning and experience of the word understand; it means to stand under. We put our own desires and needs aside and are fully present to someone else's need. Understanding does not require our agreement, but it does require our full presence. Did our youth experience a subtle neglect in this area during their most formative years? Despite frequent overindulgence in material things, were we too busy, preoccupied, and stressed to be fully present to our children? Did our own childhood hurts replay themselves in our family relationships?

Our Children as Teachers

"Nathan, quit bugging Janice." Janice had undoubtedly done something to get things started, because my son wouldn't look this angry if she hadn't provoked him in some way.

"She has asked you to stop trying to kick her, so knock it off," I said firmly.

Nate, my seven-year-old son, immediately went over and kicked Janice, a thirteen-year-old neighbor girl, a second time hard in the shin.

"I said, knock it off!" this time yelling.

Nate glared at me, ran after Janice, and unloaded as hard as he could on her shin again.

I lost it. I ran over picked him up with one arm and raised him off the ground and yelled with rage in my voice, "When I tell you to stop, you stop!" I put him back down, my heart pounding.

My son looked at me and said, "I hate you, Dad."

That cut deep, but I said angrily, "Get up to your room until I say you can come out."

I was still seething inside, but that was giving way to feeling awful and ashamed. The voice of my "inner critic" kicked in and was relentless. *I can't believe you picked him up and screamed like that. You call yourself a psychologist. Look what you've done. What kind of father are you? Your own son hates you.* The litany of self-incriminating self-talk with varieties of self-hatred proclamations was intense and continued for several minutes. I eventually began to speak back to the critic, as I had learned in my training, the value of cultivating opposite thoughts and sentiments.

"You are still loveable and worthwhile, you just made a mistake," I began to repeat over and over and over inside my head.

"Not when you shake your son like that. It's totally unacceptable," countered the critic.

"I know it's wrong, and I need to apologize, but I am still loveable and worthwhile."

The internal heated debate continued for several more minutes until I began to internalize that I really could not lose my worth no matter what. I detached from my self-hatred enough to smile at my "loveable and worthwhile" chant. It began to sound like a version of Stuart Smalley on a *Saturday Night Live* skit: "I am special and doggone it, people like me."

With the newfound detachment, I reflected on the source of my anger.

Tears came into my eyes as I suddenly realized the anger stemmed from all the times my father cut me off in mid-sentence, as I protested against being hit with his belt before one of my spankings. My dad, who overall was a loving father, at times became so angry, he was incapable of listening. He also often was not there to listen because he worked up to eighty hours a week, and was unavailable to my needs as a child. When my son did not listen when I asked him to stop, he triggered the pent-up hurt that came out as anger for all of the times I was not heard, and my dad's absences when I needed him.

I was calm now, and went up to my son's room and offered a sincere apology, because I had taken ownership of my feelings that had driven my misplaced anger. It was different than the apology my father had offered me, coerced by my mother, after he had left deep welts on my legs from his belt: "I'm sorry I struck you so hard, but I wouldn't have done it if you hadn't . . . "

I later learned the hurtful things Janice had said to my son that had launched his anger. If I had investigated the whole story, I could have prevented my overreaction with all its fallout. Despite my regrets for how I responded to my son, I am grateful that the scenario that unfolded revealed a longstanding unconscious hurt from my own childhood that I could begin to address. It's important to realize anger is hurt in disguise, and behind every hurt is fear. The fear comes from the concern that we will be hurt again. Most anger is the protective energy designed to keep you from experiencing more hurt. It also indicates developmentally where we created notions of ourselves as being inherently flawed, unimportant, or inadequate in some way. In other words, anger surfaces when a person is feeling unloved or unlovable.

This is the source of our defensiveness and much of our emotional reactivity. The pains of our childhoods created the ego's identification of itself as flawed or unimportant, making us reluctant to touch that pain and heal or detach from it. It's important to realize there that we have pain, but *we* are not the pain. The personality is not us. We have a personality but *we* are not our personality. The personality is the sum total of all our thoughts and habits; and some of them are painful. It is the roles we play, a conditioned limited self, a story of who we think we are. The mask worn in Greek theatre to hide people's true identity were called personas. We should not confuse our personality for us. Paracelsus said, "You are a special heaven, whole and unbroken." Paracelsus is distinguishing between our real self and the roles and attachments of the personality.

There is a refuge, a center, a soul, a spirit within youth and all human beings that words cannot capture. There we have no fear, stress, defensiveness, or hostility. We experience an expansive joy and a center of total contentment, much more satisfying than fleeting moments of fun. To bring balance to our self-preservation urge, we have to go beyond the ego's myriad "little selves" of the personality that are limiting and filled with fear, anxiety, and pain. There is a self within us that transcends the ego's fear. There is a fifth urge that is not primitive, but is also inherent in all humans. It is the urge to experience our transcendent self. It is difficult to find that self when most of the messages of the economic culture reinforce the ego's desires for self-aggrandizement and encourage external ephemeral notions of happiness. The economic culture might exacerbate our wounds, insecurities, and fears, but it offers nothing to heal them, and obfuscates this preeminent urge for self discovery. How we find that self and center within us will be explored in Chapters 18–20.

Anger and Love

When we are working with angry young people, we have to help them identify and bring forward the sources of their anger, increasing their awareness of the hurts and attachments that underlie that anger. Simultaneously, it helps youth enormously to feel our love, even as we help them to examine their dysfunctional and painful coping habits. One of my spiritual mentors says, "No situation is improved by the withdrawal of love," and this has been my practical experience when working with youth.

It is easier to not withdraw our love, even if youth are acting obnoxious, when we have deeply internalized the fact that their true self is spiritual. This allows us to separate their problematic behavior from their inherent worth. They are still responsible for the consequences of their actions, but withdrawing love is not necessary or beneficial.

Students, clients, and children, over time, feel the difference between their inherent worth and their behavior through our love and acceptance of them. They are then more open to honestly examining and changing their dysfunctional behavior.

It was extremely difficult for me to separate worth from behavior when I counseled psychopaths. Even when I was successful in loving them, it often mattered little in terms of changing their manipulative behaviors. Every psychopath I ever worked with, once their childhood was fully revealed, was so profoundly wounded early in their life that they survived by closing down all feeling. If you cannot feel, you cannot empathize and you will care little about how you are hurting others. Therefore, it is impossible for psychopaths to form authentic and close relationships. By closing down all feeling, they have also effectively killed any access to their conscience and the worst thing we can do in life is to lose our conscience.[61]

The Psychological Roots for Losing Conscience

John was sent to therapy at age sixteen after he had totaled his neighbor's car, cut open the bottom of another neighbor's swimming pool, and blew up part of the chemistry lab at his high school. He was court ordered to therapy. His adopted parents shared John's general background, informing me that he was neglected by his mom, and she lost custody. They had copies of the court proceedings they were willing to share with me. When John came to his first session, I learned he had actually done much more than even authorities knew. Almost every night he dressed in black, head to toe, sometimes charcoaled his face, and went about burglarizing neighborhoods. He had been doing this since he was fourteen. He rarely kept any of the stuff he stole; giving it to friends, or throwing it away. He did it for the challenge, the excitement, the rush of adrenaline.

Despite a history that alerted me to his antisocial character, I still felt over the course of several months that we were making some progress. John never missed a session, even after he satisfied his court obligation. This was not the case with past psychopathic clients. One day, after John

---

61.   Inner Dialogue, Swami Rama. Pamphlet Chapter 11.

had turned seventeen, I asked him what his dreams or goals for his future were. He had cut back on his burglaries, but that seemed to be a calculation that the risks were too high, at least for now. I pointed out he wouldn't have much of a future if he didn't change his course long term. He said: "I have narrowed down my career options to two choices. I either want to be a cook, because I love cooking, and eventually I want to own my own restaurant. If the restaurant thing doesn't pan out I want to be a hit man. I already am connected to people who do that."

I spontaneously asked: "Would you kill me for $50,000?" Without hesitation or a change of expression, he said, "I'd take you out for a few thousand." So much for the progress I thought we were making. I wasn't totally shocked by John's answer, as I had received a copy, later than promised, of his court records. I was surprised his adopted parents had neglected to share the following disturbing information early in our therapy. John had been taken away from his mother around age four. His older brother, who was a dozen or so years older, was in a state penitentiary by age eighteen. John's only memory of his brother was watching him stick a pencil through a hamster, and watching it struggle.

I had asked John in previous therapy sessions about the numerous marks he had on his hands and arms. He had no idea how they got there. His mother had not only neglected John but, also abused him. He was often sent to his room for the day and received a single apple for nourishment. If he really irritated her, she would call him over, take his hands and occasionally his arms, and put her cigarettes out on them. The court records also documented that when she was upset with him, she punished him by putting his hands in the toaster.

John, as a preschooler, had no choice but to numb himself and close off from feeling in order to survive. His current antisocial behavior was now spreading his childhood pain to the world. When your own mom uses your hands as an ash tray before you turn four, a child cannot make sense of that. So John completely buried all feelings, and with them he buried his conscience. It became clear in time that no real progress was going to be made. John wanted an audience, someone to listen while he excitedly shared his exploits. I was an audience of one. I tear up as I write this, realizing no one was there to listen and protect John when he most needed it.

Youth with less dramatic histories than John also avoid touching their pain. This is particularly true of males who learn distorted notions of masculinity from media and other cultural sources. For males, feelings are often experienced as a sign of weakness and a source of shame. This avoidance of uncomfortable feelings is reinforced by the childhood template of seeking pleasure and avoiding or escaping pain. This template is constantly reinforced by the economic culture's drumbeat for hedonistic pleasure seeking, and the distorted video and media images that reinforce macho masculinity.

Balance, The Key to Greater Contentment

Avoidance of pain and seeking pleasure are the two sides of the coin of attachment; they travel together. Avoiding pain and seeking pleasure are trumpeted by the economic culture, but pleasure and pain are part of the dualistic nature of the universe. Pleasure and pain are just one representation of the polarities inherent in life: east/west, good/bad, up/down, light/dark, and thousands of other dualities are not antagonistic, but are actually complementary aspects of a greater unified whole. In practical experience, this means the intense pursuit of pleasures will always result in pain. Many people and particularly young people think in black-and-white terms, this is good and that is bad; so it is hard for them to appreciate that seemingly opposite qualities are inseparable. They are actually opposite poles on a single continuum.

There is value in being less absolute and rigid in one's thinking, and cultivating more acceptance of life's inherent polarities. One day in my psychology class, we were brainstorming what made for a successful dating relationship. "Honesty is absolutely the main key to any good relationship," a student proclaimed, and was joined in support by many classmates.

So to get them to pause and reflect for a moment I said, "I want you all to be totally honest in all your relationships. If you think something and you believe it's true, I want you to say it. Share your honesty at all times, in all relationships, and in all places."

Students began to backpedal. They were realizing that when honesty is pursued without restraint or balance, it becomes brutality.

This realization spawned the phrase "brutally honest." This kind of brutal honesty won't enhance, but will actually destroy relationships. "If honesty isn't always good how do we know when to be honest or not?" someone asked.

"That's a great question. Honesty has to balanced and led by nonviolence. If you let nonviolence guide or inform your honesty, communication stays balanced and your honesty is likely to be more fruitful," I suggested.

In teaching and counseling, I am often amazed that once I have established a relationship with young people, loved and accepted them enough, how truthful I can be with them. I am amazed by how emotionally nonreactive youth are to the hard realities I am pointing out, as long as those hard realities are softened with love. Our conscience and intuition helps inform us as to the how and the when of our honesty. Nonviolence is really a pseudonym for love, and in combination with honesty, it leads to more harmonious and authentic relationships.

Students, trapped by the same habit of absolute black-and-white thinking, made similar comments about trust as they had about honesty. "Trust is the foundation of all good relationships," someone again confidently proclaimed.

"Obviously trust and honesty have value in a relationship, but again they are part of a trust/distrust continuum or polarity. If you're totally and naively trusting with everybody, you are likely to be taken advantage of and not respected; and your relationships, if not destroyed, will be painfully imbalanced," I offered back. Practicing 100 percent dishonesty or honesty or 100 percent distrust or trust, either of the extremes on a continuum leads one to the same place: painful and broken relationships.

What we are actually seeking, in order to create harmony in our relationships and in our lives, is a dynamic balance of these polarities. It is counterproductive and impossible to attempt to eliminate these polarities in ourselves or the universe. They are complementary aspects of a greater unified whole and they have their place in creation. We need to use our discriminative wisdom, our intuition, to make balanced decisions and not rely on a "one size fits all" approach to life. There are situations, for example, to not speak the truth because it would be too hurtful to someone in that moment, and our conscience immediately informs us that it would be wrong. We all realize that there are times we have to be flexible with our normal standards or rules. If our minds are quiet and unstressed we can easily discern the guidance our conscience and intuition are continually providing. A cookie-cutter notion of how things should be in all situations and at all times will not create peace and harmony in our relationships. Acceptance, balance, intuition, and love are what is needed to create healthy relationships, and also to work effectively with rejected aspects of our own personality.

The Four Primitive Urges and Balance

Balanced choices relative to the primitive urges of food, sleep, sex, and self-preservation are also essential. When we have a balanced regulation of these urges, we don't experience negative emotions, and the natural joy and peace of our spiritual self shines through, unencumbered. Buddha called this balance the Middle Way. Aristotle called it the Golden Mean. In Christianity, this same idea is expressed in the story of the Garden of Eden. Don't bite from the "Tree of Good and Evil," the extremes on a continuum, or you will "fall from grace"—lose your joyful balance. Greek philosopher Epicurus understood the value of balanced choices: "Be moderate in order to taste the joys of life in abundance."

The saying "too much of a good thing is harmful" makes sense from the perspective of balance being a source of joy and harmony, but it runs counter to the economic culture's messages. A biblical phrase that confounded me as an adolescent was "not to resist an evil person" (Matthew 5:39). I now have a better understanding of what that paradoxical phrase means. If we attack evil with a personal, self-righteous emotional vengeance, we lose our balance and exhibit the same characteristics as our "enemy." By resisting evil in this ego-driven way, we lose our capacity to love.

The message of the traditions of Buddhism, Christianity, Greek philosophy, and other religious traditions, is to seek balance in all things. The imbalanced messages of the economic culture and the pleasures of the senses they promote, if pursued with too much attachment or egoism, will bring pain. Sensory pleasures come and go. If you cling to those pleasures, the coming and going will be experienced as loss and will create suffering. This is why Plato said, "The noblest victory is the victory over pleasure." And Christ urged, "Do not lay up your treasures on earth where moth and rust destroy" (Matthew 6:19–20).

Exploring with youth the importance of balance as a key to greater happiness is worthwhile and helpful. Contemplating the value of not rejecting or clinging to extremes on these polarity continuums yielded practical benefits. The chemical highs that some were seeking, according to this model of balance, they realized were actually causing their own suffering. The pleasures of excitation are always followed by the dissipating shadow of pain. This is inescapable. Highs are followed by lows. This growing awareness over time led to decreased drug use for many of the more introspective young people. Increasing numbers of students and clients were beginning to understand that seeking balance in their lives might bring about a deeper and more lasting satisfaction.

Experiment:

Harmonizing and Balancing Emotions through Cultivating Compassion

It is often said that when we give, we receive. There are times when we are overwhelmed with hurt, anxiety, grief, and sorrow. Negative thoughts often feed our painful emotions and keep us stuck in reoccurring pain. There is a practice which has variations in many different spiritual traditions that utilizes the "heart center." The heart center helps to quiet the negative thinking that amplifies our emotional pain. It also helps to heal and transform our personal pain while simultaneously bringing salve to the world's wounds. The process is described in Pema Chodron's book *When Things Fall Apart*. This is a modified form of a practice called Tonglen. Science is showing that the heart has a mind, an understanding and intelligence of its own. There is not enough time to explore the research supporting that, but this experiment can provide a practical experience of the Heart Center as a source of healing and comfort.

1. First, connect with the heart center and feel it as an expansive source of love and compassion. It is both a personal space of love and kindness and a universal heart of compassion and love. In Christianity, when we see pictures of Jesus or Mary, frequently they are pointing at their hearts. Buddhists call this center the heart of the Buddha. Experience a deep feeling of love and kindness in the heart center.

2. Inhale your painful emotion, and the pain of all others who are experiencing similar suffering, into your heart. Feel compassion and kindness toward yourself and all who are suffering like you. Let your exhalation carry these feelings of love and compassion out to all living beings who are suffering.

3. Allow the breath to flow smoothly, naturally, and diaphragmatically without jerks or pauses. The suffering that is drawn into the heart with each inhalation is transmuted through your intention of love. Virgil said, "Love conquers all." The Bible says, "Perfect love casteth our fear" (I John 4:18). Continue the practice until there is a sense of harmony or healing.

4. **Optional.** Add this step at the end if your painful emotions are accompanied with negative self-talk. Challenge the validity of those messages through detailed analysis and self-dialogue. The overgeneralized, all or none aspects of these messages need to be challenged as unhealthy, and fundamentally not true. They are detrimental to happiness. Challenge notions of not being good enough, or stupid, etc. At first this dialogue can be free flowing. Eventually reduce this dialogue to short statements that can quickly come to mind to stop these automatic self-negations. These short affirmations, mantras, or encapsulated phrases not only counter negative messages, but with practice, will build a new habit that is positive and healthy. Develop phrases like: "I am worthwhile even if I make a bad choice." "I am at my core a spiritual being.

Chapter 11

Unintended Ripples and Expectations of the Economic Culture

*"Silence is the language that God speaks.
Everything else is a poor translation."*

—Unknown

"Be silent and I will show you wisdom."

—Job 33:33

The pleasures of stillness and tranquility take you off the roller coaster of pain that accompanies the desires of the senses. Stillness and silence of the mind offer real peace, contentment, and a subtle satiating joy. They create a dynamic balance beyond the pain and pleasure polarities. "Be still, and know that I am God" is a biblical injunction touting the virtue of stillness. The *Tao te' Ch'ing* says simply and profoundly, "The greatest revelation is stillness." Stillness and tranquility are beyond polarities and have no counterpoint; they are transcendent and unified.

This does not mean we cannot enjoy pleasures of the senses. They can actually be enjoyed more fully from a place of stillness or silence,

147

which allows greater concentration, resulting in greater satisfaction without the clinging and attachment. Each moment is its own satisfaction when the mind is serene. The serenity that silence offers allows us to let go of our mind's superimposition of ideas as to how things should be, and accept and more effectively engage with what is. "Attachment is the greatest fabricator of illusions; reality can be attained only by someone who is detached," is how Simone Weil expresses the notion that our attachments create illusions that throw us out of balance, thus creating our own suffering.

Little stillness or serenity is found in the world. Even when you go to a health club to de-stress, there is constant music vibrating your senses. It is harder to find quiet places. People seem intent on unnecessarily exposing themselves to noise of one kind or another, not seeing its connection to their stressed mind. French philosopher Blaise Pascal, in the seventeenth century, famously and quite correctly said, "All of our problems come from our inability to sit quietly in a room alone." More and more people seem to need their television or radio on as company, or because they can't fall asleep without noise due to over-stimulated senses that now find natural silence unsettling. Yet the sweetness of sleep ultimately beckons all of us to silence and away from the hurly burly of life. In sleep we seek refuge and restoration from the constant clamor of the economic culture. In the unconscious silence of delta sleep, where the brain waves slow and the mind's chatter stops, we lose contact with the external world and find a deep restoration.

This same restoration and refuge can be found consciously by creating emersion in silence while fully conscious. We can do this through meditation and mindfulness, which are often facilitated by a retreat in a natural setting. We explore the benefits of meditation in Chapter 19.

When I mention to people that I am going on a Silence Retreat for ten days, many reflexively say, "I could never do that." They say it quickly and with some apprehension in their voice and consternation on their face, both expressions of fear. This is understandable because the noise and busyness of the economic culture has been internalized, leaving dissonance, tension, and an almost constant chatter in the mind. It is hard for us to be at ease with our own minds when they've been wound so tight. In this wound-up, stressed, and disturbed state, peace of mind becomes an alien. When we spend time in silence, the unconscious mind will inevitably reveal some of its contents that have been kept hidden and at bay by our frenetic external pursuits. The fear of facing our hurts, anger, fears, and insecurities is the primary reason people recoil at the thought of a prolonged silence and is also a significant factor in why we continue to make ourselves busy. Blaise Pascal again said it well, "Distraction is the only thing that consoles us for our miseries, and yet it is itself the greatest of our miseries."

The good news is that silence reveals more than unconscious pains. Thomas Merton, a twentieth century Christian monk, said, "It is in the stillness and silence of nature that God most easily reveals Himself." Many people, including youth, despite the noisy seductive messages of the economic culture, still seek refuge in the greater silence and peace of nature. The external silence brings an internal quieting. Yet, avarice and consumption promoted by the economic culture, along with population growth, is shrinking natural environments by millions of acres each year. So the natural environment, that we are deeply connected to and part of, is less accessible for youth to experience its healing and restorative powers.

Psychologist Carl Jung predicted, as early as the 1940s, that America would soon have an explosion of drug problems because youth were losing their connection to nature. Urbanization, suburbanization, deforestation, and mass migration from the farms have made relationship to the land less tangible and less penetrating. There are, however, a growing number of programs recognizing the healing and transformative power of nature that are bringing at-risk youth into natural settings. In nature, young people experience the natural rhythms of life, rather than the frenetic youth culture. Nature effortlessly communicates the message that we're unique, but also part of a larger whole. Outdoor settings beckon youth to stress releasing activity in contrast to the stagnant, sedentary life of video games and media programs. Naturalist John Muir said it well: "Climb the mountains and get their good tidings. Nature's peace will flow into you . . . while cares drop off like autumn leaves."

The silence of nature provides the space and time for youth to observe their thoughts and touch feelings that are often avoided or drowned out by the hyper-frenetic economic culture. Their quieter, more reflective minds, largely absent peer pressure, facilitate becoming more open to examining destructive or imbalanced habits. Anxiety and stress melt away in this natural setting and the mind gradually quiets down. This permits a more neutral examination of their harmful conditioned habits, laying the foundation for change.

The effects of being immersed in nature include, but also transcend, simple stress reduction. Well over a hundred research studies document nature's stress-reducing properties. Recent research documenting some of nature's transformative qualities is summarized in the health section of the September/October 2010 *AARP Magazine*:

> To fix what ails you, take your workout outside. New research from England's University of Essex finds that just five minutes of "green exercise"—cycling, gardening, fishing—can boost your mood and self-esteem. The study jibes with previous research showing that outdoor walks battle depression better than mall walks do. Add to that the other benefits of outdoor activity—greater exposure to health-promoting vitamin D (from the sun), enhanced cognitive functioning, increased compassion (test subjects were more considerate after viewing images of nature)—and more time outside could mean spending less time in a doctor's office.[62]

I was encouraged recently when I saw a psychiatrist on television advocating for a new diagnosis, environmental deficit disorder, for people stressed out from the growing bright blight of urban and suburban settings. He may not have been totally serious about adding a new diagnostic category, but he was quite serious about the therapeutic value of nature. Unfortunately, over the last couple of decades unstructured outdoor activities have decreased for youth by an alarming 50 percent.[63] Programs and retreats recognizing the healing power of nature are sometimes called eco-therapy and they are a relatively rare but growing oasis of hope and transformation. They highlight the importance of protecting and restoring natural areas, so they can be experienced by future generations of youth.

---

62. AARP Magazine, You & Your Health Section, Sept/Oct 2010, 18.

63. Last Child in the Woods by Richard Louv. Algonquin Books of Chapel Hill, 2005.

Emotional Imbalance and Addiction

It is understandable why young people, out of touch with nature and born into the omnipresent economic culture, are seduced into avoiding or numbing their pain through material pursuits, drugs, and events. Yet, ultimately we all have to transcend the pleasure/pain template, if we are to be happy. We need to guide and encourage youth to examine their insecurities, hurts, fears, and the ego's misidentifications and image concerns that drive their destructive habits. Psychiatrist Eric Fromm said, "What we run from runs us." The pain young people are running from often runs them into addictive behaviors. These addictions might be legal or illegal drugs, food, sex, a person, video games, or Internet pornography. My experience supports Eckhart Tolle's statement:

> Every addiction arises from an unconscious refusal to face and move through your own pain. Every addiction starts with pain and ends with pain. Whatever the substance you are addicted to . . . you are using something or somebody to cover your pain.[64]

When we are willing to sit quietly with ourselves and face our hurts and fears, we release the energy that binds us to them. That energy is now integrated into our personality creating more balance and harmony. It allows us to experience more of the interior fullness of our spiritual self. In that fullness, there is no craving. The need to overeat, oversleep, indulge in addictions, or overconsume, to bolster a wounded sense of self, evaporates. The primitive urges automatically find their natural balance.

Expectations, Entitlement, and Emotions

The images in video games and other media sources make it particularly difficult for adolescent males to open to their pain. The theme of most videos and movies, when an injustice has been perpetrated on the

---

64.   The Power of Now by Eckhart Tolle, Namaste Publishing Inc., 1997, 36.

hero or heroine, is payback—payback with a vengeance. Pseudo notions of toughness have become synonymous with being masculine. Vulnerable feelings of sadness, hurt, and fear for males are viewed as weakness. They are often experienced as shame. These emotions are often funneled into one emotion: anger. Anger is a more culturally acceptable emotion for males, but it is a secondary emotion that masks other emotions. Frequently these hidden painful emotions are turned inward and become depression. This can lead to a psychic numbness as repressed feelings wall us off from pain, and we literally feel nothing. The process of suppressing painful emotions unfortunately also encapsulates our positive emotions, and we lose our joy and enthusiasm.

Anger can also be understood as expectations being dashed on the rocks of reality. Life sometimes flows in a direction different than our expectations. Various societal forces have led to a sort of entitlement mindset in many youth, including the media which constantly creates expectations of the importance of doing whatever feels good to *you*. These entitlement expectations are frequently not going to be realized. When youth's expectations are thwarted it can trigger strong emotions that seem way out of proportion to a relatively benign stimulus. These hidden entitlement expectations are often unconscious, and some youth are surprised and feel awkward about becoming so emotional when the world says NO. Other youth, whose entitlement expectations are so strong and so unconscious, feel perfectly justified in their emotional reactivity.

A teaching colleague recently shared a story that demonstrated this kind of entrenched entitlement. A nineteen-year-old female college student, who was making minimal effort, received a "C" in his class. She demanded a meeting with his supervisor to argue she should have received an "A." When the supervisor supported the professor's rationale for the "C," the young person stormed out of the meeting, saying to both of them, "I paid for that 'A,'" and then added somewhat menacingly, "Now you're going to have to deal with my mom!"

There is also a growing culture of victimization affecting our society and growing numbers of youth, due to unrealistic expectations of what life owes them. If life shouldn't be hard, then when it is, they are going to feel more victimized and carry a sense of unfairness or "why me?" Another factor feeding youth's victimization is the expectation that anyone who tries to set limits for them, in an economic culture that obliterates limits by pushing extreme individualism and hedonism, "deserves" to be challenged. This expectation that their grievance or demands need to be addressed has an embedded timeline expectation. Given our culture of immediate gratification, my grievance needs to be addressed, NOW.

Culturally Internalized Entitlements

Tom and Dan were nice young men, had IQs around seventy, and both were concrete thinkers. This true story is a prototypal expression that illustrates how they both had innocently internalized the values of the larger culture. I can smile now as I recount this story because it seems so absurd. Tom and Dan both had problems in the past respecting the boundaries with their therapists and teachers, because they were too invested in trying to become their close friends. As a result, they had been instructed that only in extreme emergencies could they ignore those boundaries.

My home phone rang and it was Dan who seemed to be hyperventilating. "What's wrong, Dan?" Dan was a student that I was currently counseling at school. "It's Tom! He is suicidal!" Tom was a recent graduate that I was now seeing in therapy at the request of his father and social worker. Students occasionally found my phone number because it was a public number as a result of my being on the city council. "I just got off of the phone and I think Tom's in danger!" Dan sputtered through his anxiety.

I thanked Dan and told him I would take it from here. I called the police, gave them Tom's address, and then called Tom's house. No one answered the phone. I only lived a couple of miles away, so I decided to drive to Tom's house.

I arrived before the police, and Tom came out with a smile on his face, and with an upbeat voice casually said, "Hi, Jim. Could you give me a ride over to Dan's?"

"I thought you were suicidal," I exclaimed.

"Oh, I was, but I am feeling better now," Tom said with a straight face.

It turned out the two of them had concocted this "crisis" so they could get together. They wanted to avoid walking three miles on a hot day. They knew they couldn't call me to ask for a ride. But they also knew I would likely come if I knew there was an emergency. They had no hesitation, whatever the intrigue or deception, in using me for their private taxi.

Tom and Dan's internalized entitlement values, self-absorption, impulsivity, and their desire for immediate gratification in an attempt to get from point A to point B, all came together in this drama. They needed a crisis so they could respect the boundary rules we had set up earlier. This led them to concoct an emergency that would then make it acceptable to ask me for a ride so they could avoid the heat.

Additional Tentacles of Anger

Often youth become "crusaders" on behalf of friends who they perceive are being unfairly treated. They get in other people's faces or involved in their friends' business, seeking redress on their behalf. Because of their own pain, they are more sensitive to their friend's perceived injustice and their ego extends itself into their lives. They are often willing to "go down in emotional flames" over slights to people they have become attached to, rather than encourage the person to advocate on their own behalf.

One of the great general antidotes for anger is to accept things as they are, particularly if you cannot change the situation. The serenity prayer of AA communicates this beautifully. The first sentence in Scott Peck's best-selling book *The Road Less Traveled* is "Life is difficult," a paraphrase of Buddha's first noble truth. The second sentence of the book is, "When you accept this, life gets a little easier." Accepting the truth that life is hard is difficult for some young people. In too many cases, parents' wealth has been passed on to them with little "sweat equity" of their own. Frequently, material gifts flow to children to assuage parents' guilt for their absenteeism due to long hours away from home. This overindulgence sometimes happens even in financially strapped homes.

I was guilty of this when I was on the city council, teaching full time, going to graduate school, and interning at a mental health clinic, all while raising two children. I rationalized away the impact of my busy schedule, as my wife and I had jointly decided to have her stay home with the children. We were committed to avoiding daycare in order to have a primary bonding person present during our children's formative years. My schedule kept me too busy to be aware of the hurt I had buried, which I referenced earlier, regarding some aspects of my relationship with my dad.

To the world I could present myself as the next Gandhi. At home it was harder to avoid family triggers that occasionally brought forward my emotionally reactive "drill sergeant" persona. He was a beleaguered fellow, about my height, whose role was to protect me from childhood hidden hurts, which I projected onto my children as anger. I hated this dark side of my personality. Staying busy kept me away from home, allowing my hurts to remain largely dormant. Incidents like picking up my son and screaming were very rare. My anger disguised the actual hurt of not feeling respected or important because of my dad's frequent absence from my life.

It is often in our most intimate relationships that these hidden identifications, these "little selves," like my "drill sergeant" persona, are revealed. These identities, like Ron's "bad ass," are made up of unacceptable or over-identified aspects of our ego. Martha K. Grant beautifully portrays this entourage of different ego identities in her poem "The Committee":[65]

The rude one is only one of many
Who populate my inner committee,
An unruly group of stubborn complexes
Who try to run my life.
My vigilant effort to tame these insubordinates
Is ongoing, endless.
I've wheedled and flattered
And when that didn't work
Actually reasoned
With the most recalcitrant members
But it only makes them more determined.
Besides, they have my number.

---

65. Why Good People Do Bad Things: Understanding our Darker Selves by James Hollis, PhD, Martha K. Grant's "The Committee." Penguin Group Inc., 2007, 33, 34. Reprinted with permission.

They've sat too long with my therapist,
Wringing their collective hands in commiseration,
Checking sympathetically,
When all along they were gathering ammunition.
Now they are doling out assignments—
I can hear the papers shuffling—
And what's more,
Calling in new recruits from the streets.

I unconsciously attempted to furlough my "drill sergeant" by staying very busy to minimize his opportunities to seize control of my personality. Yet, unless we become fully conscious of these hidden selves, they end up holding the marionette's strings that trigger our emotional dances. If we remain unconscious we not only continue to further calcify these entities, but additional "recruits off the streets" will be created by our minds.

Children intuitively know that what we love or have interest in is where we spend our time. If parents "love" sports they spend a lot of hours watching sports. If they "love" their car, they wash, polish, or tinker with it a lot. So, like my dad, I was showing more interest in my jobs than in my children, due to unconscious fears and unmet needs from my childhood. When my children didn't listen, hurts from that childhood brought forward anger. It didn't happen often, but I was surprised how mad I could get. The "drill sergeant" was one member of my "committee" that I had yet to make peace with and integrate into my personality.

I often dissipated the energy of my anger by walking in the woods that surrounded my home so that my children would not bear the brunt of that energy. The healing energy of that natural setting quickly transformed and harmonized my emotions. Over time, I healed much of the hurt and gradually let go of the crazy idea that my kids would always listen. Every time I got angry I would examine the hurt or fear behind it. I would allow it to come forward and feel acceptance and compassion toward that wound, toward that ego-identity, rather than avoid or project it. Gradually this allowed me to stay more neutral and be more effective and consistent with my limit setting.

Limit Setting in a Culture without Limits

Children need to push limits to some degree, as it is part of their growth. Our role as parents is to set reasonable limits; kindly, firmly, and consistently. The economic culture is riddled with messages that constantly challenge or outright ignore parental and societal limits. It loudly proclaims the joys of hedonistic pursuits making individual "freedoms" sacred, while the collective needs and the joy of serving others are rarely even whispered.

Limits provide security and safety that are critical for children's emotional development. If reasonable limits are not set, a child will have too much power, which ultimately will overwhelm them. Without the security and safety that limit setting provides, children will struggle with emotional control. The art of limit setting has taken a beating due to the stress-producing pace of the economic culture. When we are stressed we sometimes "cave in" to avoid conflict or we impose limits with emotional and mental rigidity. We withdraw the love that should imbue every setting of consistent and firm limits. Love is what causes children to internalize and ultimately honor the values and expectations of their parents, even as they protest against those limits because of dashed expectations. Compassionately setting limits not only increases the probability that children will internalize parental values, it is essential for their emotional security.

Limit setting suggests that there are certain ideals or values people need to respect. The main regulator of negative emotions, that limits the intensity and range of one's emotional expression, is our internalized values. If, for example, you have the value that it is not acceptable, as a child or adolescent, to swear at your parents or other adults, this will naturally limit the frequency of it happening. I have observed many young people who routinely swear. Yet when they go into a church, or hang out with Grandma, they never utter a vulgarity. They have internalized a value based on context, where swearing isn't acceptable; and that limits even its unconscious or emotional expression. So reasonable limit setting helps children feel secure and helps them internalize important ideals and values that will help them manage their emotions. This is much more challenging when the economic culture's values of self-absorption and hedonism have permeated the culture, corrupting centuries-old traditional values of unselfishness, service, and civility toward others. This has contributed mightily to young people's struggles with emotional control and their resistance to reasonable limit setting.

To assuage my guilt for my absence and my anger, like many busy parents, I occasionally bought things, paid for events, or ignored behavior in my children that I shouldn't have. Youth who receive too many material bribes or escaped consistent limit setting, later struggle when life gets hard or more is demanded of them. They have had little experience or training for accepting the reality that challenges and difficult times are built into the fabric of life. Youth's hidden expectation that things should come easily, and that *no* does not really mean *no*, is a significant source of their frustration and anger.

This largely unconscious expectation also makes it less likely that the perseverance and dedication required to successfully engage a challenge will be sustained. Young people seem to struggle with staying engaged when things get hard, and they end up quitting prematurely. Perseverance and sacrificing smaller pleasures to accomplish something greater is a prerequisite for growth. The growth we experience through overcoming challenges makes us feel alive. This is missing in many youth's lives. Thrill seeking has become a poor and transient substitute for the energizing and positive feelings experienced when one accomplishes something difficult. More young people appear to be engaging in high-risk behaviors in order to create some sense of aliveness.

Challenges or demands on them often elicit a complaint, passive-aggressive resignation, or outright anger and even rage, because these demands run counter to their expectations. Insufficient limit setting in childhood ends up creating adolescents who have a heightened desire to be in control. When people expect more of teenagers or attempt to impose limits, the feeling of not being in control can trigger fear in them. This fear, combined with an often unconscious fear that they might fail to meet the growing expectations that come with being an adult, often expresses itself as some form of resentment. Projection often takes place, as there is a need to create an enemy to avoid taking responsibility for stepping up to life's increasing demands. Suddenly, what seems like a legitimate request from a person of authority elicits resistance, anger, and often outright hostility.

Anger and depression are closely related, and frequently anger masks depression. If one's perception is that something is not right with the world, and that person feels that it is another person's fault, the person expresses frustration or anger. If a person's perception is that something is not right with the world and it's their own fault, the person will experience depressed feelings. Whether turned inward on ourselves or outward toward others, the psychology of blame becomes the avoidance of pain. Blaming keeps us from experiencing and naming the specific underlying feelings that are behind our pain. Blaming oneself leads to an amalgamated depression that insulates us from the awareness of the specific painful emotions that are driving our depression. Blaming others brings anger and, as mentioned earlier, is a secondary emotion that also blocks the direct experience of our hurts. We need to develop the courage to feel the hurt behind our anger and depression, and nurture with the appropriate psychological salve what the direct experience of those wounds suggests.

There are a variety of experiments that can help young people successfully let go of their often unconscious conditioned expectations. If the techniques offered are practiced, they can help free people from the almost automatic negative emotions triggered by their attachments and expectations. One of these experiments is called the "Director's Chair" technique. I taught it to a twelve-year-old client who was developing acid reflexology problems. His doctor sent him to me when the prescribed medicinal interventions weren't working.

The "Director's Chair" and Emotional Neutrality— A Case Study

"So, Michael, I understand that you're having some problems with acid in your stomach and chest region."

"That's for sure," Michael said, with emphasis.

"Your doctor thinks if I could help you lower your stress levels, it might help. Would you like to lower your stress?" I asked.

"Yes, I would, because I am really stressed out," the anxiety in his voice was obvious.

"What are the stresses in your life?" I asked.

"My mom and my brother are driving me crazy! Did you know my mother comes to this clinic because she's depressed?"

"Yes, I knew that. What is it about your brother that gets to you?" I inquired.

"He just got kicked out of the Army and he has a really bad temper. When he and my mom get into it, watch out!"

"Do they fight a lot?" I asked.

"Every day they fight. I try to stay away from the apartment until supper or I go to my room when they start screaming. But, I can still hear them, and my stomach starts churning and burning."

"Why did your brother get kicked out of the Army, Michael?"

"He had schizo . . . something and was acting weird—and he IS weird," Michael said forcefully.

"Was it schizophrenia?" I asked.

"Yeah that's it! He sometimes hears things I don't hear," Michael replied.

"Tell me about their fights. What do they do and say?" I inquired.

"Something ticks them off and they start screaming and throwing things; shoes, plates, stuff like that. I try to get in between to protect my mom, but he orders me to the couch. I try to go to my room; but when he is really mad, he won't let me. So I have to watch and listen, and I can't stop it, and then my stomach starts hurting," Michael said with frustration and sadness in his voice.

"So there really is nothing you can do, is there Michael?"

"No there isn't," he said with resignation.

"Well, I have some good news for you, Michael. I know some high school students who have problems like yours. They can't change their situation, and they are too young to leave home. So they are frustrated and stressed just like you. But, they have learned to decrease their stress by using something called the 'Director's Chair.' Do you know what a director's chair looks like, Michael?"

"Yup, it sits up high and they say 'roll 'em' when they want to start filming," he offered.

"That's right. Can I teach you the Director's Chair technique to help you with your stress?"

"Yes, if it will help," he said with some enthusiasm.

"Well it has helped a lot of my high school students so I think it can help you, too. Wait a minute, how old are you?" I asked with concern.

"I am twelve," he said firmly.

"Oh nuts, you looked older than that. I have never had anyone successfully use the Director's Chair younger than fifteen," I said to bait him.

"Well, I am mature for my age, so I bet I could do it," he replied with a little bravado. He had taken the bait.

"Well, I suppose it's worth a try, because you do seem mature. Every time you see the tension begin between your mom and brother, I want you to imagine it's just a movie, and you're the director. Imagine yourself sitting up on that tall chair and say, 'Roll 'em' to yourself. You might want to give the movie a title based on the lead characters: your mom and brother. Before, you only had a bit part as the scared brother. But, now you are the director. What does a director want from his actors, Michael?"

"He wants a good performance," he said tentatively.

"That's right. He wants your brother to act angry, and your mother to have a pretty intense reaction. What do you think would be a good title for your movie, Michael? Any ideas?"

"Well my brother's like Godzilla so . . . how about *Mom Meets Godzilla?*"

"That's great," I said. "So, as the director you're actually hoping the fight scene is intense and realistic. You are just going to observe the action. You told me earlier you liked Blizzards, and I will buy you the biggest Blizzard you can find, if you can stay as the director and not become the scared little brother. I don't think you'll be able to do it, because you're so young, but maybe you'll surprise me," I said, further setting the hook.

Michael sat silent for several seconds and then said, "I don't want to be the director!"

I immediately thought I had just wasted a therapeutic hour for nothing.

He then said, "I want to be the camera man, because a camera man can swoop in and out to get close-ups and distant shots, and I can still watch the show."

I replied, "That's terrific, but I still don't think you'll get your Blizzard, because this won't be easy."

As Michael left my room he said, "We'll see," flashing a big smile.

Michael returned for the next therapy session and announced he had changed the title of his movie to *The Bitch Meets Godzilla*. He told me he had never realized how often mom put his brother down. "My mom really is a bitch at times, and I can see why my brother gets mad. I try not to laugh because now I realize they both act like children. They try to get me to pick sides, but I can see they're both to blame. When things get intense, I just zoom out. They are both going to win an Academy Award!"

Michael earned his extra-large Blizzard. I learned from Michael's mother several months later that he had recently gone into her bedroom and called 911 when his brother threatened to get a knife during an argument. The police arrived and Michael's actions ultimately led to his brother getting additional help for his mental illness. Michael obviously had continued to practice his version of the Director's Chair technique. This helped him detach from his ego's identification as mom's rescuer. He saw things more objectively as the camera man, a neutral witness to the dysfunction. This neutral witnessing did not inhibit him from calling the police. The Director's Chair technique helped Michael detach and be more clear-headed about what needed to be done. As a result, Michael was less stressed and happier, and his newfound neutrality also ended his acidic health issues.

There are two other experiments at the end of this chapter that can help establish neutrality in situations that normally hook us emotionally. If practiced, they help change our habitual unconscious emotional reactions in situations that we have little power to alter, except through making an internal mental shift. There are many varieties of therapy, but all successful therapies have one thing in common: they involve detachment. We learn how to let go of the overextensions of our ego, with their accompanying attachments, expectations, and hurts. We are able to change and establish new habits, while experiencing healing and greater freedom.

Choosing Our Emotions

There is fertile ground and great hope for decreasing young people's painful emotions. There is a growing recognition that the economic culture's model of happiness does not deliver on its promises. Let me give a hint of the power we all have to not only control, but to even choose our emotions. We live in a culture that has imprinted the perspective that emotions are automatic reactive responses to challenging or "unfair" external events. Therefore, we are powerless to change our emotional habit pattern, and we feel victimized by these "unfair" situations. The following example was shared by Dr. Arya when I was twenty-six, and it provided hope that I didn't have to live as a victim of circumstance.

> The phone rings. You've been arguing rather heatedly, let's say, with your teenager. It rings just when things are getting intense. A friend whose call you've been expecting is on the phone. Immediately, there is a change in your voice and attitude. "Hello? Oh, hi . . . Yes, I look forward to it—pick me up at 7:00—can't wait." You hang up the phone, and you're right back at it with your son or daughter.

What this reveals is that you made a choice to be pleasant, even playful, because your mind made a quick discrimination that your friend didn't deserve your wrath. You were not faking. There was an emotional shift reflected in your voice that responded immediately to the change in your intention. We have the power to choose emotions and quickly let go of negative emotions in even a more conscious way than this phone example suggests.

Two Detachment Strategies to Pacify Negative Emotions

In addition to the Director's Chair technique, here are two other detachment strategies that helped many students and clients. These techniques proved effective in detaching from strong emotions, particularly with young students and clients, who seemed more open to trying these experiments.

1. Brain Tumor Technique: A Case Study

This technique is useful when dealing with a person that frustrates or angers you—someone who seems to frequently push your buttons, whether a boss, coworker, or family member. This technique recognizes the reality that there is always hurt behind anger. If you can relate to the other person's hurt and pain rather than some irritating behavior, it helps you detach. It starts by imagining the person who has "provoked" you with a brain tumor that is growing rapidly, is inoperable, and will likely soon cause death. You are now aware that this person has been acting in an increasingly hostile or irritating manner because their growing tumor has altered the brain's chemistry and its function. The person can't help themselves. Nancy employed this technique very creatively.

> My dad was being a jerk. I asked him days before if I could use his car to go out with my best friend to a movie. He said yes, than started changing his mind. He told me I never put gas in his car and I always left the inside a mess, and he was "sick of it!" This is one of his favorite phrases that ticks me off. My dad and I always get into these stupid fights, and I sometimes end up slamming doors and saying "f . . . it!" I could feel steam coming out of my ears. Then suddenly, I remembered the Brain Tumor idea you suggested earlier in the week. I imagined an oozing, bloody, expanding and pulsating tumor inside my dad's skull. It looked like it was about to explode, and would kill my dad. My dad does have health problems, and despite our fights and the fact that I do think he can be an ass sometimes, I wouldn't want to lose him. So I put a top hat on his tumor, gave the tumor legs and arms with a cane, and a face with a big smile. I had the tumor dance right out of my dad's skull. My dad kept saying stuff, but surprisingly I didn't argue back because the dancing tumor had lightened my mood. I actually apologized for not helping out with gas and the times I left taco bags in his car. But I also was able to tell him, calmly, that I really hated to disappoint my friend because she was expecting me soon. He exhaled kind of loud and said, 'All right, but, don't leave the car a mess!'

Nancy was creative, honest, and had enough positive connections to her father that this detachment strategy worked. Sometimes so much damage has been done to a relationship that students report that they cannot let go of being glad that the person they were conflicted with had a brain tumor. However, in most cases, compassion arose and they sensed the pain and struggles the other person was having.

This more empathetic and detached state helps one see reality more objectively in several ways. It reinforces the truth that hurt drives our anger. It also demonstrates that the "prickly" behaviors of the other person are less about us and more about that person's problems or lack of awareness. Most importantly, it illustrates that we have a choice as to how we react. With practice we can get better at stepping out of our habitual emotion reactions. In this more neutral place, we can sometimes gently and sincerely offer an opposing perspective while modeling how to share feelings and differences in a more positive manner. We are able to quit judging and reacting to others long enough to discern when we're most likely to be heard. We realize that by delaying the sharing of our perspective for a more opportune time, we increase the likelihood we will be heard.

2. Detachment technique: "Interesting, There's Anger in Me."

Phil Nurenburger, a psychologist and engaging speaker, told a story at a Yoga Congress and the story itself suggests when to employ this technique.

> Phil had a cousin around twelve whom his mom was insisting he entertain at a family gathering. Phil was a few years older than his cousin, and had no interest in doing anything with him, but eventually he "hatched an idea" and gave into his mom's request. Phil's home had a relatively steep sloping backyard. He invited his cousin to race with him down the hill. His cousin was excited to be with Phil, and about the running.
>
> They went tearing down the hill, feet flying and exhilaratingly losing control. What Phil knew, and his cousin didn't, was the long grass at the bottom of the hill concealed a drop off into a muddy creek bed. Right before hitting the tall grass, Phil yelled out, "Watch out!" and Phil veered away. It was too late for his cousin, whose momentum carried him into the long grass and beyond. He was not injured, only scraped a bit and muddied.

Phil's story is a metaphor for our anger. It is difficult to veer out of the groove of anger once it has gained intensity and momentum. However, the technique of saying continuously over and over,

"Interesting, there's anger in me," can help us detach from the groove of anger even after it gets rolling and is gaining momentum. Sometimes it is helpful to use the third person and substitute our first name: "Interesting there's anger in Sue," or Fred, etc. This provides the perspective of a witness that can help us step back from our anger.

When someone does something that angers us, the language of the ego says: *I'M* mad! This ensures that we will totally identify with our anger, and it takes over our entire mind. The anger and "I" become inseparable. It is fine to have emotions, but we don't want to *be* our emotions. So by using the word "interesting" and "in me" or "in Sue," over and over again, we can begin to separate the feelings from us. The word "interesting" is a detaching word, a neutralizing word, and it helps shift our mind to a neutral witness. We become more like a scientist studying our anger.

The more one practices this technique, the easier it is to let go of one's anger. Initially it can take hundreds of repetitions.

"Interesting, there is anger in Jim."

"Interesting, there is anger in Jim, his heart is pumping so hard his aorta is about to explode."

"Interesting, there is anger in Jim, he's about to tear every strand of hair from his scalp."

"Interesting, there's anger in Jim, but, hey, his ears and toes aren't angry; they seem to be doing fine."

"Interesting . . . ," you get the idea.

Students repeating phrases like this often report that they eventually broke out laughing, and their anger just dissolved. It is possible to change and hasten a return to balance by detaching from our old habits, expectations, attachments, and identifications. Many of these habits developed as unintended consequences of living with the values and stresses of the economic culture. We examine the nature of change in Chapter 15, but without practicing some means of detachment, old habits will die hard.

Chapter 12
Disintegrating Values and Relationships in the Economic Culture

"If we try to listen, we find it extraordinarily difficult because we are always projecting our opinions and ideas, our prejudices, our backgrounds, our inclinations, our impulses; when they dominate we hardly listen to what is being said . . . One listens and therefore learns, only in a state of attention, a state of silence, in which the whole background is in abeyance, is quiet; then, it seems to me it is possible to communicate."

—KRISHNAMURTI

"My advice to you is to get married. If you find a good wife, you'll be happy; if not, you'll become a philosopher."

—SOCRATES

We have been discussing how the values and messages of the economic culture affect youth, and how our ego's unwillingness to examine its insecurities and attachments leads to many painful emotions. It creates the conditions for expanding the power of the media's image making and encourages advertisers' manipulations. The suggestions and values represented in the media create stress and confusion about life's purpose, compounding the suffering of our youth.

Hedonistic advertisements encourage young people to do what feels good and ignore parental and cultural limit setting. We have created a generation gap through media messages portraying friction and misunderstanding between generations as inevitable, and it has become a self-fulfilling prophesy. The generation gap is relatively nonexistent in many other parts of the globe. The reality that youth will spend significantly more time together during adolescence doesn't equate in less-developed countries to a drastic increase in friction with parents. We will see whether the phenomenon of a generation gap becomes more universal as the economic empire and media messages reverberate across the planet.

Extreme individualism, pushing limits without concern for its effects on others, is increasingly the norm. Cars overloaded with large sub woofers vibrating and blasting neighborhoods, jarring a child or an elderly person out of a nap, become "collateral damage" to "my" fun. There isn't a hostile intent, but a deep self-absorption that doesn't consider the larger village.

The Economic Culture and the Elderly

A T-shirt on a five-year-old at an Ashram in India where I was recently doing five weeks of silence read: "If the music's too loud, than you're too old." This T-shirt reveals much about the cultural shifts we have been exploring. Old people need to get out of the way. They are rarely viewed in our culture as potentially possessing more wisdom through having observed and experienced life over a longer period of time. In a youth-centered culture, where moral, ethical, and spiritual values are replaced by economic considerations, this should come as no surprise. The elderly rarely have a place of prominence in the culture, as they are less important in the consumption demographics except in areas like healthcare and scams. The idea, however, that the elderly should hold an important role in advancing the culture is not even considered. The geographical scattering that has splintered the family, often as a result of pursuing the goals of the economic culture, has contributed to the isolation and loneliness experienced by many of our elderly. In the economic culture, when you have lost your economic role, you have lost status and, all too often, purpose and meaning.

It would be worthwhile to consciously create forums to seek some of the elderly's counsel in order to tap their insights, knowledge, and wisdom. We need to systemically create meaningful opportunities for our elders to contribute something valuable to society. Not one retired teacher, that I am aware of, participated in an exit meeting designed to explore their suggestions for improving the education system they had worked in for decades. We could be creating systems in our education institutions for exceptional and interested retirees to mentor new teachers and participate in building a better education system.

These kinds of dialogues and opportunities should be present in all fields. The fact this rarely occurs gives support to the perception that at a certain age you are "devalued." Elders may remain as sympathetic characters, but that is very different from being respected for the gifts that still remain. There is not an obvious economic windfall for tapping wisdom and sustaining purpose in our elderly. This loss of intellectual "capital," and the lack of opportunity to extend purposeful living, needs to be reversed, as it would significantly ameliorate our elderly's epidemic of loneliness. Each retired individual is currently left on their own to figure how to battle against the economic cultural message that "your time has passed." It is wonderful and admirable that many elderly seek purpose through volunteer opportunities, but we are underutilizing this tremendous resource.

The Economic Culture: Youth Centered vs. Youth Needs

Despite the growing population of elderly, America is largely a youth- or child-centered culture, including the economic culture's efforts to condition children's consumption habits. Don't assume, however, that this child-centered focus bestows a benefit on our youth. Many young people are more lost and less happy than ever before. The importance and attention paid to youth by the economic culture is rarely driven by good will and noble intentions. Profit is the obvious focus of the economic culture. This is an appropriate focus if this motive was paired with positive societal goals, and not just an effort to increase consumption and distractions for personal greed. The expectation-embedded messages in the carnival pitch to our youth boil down to: "Your individual desires are preeminent, they will make you happy, and they need to be satisfied sooner rather than later." To change these egocentric expectations, we need to pair the profit motive to societal goals that create systems that tap the wisdom of our elderly, and the purposeful creativity of our youth.

Many exhausted parents assuage a gnawing guilt about their absence from their children's lives by purchasing fool's gold for them. Objects and events bring some pleasure, but the pleasure soon fades, and another desire quickly replaces it. The new itch intensifies and it seems that it can only be scratched through another acquisition, setting in motion a process that is insatiable and leads to no lasting satisfaction. What children really need is our time and full attention. They desire our involvement with them much more than things, assuming their addiction to objects is not too far along. Frequently, as parents, our unresolved childhood issues often fuel the tendency to express love through things or special events.

I am amazed, when working with youth, at the enlivening transformative power of something as simple as sustained eye contact and interest shown through listening and relaxed attention. I have found this to be the real elixir youth are craving, sometimes desperately so. Eckhart Tolle highlights the power of giving authentic attention: "Attention dissolves the barriers created by conceptual thought. It joins perceiver and perceived in a unifying field of awareness. It heals separation."

Instead of supplying external enticements, parents can be present through teaching and modeling for young children the appreciation and connection gained through helping with family tasks. Developmentally, children are naturally egocentric and this requires us to nurture their unselfish impulses. I have seen the engaged faces of young children participating in a shared effort to help prepare meals, set tables, say grace, or even when helping to wash the family's dishes. This collective family effort, experiencing the connection created by pulling together, is one of the antidotes to the fragmenting effects of the extreme individualism and selfishness embedded in the messages of the economic culture.

When there is a multigenerational family gathering for events like Thanksgiving, conversation and connection is frequently interrupted by texting, cell phones going off, and video games emerging. Many adults have capitulated to the child-centered expectation that this is just the way it is. In other homes, the opposite imbalance occurs where children's help is enlisted like forced labor. This, and the other extreme where little help or effort of any kind is required of the child, interferes with the potential for deeper family bonds. The demanding approach brings resentment, and the no-expectations approach reinforces the unconscious entitlement mindset. This is why it is so essential to model, teach, and enthusiastically reinforce young children when they contribute to family needs and cohesiveness.

The Withering of Social Skills: Relationships in Peril

Many youth and adults are increasingly lost in their individual world of videos, movies, television, virtual realities, and computer games. They do not develop the necessary social skills to initiate, sustain, or give the requisite time required for creating psychologically intimate relationships. Growing numbers of people literally lose contact with daily reality and with their primary relationships in their pursuit of virtual realities. They are more interested in creating an online life that brings some connection, but also allows for people to project and exaggerate underdeveloped aspects of their personality, attempting to satisfy unmet relational needs in their daily lives. They escape facing and working on their insecurities and fears. They also escape many of the very real emotional challenges and difficulties inherent in developing greater intimacy in the family and other significant relationships. People often become so addicted to building the scaffolding of their virtual world, they are willing to let their real jobs, marriages, and families fall apart.

The cumulative effect of the hectic lifestyle of the economic culture and the desire to escape its stress through technological immersions into other realities is that relationships suffer. The result is that many relationships are less psychologically intimate as people's individual interests take priority over relational connections. This increases couples' disappointment, leading to an estrangement that creates serious relational conflicts and more frequent ruptures of those relationships. Parents know from experience, what research also reveals, and that is just how difficult divorce and family stress can be on children. If we are going to bring more cohesiveness and harmony to our society, we will have to address the causes of increased family stress and the intensifying pressures on couples' relationships. This needs to be a higher priority than increasing Christmas sales over the previous year.

Many young people carry an idealized notion of marriage shaped by the romantic ideals of relationships portrayed by Hollywood. They resist the reality that there will inevitably be friction in any long-term relationship. When couples merge from two different family systems, the differences in perspectives and expectations will inevitably lead to some frustrations. Commitment to work hard on developing the skills necessary to resolve conflict surrounding these differences is often absent. Conflicts triggered by differing expectations and fueled by each person's childhood insecurities often lead to defensiveness and poor communication.

The self-indulgent emphasis of the economic culture deepens each individual's unconscious attachments and expectations. This serves to intensify conflicts. An individual's pleasure, comfort, and desires can become preeminent in the relationship and their partners' needs become secondary. Making these differing underlying expectations conscious, communicating them kindly and skillfully as you work to compromise and resolve these differences, is very challenging. How well couples execute this process of communication and compromise will determine the quality of their relationships, as well as the harmony or stress experienced by the children raised in that family. Isolating oneself on the computer, losing oneself in games and videos, or constant television viewing atrophies the social and communication skills essential to long-lasting and satisfying relationships.

The Chinese word for conflict is a combination of two characters—danger and opportunity. Accepting there will be differences to resolve due to differing expectations born of our childhood hurts, and internalized desires from the economic culture, helps couples move in the direction of opportunity. Long-term relationships almost always bring forward unmet needs from our past. Relationships provide the opportunity to increase our awareness of these, so we can heal and integrate our hurts, which contributes to our individual happiness and to more harmonious relationships.

The realization that conflict has a self-awareness opportunity in it is obscured not just by Hollywood movies and eHarmony commercials. The opportunity for self-awareness that helps us identify and heal our childhood insecurities is buried under the avalanche of the self-absorbed messages of the economic culture. Arguments of couples usually degenerate into what each person is not getting, rather than what each person can give to the relationship. Alfred Adler, the famous psychiatrist and contemporary of Freud, said, "Relationships flourish when *each* person cares more about their partners' needs than their own." Unrealistic and unexamined selfish expectations always escalate emotions and increase relational conflict.

If a person understands that some conflict or disagreement is inevitable, this in itself will soften their overall expectations of their partner. This acceptance can decrease defensiveness and increase the opportunity for increased self-awareness and growth, which strengthens and enlivens the relationship. Expectations turn relationships into a contract, a business relationship. If you do "this," then I will love you; but if you do "that," then I will withdraw my love. Life is relationships and relationships imply sharing. Communicating the desire to resolve differences kindly at the beginning of a relationship can help provide each partner the assurance, confidence, and security needed to stay engaged when conflict emerges.

One practical way to decrease expectations and the strong emotions they evoke is to have couples practice shifting their own needs to preferences. Preferences lower expectations and bring less resistance when couples are exploring differences. They allow for less attachment to a particular outcome and are more empowering than a need orientation.

Accepting the reality of some friction, and shifting needs to preferences, can help couples approach their differences with more love and
compassion. The opportunity for growth is enhanced, and the likelihood of danger recedes. Shifting needs to preferences, when practiced
over time, can drastically improve communication. Developing compassionate nonviolent communication to safely share fears and resolve
differing expectations with one's partner can deepen one's unconditional love, which then often generalizes to the rest of one's life.

Parents and others who work with adolescents and young adults
need to help youth examine ways to shift from the self-*ish* values of the
economic culture. The art of compromise and dialogue is not embedded
in movies, ads, or TV sitcoms; but they are the birthplace for many of
our expectations and our desire for instant gratification. Examining and
detaching from our internalized economic values of extreme individuality, impatience, and hedonism is difficult. Many of youth's relationships
painfully rupture in the first few years, and many of the seeds for that
rupture were sown by the implicit messages of the economic culture.
Without consciously working on one's attachments and expectations,
people end up in conflicted and loveless marriages, where alienation
and loneliness pervade their shared living space.

Loneliness and isolation are not just the world of many of our senior
citizens or conflicted couples. Loneliness, isolation, and alienation, as
we shall see, are growing, and becoming increasingly oppressive for
young people.

Experiment:

Letting Go of Expectations—Do I Have to Have This to Be Happy?

A simple but very useful and practical experiment is to notice each time one's upset is triggered by a particular situation or a particular behavior of another person. Identify the hidden expectation or attachment and ask yourself: Do I need to have this go a particular way for me to be happy? Could I theoretically remain happy even if things go "badly"—not according to my expectations? Usually, your own intuition and discriminating wisdom will help you realize it is possible, even when things are very difficult, to let go of the expectations and attachments that are driving our negative emotions. We can then ride through these challenges with some degree of equanimity. At some deeper level, we know we have that strength. Again, like all new habits, this requires practice to improve and potentially gain mastery over our emotional reactivity.

Chapter 13
"Hello, I'm in My Room—
Is Anyone Out There?"

"Me is the seed from which the plant of loneliness grows."

—Dr. Urshabudh Arya

"At the innermost core of all loneliness is a deep and powerful yearning for union with ones lost self."

—Krishnamurti

External consumption and self-absorption cannot satisfy the longings of the soul. More and more youth are experiencing an existential depression, but continue to look for external and often media-driven salves for treatment. Youth are lost in videos, online games, cable shows, social media such as Facebook, tweeting, texting, sexting, and on pornographic websites, desperately searching for ways to lessen their growing despair. Exhausted parents struggle to adequately supervise these activities, and these electronic entertainments often also become de-facto baby-sitters so parents have some downtime for themselves. Many parents are stuck in their own addictions. Sixty-five percent of the residents in American households play video or online computer games, and addiction is occurring across all age groups in those homes.[66]

---

66. Dr. Phil Show, 2011.

Technological Distractions and Risks

Young people between eight and eighteen spend over forty-four hours a week, on average, with videos, chat lines, Facebook, and online gaming.[67] This doesn't include texting, tweeting, or phone conversations, which would bring the number to over sixty-three hours of media and technological involvement every week.[68] Most of this goes unsupervised as parents struggle to monitor the unrelenting onslaught of the consumer culture. One-third of young people end up looking at pornographic sites, 42 percent report having been bullied on the Internet, and 16 percent say they would meet their online virtual friends "without hesitation."[69]

The desire for connection often drives a blind trust, despite the fact that 69 percent of them have received sexually suggestive or offensive messages online.[70] Addictions to social media, sexting, porn, video, and gambling games can be as powerful as drugs. These addictions develop in a family setting and once developed, further compromise family cohesiveness, while eroding the mental health and even the hygiene of those stuck in their addictions. These problems are likely to intensify as one quarter of today's three-year-olds goes online daily.

Forty-plus hours a week engaged mostly in fantasy is tragic if only because of what it replaces in young people's lives. For many, this eliminates or severely restricts exercise, connection to nature, psychological intimacy with family members, healthy social interaction, reading, service to one's community, and a more penetrating self-awareness. In short, it eliminates balanced, purposeful, and healthy living.

Parental supervision is sometimes lacking because they, too, are pursuing their own technological interests and conspicuous consumption. For example, since 1950 houses' average square footage has almost tripled. This happened even as the average number of children in families during that same time period decreased by over half. This reflects our desires, not our needs, as we adults got caught up in our ego's desire

---

67. "Too Cruel for School" by Peg Tyre, Family Circle, Oct. 1, 2010, 42.

68. Ibid.

69. Ibid.

70. Ibid.

to be *SOMEBODY*. What we gained in square footage, we lost to increased stress, decreased personal growth time, and a lack of family cohesiveness.

New videos and games allow youth to view carnage more realistically and experience it more intensely. Hundreds of studies have shown that this desensitizes people to violence. There is growing concern even in the military about this desensitization. Significant increases in mistreatment of innocent civilians by American soldiers in Iraq and Afghanistan has resulted in the military investigating the causes for this growing abuse that was perpetrated mostly by young soldiers. The army wants to determine whether there is a link between the violent dehumanizing images in games and videos, and increases in callous and abhorrent behavior. Desensitization and violence is occurring not only abroad, but senseless acts of violence are increasingly within our own borders.

Social Isolation, Diminished Social Skills, and Loneliness

There is another insidious effect of these ubiquitous games and videos in addition to desensitization. More young people are spending time at younger and younger ages alone with their games, videos, card collections, etc. Their ability to relate to real people is being profoundly compromised by this social isolation. We learn through doing; our social skills do not develop in a vacuum.

The hours locked away in their rooms makes it challenging for many to connect to others. Their poorly developed social skills make reaching out and interacting with others awkward and anxiety producing. The inability to establish true friendships and psychologically intimate social connections isolates growing numbers of young people. This creates a negative feedback loop, where their anxiety and awkwardness make taking the risk to reach out to others less likely, intensifying their isolation. When they take the risk and attempt to connect face to face with peers, their poorly developed skills create a greater risk for rejection and loss, which can trigger further withdrawal.

Occasional negative outcomes in establishing peer relationships, including occasional rejection, were part of the learning curve for most of us growing up. Studies of people whose main relationships are virtual reveal that rejection increases their defensiveness and further intensifies their isolation.[71] This withdrawal can be triggered by online rejections and bullying, which is not an uncommon occurrence, though it usually remains hidden from parents. Youth's defensiveness often spikes when parents try to intervene to minimize their child's withdrawal from family and social interactions. Youth don't want to be interrupted from their increasingly addictive pursuits. Their kinder and positive communication skills atrophy, along with their interest and motivation in participating in relationships and civil discourse.

Youth's isolation and its impact on social connection and intimacy produce a profound loneliness. Being alone or choosing solitude is not what is being described here. Many of us love alone time. Being alone does not equate to loneliness. Young people's loneliness and isolation, that at first glance seems self-imposed, is often part of an addictive process involving online gaming that erodes and blocks the development of their social skills. Yet, the desire for connection remains and, because it isn't occurring, a quiet desperation gradually intensifies. This feeling of disconnectedness can turn inward feeding depression, or outward, expressed as hostility, distrust, and even paranoia. Either way, it compromises any sense of a purposeful and meaningful existence, and destroys hope for many young people for a positive future. The way adolescent brains interpret peer exclusion and isolation helps us understand how overwhelming their despair can become. "Some brain scan studies, in fact, suggest that our brains react to peer exclusion much as they respond to threats to physical health or food supply. At the neural level, in other words, we perceive social rejection as a threat to existence."[72]

Youth sitting alone, losing themselves hour after hour in videos and virtual worlds, may be triggering their self-preservation fear. This primal fear we now know registers in the brain and likely in the hearts of

---

71. "All the Lonely People" by Brad Edmondson, AARP Magazine, 2010, 56.

72. "Beautiful Brains" by David Dobbs, National Geographic—The New Science of the Teenage Brain, October 2011.

isolated youth. This leads to a deep-seated fear where youth worry that more satisfying and intimate peer relationships will never occur. This deepening fear drains hope and energy, often ending in depression.

In studies on loneliness, the people with one of the lowest rates of loneliness were people diagnosed with cancer. Bob Riter, a cancer survivor himself and director of a Cancer Resource Center in New York, explains this in a 2010 AARP article. He stated that people with this life-threatening diagnosis are often thrown together, much like soldiers in a war zone. They end up creating, through their common struggle, a deep connection, a bond that decreases their loneliness.[73]

This is suggestive, in terms of what is missing in many young people's lives. Growing numbers of youth have as their closest friends Internet people they have never met in person. It's easier to show a pseudo self-confidence when relationships are more virtual than real. I have had many students express how deeply in love they were with their "online soul mate." But, this "love" was more a longing for connection in the hope of ending their loneliness and alienation. It was an attachment born of loneliness, not love. Their "love" was an expression of an internal desperation. Psychiatrist Jacqueline Olds, in the same AARP article on loneliness, puts it this way: "We've known for a long time that people who don't feel connected to something outside themselves feel a malaise, as if there's a hole in their lives."[74]

These online romances reflect youth's longing for social connection, but the isolation hole they are falling into is collapsing their hopes for intimate relationships. Researchers have found higher educational levels or higher incomes do not decrease loneliness rates. Liv Ullman said, "Hollywood is loneliness beside the swimming pool." Many of the youth I counseled spent long hours isolated in their rooms playing videos, gaming, or on Facebook; they were not poor, but they were miserably unhappy.

---

73. "All the Lonely People" by Brad Edmondson, AARP Magazine, 2010, 84.

74. Ibid.

The Costs of Loneliness

Research points to serious medical problems that accompany lone-liness. Problems include higher rates of obesity, sleep disorders, chronic pain, higher cortisol levels, high blood pressure, 56 percent higher anxiety levels, emotional control problems, and earlier deaths.[75] At first glance, this seems almost counterintuitive. These young people are not engaged in obvious anxiety or stress-producing activities as they sit at home "having fun." But, the real fear is just below the façade—the fear of remaining isolated, disconnected, and with few prospects for a real relational future. This fear we now know registers in the brain as a deep-seeded self-preservation fear. Loneliness or isolation from peers is perceived as a threat to their very existence. This fear stokes their stress levels, which is reflected in higher levels of the stress hormone cortisol, higher blood pressure, and other physiological measures of anxiety. These health risks can hasten young people's deaths.

Studies reveal that people who are lonely have more difficulty managing their emotions. This is reflected in their tendency to over-react to small annoyances and express more overt anger.[76] We see a lot of this in young people, and I suspect these are really signs of depression fed by isolation. An additional consistent finding is that people who regard themselves as deeply religious or spiritual report much lower levels of loneliness. This may reflect a connection to a divine reality, but likely also illustrates the benefits of belonging and feeling part of a community.

A growing body of research on factors that increase happiness has a sense of belonging and community right at the top of the list. Denmark's government actually facilitates getting people together who have similar interests. They provide transportation and communica-tion conduits, and even provide financial incentives to connect people. This facilitation has resulted in 92 percent of Denmark's people belonging to social clubs.[77] Perhaps it is not surprising then that several

---

75. Ibid.

76. Ibid.

77. A New Day A New Me, "Own: What is the Happiest Place in the World?" Sept. 21, 2011. http://a new day a new me.com.

studies have rated Denmark as the happiest country in the world. The most recent report is an October 13, 2011, study done by the Organization for Economic Development (OECD), which rated Denmark number one in happiness among forty countries studied.[78] On the other hand, for those left disconnected and alone, it is harder for them to experience contentment or conceptualize a hopeful future.

Many of the youth struggling with loneliness who I worked with as a therapist and a teacher had "lost their faith"—first in themselves, then in others, and finally in God. Perhaps their faith wasn't really lost. Young people chasing the pursuits of the economic culture results in more superficial and unsatisfying connections to others, and leaves little time or energy to explore something transcendent—something that might awaken or deepen their faith.

Technological Sophistication, Social Skills Emaciation: A Case Study

Bob, a student I had known for three years, was twenty years old with a high IQ. He had been in my men's group, a DBT group for emotional regulation, and a group we called: "Love, Superglue, and You." This was a relationship group to help young people distinguish between healthy loving relationships and dependent attachments. He had never had a girlfriend, but he suddenly announced after one of the groups: "I'm thinking about getting married.

"To whom?" I asked.

He was unusually animated as he discussed a sixteen-year-old girl from Alaska "who," he gleefully shared, "is really into me."

But, marriage, after only a two-week Internet relationship, seemed extreme. Bob had always resisted going to work because of his social anxiety. He said he was now willing to take on the challenge in order to provide for her. He revealed in the course of our conversation that she had cancer. When I inquired about the details of the cancer and her prognosis, he said he hadn't asked as she didn't seem too concerned about it. I would have thought that question might have arisen, given they were discussing

---

78. Ibid.

spending a lifetime together. Yet after only two weeks of Internet communication, he was convinced she was "the one," and was going to tackle his reticence about working.

Bob had spent much of his adolescence and young "adult" life lost in computer and video games. In childhood, he disappeared for hours playing with Pokémon cards and watching cartoons. He was allowed to do so. He was now absolutely convinced that the Internet had led him to the love of his life. Two or three weeks passed where Bob was suddenly absent from school. I heard from his work coordinator that he had made no job applications, and he was not responding to phone calls. Bob finally returned, and I asked him where he had been and about his lack of effort to secure a job, given his desire to provide for his future wife.

He said with a flat affect and no eye contact, "She dropped me; she apparently wasn't as in to me as I thought."

This illustrates not only the risk of a virtual relationship, but also a young life spent in isolation with fantasy games. Bob was sincerely disappointed, he seemed depressed and even more cynical after his loss. His despair, however, was driven more by his unrealistic attachments, expectations, and fantasies that grew out of his loneliness, than by the girl's decision.

In essence, Bob was delusional, not because he was mentally ill, but because he had spent sixty hours a week alone with his games, isolated in fantasy and avoidance for years. He had little experience as to how to nurture a fledgling relationship, or what a meaningful relationship looked like. He had never developed those skills, and this tragedy plagues many youth. This young man was desperately longing for connection, but the skills and life experience necessary to make that a reality were literally "missing in action." Bob was hospitalized twice for suicidal ideations and gestures in the year following his Internet rejection.

Another student I counseled, after only a two-week Internet "rendezvous," decided to drop his real girlfriend. He shared with me that he was now engaged to his new Internet partner. I did not even ask how this engagement was accomplished since, having been down this road before, I was skeptical that this relationship would last. When I asked him her name, he said "Susan." When I asked the last name of his fiancée, he paused a long time and said, "I don't know."

These stories illustrate how deep the longing for connection and relationship is in youth, and in all people. Unfortunately, the skills to make this a reality have atrophied, lost in the fantasies and self-indulgences of the economic culture. I am not advocating ending these social network connections completely. Facebook, chat rooms, texting, tweeting, and even gaming that preferably involves other people have their place. Many people have made online connections through the Internet that have resulted in life-long relationships and 96 percent of teenagers are on social networks. There is nothing inherently wrong with these activities, and without them many youth would have little social discourse. It is again a question of balance. When almost all of one's discretionary time is lost to technological diversions, what other elements of life are being sacrificed? Writer Peter M. Leschak, a long-time Facebook user, shares why he decided to "delete" Facebook:

> Facebook's . . . mesmerizing growth and reach and its power to hijack attention and focus to mostly trivial concerns make it a fat target for deletion. Facebook is a burglar of time, and as a living human, time is the only thing you own for sure until you die. Almost any activity short of crime is healthier than festering in front of a screen, especially when you don't have to. . . . We're keenly aware of the narcissm of the social network—the "Look at me! Look at me!" spirit of pictures and posts and the shallow caricature of a Facebook "Friend." But more telling is the detachment from outer reality fostered by residing online. Facebook is one more inoculation against "being here now." I submit that you cannot "be" online in the same sense you can "be" outdoors or "be" with people or "be" in pain or "be" in love. Cyberspace is a narrow communications channel, that however useful for limited information exchange, offers only a fleeting illusion of being connected to anything but the computer itself.[79]

We need to recognize that forty to sixty hours lost in videos, games, and Internet pseudo-relationships every week is not a life well lived. The diminished social skills and avoidance of reality come at a cost, and delay meaningful living.

---

79. "Goodbye to a trivial pursuit" by Peter M. Leschak, Star Tribune, March 4, 2012.

I have had students get very angry and even suffer panic attacks when their cell phone was set aside during classes, or when I required it be turned off during a therapy session. One student carried a doctor's notice that allowed her to periodically text while at work to abate her panic episodes. This demonstrates both a longing for connection as well as an unhealthy dependency, and perhaps a codependency on the part of the doctor. CNN reported a study in February 2012 showing that 66 percent of adults in the United Kingdom said they were very anxious or even panicky if they were without their cell phones. The younger adults' percentages were even higher. They have named this growing phenomenon "nomophobia." We cannot let our youth lose themselves and sacrifice much of their potential and future due to poor social skills lost to their tech and text obsessions.

Learning to Relate

I cofacilitated a high-functioning Asperger's group for a few years at Transition Plus, a program for at-risk young adults. Many of these students proclaimed during the first group gathering that they would be happy alone. Happy, assuming that someone would provide them a house or an apartment, food, and the finances to engage their individual interests. However, as they gradually felt more comfortable in the group, many revealed a crushing loneliness and a desire for connection. They wanted deeper relationships, particularly with peers. Unfortunately, they had little idea as to how to make that happen. Many for years had withdrawn into cartoons, media and tech options, or read fiction with powerful protagonists. Almost all had also been teased, shunned, or bullied at early ages because of their social awkwardness.

Our group became a practice ground for developing the social skills they lacked. We went to coffee shops, out to eat together, and even attended a play on Asperger's syndrome together during non-school hours. By the end of the year, many had exchanged phone numbers and interacted comfortably and playfully in the hallway before us "old people" arrived to facilitate the group. Several students began going to events together, independent of the group, and created opportunities to just "hang out." This growth was wonderful to witness and suggestive of

186

the potential for isolated or relationally awkward youth to deepen their peer connections.

These students needed modeling and opportunities to practice learning how to relate to people, particularly their peers, in order to lower their anxiety in social situations. Many programs and groups have been created to enhance the skills of children with compromised social skills. The earlier these interventions occur, the more the child benefits. These skills would not have atrophied as significantly for many of these young people if they hadn't been allowed to withdraw for forty to sixty hours into games and other technological enticements of the economic culture. Despite the "fun" young people say they are having, their fun does not equate to contentment; and it is rarely tied to purposeful living. Addictions and avoidance of social interactions are ultimately not enjoyable and can lead to a debilitating loneliness and other lifelong consequences. Communication skills that support building and sustaining healthy intimate relationships are being eroded and stifled by the seduction of individual consumer-based notions of happiness.

Bullying, Busyness, and Diminished Social Skills in the Economic Culture

There is another surprising negative effect of poorly developed social skills: bullying. In a *Family Circle* magazine article, "Too Cruel for School," the connection is made between a disturbing decline in social skills and bullying among adolescents. A 2009 federal research study suggested that bullying is becoming epidemic in schools, with 32 percent of middle and high school students reporting being victimized during the year. An estimated 160,000 students stay home each day to avoid bullying.[80]

Bullying is also exhibited through social media. Eighty-eight percent of teens said they had witnessed cruelty on cyber sites, with 15 percent having been personally bullied during the past year, according to a November 2011 Pew Research Center study.[81] The effects of emotional

---

80.   "Too Cruel for School" by Peg Tyre, Family Circle, October 1, 2010, 43.

81.   Pew Research Study November 2011, on cyber bullying.

cruelty and intimidation can be devastating. Victims feel the same intensity of fear and anxiety as they would if they had been physically attacked. In both circumstances, the self-preservation fear goes on overdrive. Bullying leads to distraction and the inability to concentrate, often resulting in poorer grades. It leads to overwhelming feelings of powerlessness and despair, sometimes resulting in suicide— "bully-cide."

In the 2009 study reported in *Family Circle*, researchers asked teachers whether children's ability to "get along" had declined over the last decade. Seventy-five percent said there was a significant drop, and the other 25 percent said there was a slight decline. One-hundred percent of these educators reported that children's ability to get along and resolve disputes had worsened. The article suggests that opportunities for young children to engage in free play have been lost to overcrammed schedules and adult-structured academic and sports enrichment activities. What has been lost is the opportunity for unstructured interaction with other children, which helps children learn impulse control and regulation of their emotions—skills critical to successful relationships.

> "We've forgotten they need time to learn how to be competent social beings; that is every bit as important as knowing algebra and grammar," says Kathy Hirsh Pasek, a professor of psychology at Philadelphia's Temple University, who has researched . . . the social, cognitive, and emotional growth that accompanies play. According to a 2010 study by the Kaiser Family Foundation, children between the ages of 8 and 18 now spend about 7.5 hours a day tethered to smart phones, laptops, or other devices, up from 6 hours in 2005. And that doesn't include the 1½ hours they spend texting or talking. It adds up to 63 hours of media every week.[82]

The article concludes that children's structured time and lack of face-to-face interactions deprive them of the subtle facial and verbal cues and the emotional skills that can only be learned through direct social interactions. The authors of these studies suggest these deficits

---

82.   "Too Cruel for School" by Peg Tyre, Family Circle, October 1, 2010, 43.

contribute to the surge in school bullying.[83] There is research going back fifty years demonstrating that bullies misread social cues. This problem is increasing due to changes wrought by the economic culture.

The busy sports and academic schedules, mentioned above, are also usually hypercompetitive and potentially charged with performance anxiety, creating insecurities at a young age. Children developmentally are naturally egocentric and through social interaction they gradually develop inclinations toward other-centeredness. Young children, when thrown into competitive environments with "winners and losers," will internalize these labels as an aspect of their egos' identity. Their value becomes conditional as it depends on performance and outcomes relative to others. Bullies' childhood performance anxieties, internalized at the time as fear and damage to their self-worth, years later are projected outward, victimizing others. Bullies exhibit a displaced need for control in the hope of gaining status by exercising power over others.

The new bullies are not the physically intimidating, low-achieving "misfits" of yesteryear. More often, bullies are often popular and academic achievers. They carry hidden wounds inflicted by the economic culture's competitiveness, busyness, and embedded performance anxiety that gets expressed as hostility toward others. I have compassion for the bullies' pain that their behavior masks. Twenty-four percent of children who bullied in middle school or high school have not healed the pain that drove their bullying, and they end up in jail by age twenty-five.[84]

When Winning Isn't Everything

"Jessica and Nathan, the basketball hoop is up and ready."

My children came running over with great excitement and started shooting baskets. Jessica was almost eight and Nathan was six-and-a-half years old. We all shot around and laughed as we chased errant shots that skipped off the driveway.

I innocently asked, "Would you like to play a game?"

---

83. Ibid.

84. "Bullying in the Digital Age—Words can Kill," CBS 48 Hours Special, aired September 17, 2011.

"Yes," they yelled in unison.

"It is called 21. If you make a shot from beyond this chalk line you get two points and if it's in front of the line you get one point. The first one to 21 wins."

"Let's do it!" Nate said with excitement.

Both of my children were athletic; but relatively quickly Jessica, being older, established a pretty large lead. I could see my son's frustration growing. He began to try to distract her. "You're going to miss, you're going to miss!" He bounced the ball at her shins and did other things to irritate her. When Jessica got to 19 points, Nate grabbed the ball and kicked it into the woods saying, "I hate basketball. This is a stupid game and I am never playing it again!"

What had happened? Just ten minutes ago, they were enjoying the new basketball hoop. My angelic son, moments ago, was retrieving balls for Jessica as they laughed together. I soon realized that by having one winner, I had not only pitted them against each other; I had caused horns to sprout as my son felt the anxiety of becoming a "loser." I let some time pass and coaxed my son to give it another try.

"I have a much better game. It is called 31. Your goal together is to get to 31 points in less than 31 shots. It may take a while because it is really hard, but challenges can help us improve."

Within minutes, a completely different "tone" took over, and my son's devilish horns receded. "You can do it, Jessica; we have 22 points and we still have 14 shots."

"Great shot Nate! That's a 2 pointer." Jessica yelled.

They high fived and actually embraced when after 29 shots they made it to 31.

We can minimize the damaging effects of children's natural developmental tendency to internalize feelings of devaluation in competitive events. The original Greek word for competition meant to "strive together." How far we have drifted from that ideal, where the challenges games provided led to improved skills because they required increased concentration and effort to achieve a common goal. Growth can occur without having to pit children against each other. With a small change, like the "31" game, we can create cooperation, mutual support, encouragement, and growth for all participants. To throw young children into competitive situations, where only one person or team can win, creates performance anxiety. Long term, this can erode self-confidence and is all too often projected onto others in some form of hostility, including sarcasm and bullying.

The decrease in time children spend playing together in unstructured noncompetitive situations has damaged children's relational skills and sacrificed their empathy. This loss, along with the sixty-three hours of media time that further diminishes face-to-face social interactions, takes a toll on young people's relational skills. This contributes heavily to the epidemic of bullying. When children at young ages are able to play together in noncompetitive ways, they increase their ability to resolve problems, accept differences, and expand their empathy and compassion. We have to understand what we have lost pursuing a frenetic hyper-competitive lifestyle if we are to reverse the escalating carnage of bullying that we have unwittingly created for our youth.

Social Isolation and Technological Addictions

Many of the video games youth are playing, often in isolation, during their seven-and-one-half hours per day of "tech time" have "levels of performance." These levels of difficulty are carefully calculated to develop a reinforcement schedule similar to gambling machines. In psychological jargon it is called a "variable-ratio schedule." Reinforcement, like the frequency of payoff with a casino's one-arm bandit, comes sporadically and unpredictably. This unpredictability, the possibility that the payoff could come at any time, is an essential factor that drives the development of addictive behavior. In the laboratory, rats on a variable-ratio schedule will press a lever essentially nonstop in hopes of receiving a food pellet, until the rat exhausts itself and dies. The key to developing addictive behavior of this kind is to give lots of reinforcement early, and then systematically decrease its frequency and predictability. This is the equivalent of early success in the easier levels of difficulty in video games, and then gradually increasing higher levels of challenge. Variable-ratio schedules like this can create an almost irresistible addiction.

To a casual observer, the rat looked to be neurotic, a "workaholic" who killed himself. But, this workaholic behavior was a byproduct of a reinforcement schedule constructed intentionally. The growing addiction epidemic to videos and gaming worldwide is spawning an explosion of treatment centers, particularly in the birthplace of many of these products: Japan. Despite this damaging reality, program designers continue to knowingly design reinforcement schedules that make addiction likely. Add awesome graphics for "realism" to these intentionally crafted reinforcement schedules, and addiction is often the inevitable result. Many young people are overmatched by this sophisticated psychological manipulation. Technology's proper role is to serve as a means for achieving a purposeful end. When it is an end in itself, it serves as a brief eddy of pleasurable distraction, allowing for the unnoticed visitation by the slow death of a meaningful life.

Programmers know exactly what they are doing, just as casino designers know there will be casualties to their version of fun. Addictive fun may give you a high, but it never creates contentment or satiates a desire. You are left with infrequent islands of fleeting pleasure, and you are often left alone.

Suggestions:
Keeping Loneliness at Bay

There is no easy solution to eliminate or reduce chronic loneliness, but the following suggestions are adapted from the article "All the Lonely People" and can help lower your risk for loneliness.[85]

1. Nurture your personal relationships.

2. Don't substitute electronic communication for face-to-face contact.

3. Take time to volunteer.

4. Join a social club or community organization.

5. For youth, try to maintain contacts with a few high school friends after you have graduated.

6. Meditation is the ultimate antidote for loneliness because it introduces you to your spiritual self.

---

85. "All the Lonely People" by Brad Edmonson. AARP Magazine, 2010, 84.

Chapter 14

The Exploitation and Expansion of Fear

"The direct use of force is a poor solution to any problem. It is generally employed only by small children and large nations."

—David Friedman

"Always remember, fear invites danger."

—Swami Rama

Perhaps the ultimate irony in Madison Avenue's notion of happiness achieved by pursuing your individual desires through external consumption is that it really isn't individuality at all. Young people are not really "marching to the beat of their own drummer." Dr. Arya, a spiritual mentor, commented on these independent choices, saying, "They look more like the independence of the *herd*." Suddenly everyone at the same moment in time chooses to use "mousse" in their hair, wear more black clothes, get more tattoos and piercings, start tweeting, get an iPod, or catapult Close Up toothpaste to the number-one bestseller.

These "choices," including staged images of rebellious youth, have been heavily influenced by the economic culture, and they are not new. They are the reason millions of earlier "rebels" like me ended up with renditions of the Beatles hairstyles, or others grew extremely long hair to mimic "hippies." The difference more recently is that these images and desires to encourage herd behavior are programmed by the economic culture to change more frequently in order to maximize profits. These new images and trends are just the latest renditions or fads perpetrated by the economic culture to manipulate our insecurities through the self-preservation urge.

The Politics of Fear and the Media's Collusion

Political ads and election materials have always had a certain percentage that contained elements of fear. Historically, the majority of candidate ads had at least a minor educational component. National ad consultants and political advisors rely much more heavily on targeted research to play on individual insecurities and biases, the fears of the ego. There is no hesitation to stoke and create fears that some calamity will befall a particular block of voters if the other candidate were to be elected. The hysteria and misinformation in these ads and on partisan talk radio, television "news" programs, and Internet chatter creates fear, suspicion, and distrust across the country. This has a damaging effect on statesmanship, the democratic process, and is also profoundly affecting our youth.

Much of the agenda for this fearmongering and distortion is driven by the economic culture elites' desire to control and expand the economic benefits that culture has provided them. Championing fear boosts ratings for television networks owned by corporate conglomerates; but that fear is also shattering civility, cohesiveness, and any spirit of cooperation. It is obscuring the need for shared sacrifice, and blocking the compassion that is needed to create more balance, harmony, equity, and justice in our society. There is little statesmanship left. Discourse is devoid of the intention to look for integrating and synthesizing the "opponent's" perspectives with one's own. These fear tactics and misrepresentations, if they were applied to our personal relationships, would shatter them.

Even the overuse of "breaking news" is designed to suggest an urgency often trying to capture attention through fear. We humans tend to project our own insecurities and imbalances so that we don't have to face them. We find enemies to blame for our hurts and fears. Fear is the mother of anger, and anger seeks an outlet. It's easier to blame, label, and demonize someone for our hurts, pain, and fear than it is to courageously face our own fears and take responsibility for healing them. If there really is a real threat to our collective security, this should catalyze more cooperation and understanding, not less.

"Journalists" themselves often drown out, gang up on, constantly interrupt, and disparagingly label someone they have invited ostensibly for an interview to share their perspectives. Many journalists' real goal is to drum home their own viewpoint to a partisan audience. Their position might suffer if they allowed someone the time and courtesy to present a different view. Instead, disparaging labels are attached to people to marginalize their perspectives. Labels by their very nature distort, oversimplify, and restrict understanding and compassion. Too much of what is called journalism amounts to a rude, dismissive bullying and not a genuine search for balance, integration, or truth.

Time for true dialogue is also often lost because commercials pushing the products of the economic culture intrude so frequently, making any sustained in-depth discussion impossible. This reduces discussions largely to talking points, killing any hope of real learning or synthesis. The lack of civility, demonizing, and short unconstructive bantering, and sometimes outright intimidation, is now seen every-where—at town hall meetings and orchestrated political gatherings. Unfortunately, this lack of civility and the demonizing of others is constantly witnessed and internalized by young people.

Fear's Impact on Youth

Young children are particularly sensitive to any feeling of angst in their parents. My daughter Jessica, around age three, anytime her mother and I were having a mild disagreement with even a whiff of a strident tone, ran between us and repeatedly said, "I love you, Mom, I love you, Dad," while kissing us.

This was her best attempt to quiet her fears and any tension between us. The fear, anxiety, and anger of parents resonates deeply within the hearts and minds of children. Fear compromises children's most basic need, the need to feel safe and secure.

Economic stress is affecting many more millions of citizens fearful of losing their homes or being able to provide food for their families. This heightens people's self-preservation urge, creating great anxiety for parents, which ripples into the psyches of their children. When you compromise a child's sense of security, you also steal their trust. This is true for individuals and countries alike. When you saturate a culture with fear, including the fear generated by economic injustice and uncertainty, trust disappears; and suspiciousness takes over the land. This distrust unravels cohesiveness and civility, pitting people against each other, leading to violence in both subtle and virulent forms.

Research shows that countries that provide a safety net, and have less income disparity, have greater trust in their fellow citizens and their government. Trust is a prerequisite for security and societal harmony, and it is being eroded by our growing culture of fear. Children suffer most in an atmosphere of fear. Christ said, "Unless you change and become like children you cannot enter the Kingdom of God" (Matthew 18:2-3). Part of the meaning of this phrase is that you need to have the openness to life and the wonder that children exhibit. Fear threatens that openness, trust, and awe in children, and in the rest of us. And, fear is becoming the calling card of our culture.

Older youth and young adults often join the cultural polarization, spouting facts that aren't facts or opinions without adequate knowledge. For the well informed and more reflective youth, a deep cynicism frequently sets in that feeds their growing malaise. This is one of the most damaging aspects of fear and negativity; some of our most gifted young people have become cynical and have lost hope. As mentioned earlier, fear thoughts deplete energy, which further feeds growing cynicism and hopelessness.

The chance to improve problems or create a hopeful future seems overwhelming (Did you know the world was going to end in 2012?), or already seems lost because no one listens or is willing to work together. The desire for ratings, short-term political advantage, and individual greed, without consideration for the long-term effects of creating a culture of fear, is damaging to the security, trust, openness, and hope of our youth. When adult role models exhibit an inability to listen and respect differences, young people are likely to emulate them.

I know we face serious problems that will be difficult to reverse. This fact, however, does not equate to fear any more than my burning car and house equated to anxiety. Our emotions depend on the mindset we cultivate relative to the challenges we are facing. Antagonistic personalized discourse and ratcheting up fear make solutions impossible. It has reached the point where the local news even uses weather to create a degree of fear, so you feel compelled to watch. The weather "teasers" before the news often sound like the sky is falling: "Looks like a potentially devastating morning commute . . ." Our growingly fear-based culture with intentional exaggerated rhetoric makes things feel overwhelming, creates immense anxiety particularly for children, and contributes to older youth's apathy and despair.

Fear and Projection

Paradoxically, our fear-based culture obliterates the very prerequisite for the change needed to bring more happiness to our lives—the need to overcome our fears and anxieties. When people feel threatened by some outside entity due to political expediency or media hype, we automatically focus our energy outward in an attempt to silence, intimidate, or eliminate that entity. We fail to look at *our* own role in creating disharmony. By demonizing, labeling, and projecting our fears onto others, we not only fail to heal the hurts that spawn our anger, we create more hostility and dysfunction in the world.

Emotional or negative judgments of others come from unconsciously recognizing a quality in ourselves that we deem unacceptable. This is often an echo of some rejection or deficit from our significant caregivers, or hurt from a childhood trauma that is difficult to face. So, we project it onto others. Certainly we sometimes witness actual imbalanced, egocentric, and destructive behaviors in others; but the emotion and judgment that accompanies our observation is revealing our own attachments, fears, and insecurities. All suffering, including fear and anger, is born of the ignorance or lack of awareness of ourselves as spiritual beings. When we are connected to that source, we have compassion for those who have lost touch with it.

An interesting study reveals the process of projection, which keeps us from examining our own hurts and fears. It illustrates that what we reject in ourselves, we project onto others. In this study, people's attitudes about homosexuality were surveyed. Subjects were asked questions designed to determine the degree of their antagonism toward homosexuals. All subjects were hooked to an array of monitoring devices and then shown rapidly displayed slides of same-sex erotic images. The subjects with the highest score of emotional hostility toward gays also showed the greatest sexual arousal to the erotic same sex images. Often when we are judging others, we are actually judging qualities in ourselves that we deny and have repressed.

Fear's Educational and Health Ripples

Fear is also a factor in our growing litigious society, wherein someone must be blamed and made to pay for our grievances. Fear drives an inordinate amount of paperwork and documentation. This paper trail is generated in the hope of decreasing the threat of a lawsuit, from outraged and self-proclaimed victims. We are becoming a nation of victims. Special education teachers live in this world. They are often left exhausted, buried under an avalanche of paperwork, insuring they will be less energetically available to the real needs of their students. This causes many excellent teachers to leave the profession prematurely. Their joyful energy and effectiveness have been lost in the bureaucracy of fear.

Fear leaves us scarred and exhausted. Fear paralyzes our creativity. Fear is also the source of our violence. Dr. Arya states this boldly: "Show me the size of someone's gun and I will show you the size of their fear."[86] The gun can be a public, sarcastic, and shaming remark, or a bazooka. Fear sabotages our happiness. It leaves us stuck in our pain and less able or willing to help others. The degree of dysfunction driven by fear is escalating in intensity and frequency, and is spreading to more areas of our lives.

---

86. "Good Memory" by Hillari Dowdle, Yoga Journal, Oct. 2008, 43.

There is a potential growing and unanticipated consequence of this culture of fear that more of us will be facing as we age. Dr. Dharma Singh Khalsa, MD, author of the book *Brain Longevity* is quoted by Hillari Dowdle in the October 2008 issue of *Yoga Journal* about this expanding problem:

> About fifteen years ago, there were four million people with Alzheimer's; today that number is 5.2 million, and we're going to see it skyrocket. I think stress and lifestyle are leading causes. Right now in America, we're being told to be afraid, be very afraid. There's so much stress and pressure in our society, it's creating an epidemic of memory loss.[87]

The article goes on to explain how constant low levels of fear damage the brain through increased cortisol levels triggered by stress, contributing to the growth of Alzheimer's. We should consider, before we participate in fueling the culture of fear, that our children's rapidly developing brain is also likely to be extremely susceptible to the damaging effects of fear.

Conquering our Fears

Taking responsibility for our negative emotions, including fear, rather than projecting them onto others, isn't the same as accepting blame or guilt. By taking responsibility, we are recognizing that we are responsible for managing our emotions. Positive change can take place only through *our* choices, and a change in *our* attitudes. William James, sometimes called the father of American psychology, stated, "The greatest discovery of my generation is that a human being can alter his life by altering his attitude."

Charles Swindoll further articulates the wide breadth of benefits and the power inherent in taking responsibility for our attitudes:

> The longer I live, the more I realize the impact of attitude on life. It is more important than the past, than education, than money, than circumstances, than failures, than successes, than what people think or say or

---

87.   Ibid.

do. It is more important than appearance, giftedness, or skill. It will make or break a company . . . a church . . . a home. The remarkable thing is we have choice every day regarding the attitude we will embrace for the day. We cannot change our past . . . we cannot change the fact people will act in a certain way. We cannot change the inevitable. The only thing we can do is play on the one string we have, and that is our attitude . . . I am convinced that life is ten percent what happens to me and ninety percent how I react to it. And so it is with you . . . we are in charge of our attitudes.[88]

There is no hint of a victim mindset in Charles Swindoll's declaration. It suggests instead an empowering ability to face and react positively and compassionately to the challenges of life. It is possible, through letting go of fear, to cultivate an attitude of love and respect for all living beings in the most difficult of circumstances. It is what all great teachers have urged and modeled. "There is no fear in love; but perfect love casteth out fear: because fear has torment" (I John 4:18). This Bible quote urges us to conquer our fear so we are capable of a perfect love. Fear blocks love and creates barriers between people. It is very challenging "to love your enemies," but it is a noble quest. It is the best we can offer a world fragmented by fear.

Peace is an inside job and it starts with us. Our contribution to peace requires purifying our attitudes and cleansing our perceptions to determine how our fear is creating negativity and violence toward others, thus undermining our capacity to love. Taking responsibility for quieting our fears, stilling our minds, and healing the hurts driving our anger is the fundamental prerequisite for growth and change. Parents can model and support children in quieting their fears, while strengthening their own courage to face life's external and internal challenges.

Facing Fears in Therapy

For many young people, therapy can facilitate this process of healing hurts that manifest as anger or depression. The therapeutic process

---

88.   http://thinkexist.com/quotes/charles_r._swindoll.

itself, however, can sometimes get stuck in blaming circumstances on others for one's pain. This might relieve some internalized guilt and temporarily lift one's mood as we more appropriately assign guilt and quit judging ourselves. Again, it may be true that someone is to blame for a hurt we experienced. However, this blame cannot keep the focus off this absolute fact: we are the only ones who have the power to alter our misery. There is a story told to me by Dr. Bob Baumer, a wonderful psychiatrist who founded the Family Life Mental Health Clinic that I worked at as a consulting psychologist for fifteen years.

> There was a young married couple moving into their first home. The grass had recently been laid and was green and plush. That night they fell asleep with smiles on their faces. Toward morning, they awoke to an awful stench. They looked outside and on their front lawn was an eight-foot by twelve-foot mountain of fresh manure. They gagged at the smell. They wondered, *Who would do such a thing?* Over the next few days, they contacted friends and relatives, and commiserated with the neighbors and those passing by about this awful injustice. This went on for days, then weeks; and every time it rained, the stench intensified. But, the manure remained. Finally after complaining to everyone they knew, when they just couldn't take it anymore, they got a truck, shoveled up the manure, and carried it away. They had suffered the odor for a long time. But this couple finally came to the realization that even though what happened wasn't their fault, they were still ultimately responsible for constructively dealing with their problem.

I still find it useful to let young people tell their story, including the manure chapters in their life. In the first counseling session, I ask them if they would be willing to tell me about their entire life—the good, the bad, and the ugly. The next one or two sessions, I listen to the unfolding of their life from their earliest memory to the present. They choose what they wished to highlight. This reveals priceless insights and begins to establish a therapeutic bond. For many clients, it was the first time they had really been listened to, and that in itself was deeply therapeutic. So telling their story can be beneficial, but the key is to not get too lost or identified with the story, as this will delay and imprison their growth.

Blaming traps us in the role of victim, leading to more helplessness and hopelessness. Therapy, which means to heal, does not start until we take responsibility for our emotions and our choices. A historical focus in therapy can be cathartic in the beginning. Its real value is in revealing patterns in the ways we learned to cope with difficulties from our past that are not working for us now. We can't change the past, but we can change how we react to the past so it doesn't continue to painfully echo into and distort our present moments. Life is to be lived in the now, but there also needs to be a forward focus, a vision of where we want to head and what we want to create. Then, the actions we take now can build the future we have envisioned.

Rehashing calamities of our childhood, if overplayed, can keep us chained to painful fear-evoking memories, so that they color and distort our present moments over and over again. Developing strategies to stay engaged with what providence is bringing forward in the present, and correcting ineffective coping strategies, is empowering. Feeling competent with some measure of control strengthens a deeper sense of worth. This increased acceptance of responsibility without guilt helps us develop a blueprint for our lives that, if we persistently follow, will help us build a brighter future.

Fear, Change, and Resiliency

Fear makes us less likely to take the risks that will lead to growth. The ego, the mind's generator of fear, can paralyze our willingness to take on a new challenge or initiate a necessary change. But, the voice of conscience and intuition whispers the needs and insights of the soul, and encourages us to let go of our ego-based fears. Fear feeds the tendency to be inflexible, and it can paralyze our willingness to change. It makes it more difficult to recover from the setbacks we all experience in life. Fear also increases the mind's tendency to focus on what is or could go wrong, and inhibits seeing positive options to resolve problems. Psychologists have a word for people who bounce back and even thrive after traumatic fear-inducing events: resiliency. In an article in the September 2011 *Experience Life* magazine, Jessie Sholl quotes Al Siebert's from his best-selling book *The Resiliency Advantage:* "Highly resilient people are flexible, adapt to new circumstances quickly, and thrive in constant change. Most important, if they **expect** to bounce back and feel confident, they will. They have a knack for creating good luck out of circumstances that many others see as bad luck."[89]

Jessie Sholl highlights some other qualities of resilient people, including being good at seeing things through another person's perspective. In other words, resilient people can empathize. Fear imprisons empathy. Perhaps this partially explains why there has been such an erosion of empathy, because we are living in a growing culture of fear. Empathy for others actually helps people struggling with a traumatic event, as they don't get as deeply lost in their own pain. This contributes to speeding their recovery from traumatic experiences.

Sholl points out that the way we look at negative events has a critical effect on how resilient we are and on how long we will suffer. If traumatic events are seen as permanent and unchangeable then we suffer more and exhibit little resiliency. If we feel we have some control over how we react and the meaning we give to these events, then we tend to bounce back quicker. Research shows this more resilient attitude positively impacts one's physical, emotional, and mental health. Fear restricts resiliency and increases human misery.

If we look at difficult experiences and label them as permanently "bad" versus "hard," then we will have a set of emotional reactions leaving us feeling victimized by "unfair" events. Youth who are overindulged are likely to be less resilient. When their life gets difficult, there is a built-in sense of unfairness, conscious or unconscious, that can make things feel overwhelming. This inhibits their ability to persevere and resiliently engage life's challenges. Perhaps this played a role in the university suicide study referenced in Chapter 1, wherein there were few intense external triggers to explain students' suicide attempts. When things got hard for these students, they experienced little resiliency and their life became overwhelming.

However, if youth can hold onto the notion that there is potential growth when difficult or even tragic events occur, they will still feel pain, but it will be tempered by other feelings born of emerging possibilities. Our attitudes and perspectives matter because they shape and

---

89. "Resiliency" by Jessie Sholl, Experience Life, September 2011, 57.

alter our experience of events. We gain power through our attitudinal choices even though we might have been powerless to alter the traumatic event when it originally happened.

Change is the nature of life; nothing stays the same. The only change we have control over is a willingness to address our imbalances and our attitudes. This is our contribution to improving the world. Gandhi said, "We must become the change we are seeking in the world." This short statement is tremendously profound. We cannot change our past, and the future isn't here yet. The future is created by our actions performed in this moment.

It is easy to get lost in "why" questions, as to how our childhood is causing us to do something now, or why a difficult event happened. But, our conclusions are speculative. At the end of the day, understanding why something happened does not guarantee greater happiness or contentment. It is more important to notice our habits and patterns and the feelings and emotions that accompany them. Repeat and strengthen the choices and habits that bring contentment, joy, and peace. Stay "kindly neutral," and face those habits that bring emotional pain until the "dark" energy is integrated into the personality, or vanishes in the light of the soul.

An eight-year-old goes to the wise elder of the tribe to share a troubling nightmare. "I dream often that there is an evil black wolf and a noble white wolf battling for my soul. I am terrified—tell me oh, Wise One, which one will win?"

The answer came quickly from the wisdom-filled elder: "It depends on which wolf you choose to feed."

Which inclinations, attitudes, and habits of our minds are we choosing to feed? Do we dwell on our fears and identify with a limited sense of self, depleting our energy and hope? Or, do we focus our minds on thoughts and actions that inspire us toward a more expansive sense of self and future? We have the power to increase our energy by the thoughts we choose to cultivate. The meaning or interpretation we attach to childhood pains needs to be examined. Our childhood interpretations often negatively shade events occurring in our lives now. "All men are like that," or "There she goes again . . . ," and hundreds of other generalized phrases keep us stuck. They end up coloring the current moment with old crayons, feeding our fear and our emotional reactivity.

The story we have created and grown attached to often becomes just another limiting identity for the ego. So, though it may be important to tell our story, once told it needs to be left behind. The historical story, and the thoughts and fears surrounding it, profoundly affects our moods and actions. People have the power to change these interpretations and the attachments that are keeping them stuck. They can focus on choices that will create the future they want to live in, and fashion in this moment the person they want to become.

This process of reframing life experiences can release our emotional eddies. The energy, once stuck in maintaining our story, can now flow and be integrated into the stream of an expanded life, bringing greater harmony and vigor to our personality. We can observe and alter habitual interpretations and end the suffering that our victim stories cause. There is an experiment at the end of this chapter that can help change and transform our negative and habitual ways of interpreting life. Through the process of changing our destructive habit patterns and cultivating uplifting ones, we make our greatest contribution to decreasing suffering in the world. When we feel more whole, integrated, less stressed, and peaceful, then every one of our actions contributes something beneficial to the world around us.

Fear and Its Spiritual Consequences

This ability to construct our attitudes and approach to life is a very empowering message to share and explore with young people. In the media, the drumbeat of fear is hurting them and fracturing our society. Fear is not caused by differences but by the exploitation of those differences. Fear pits people against "others"; it creates in one's mind the idea of "other." Fear is exploited by political leaders and the media for selfish gain. Even those who are religious, out of their own fear, create lots of "others" through their judgments. Every religion in the world asks us not to judge, but fear makes that impossible. Fear blocks our connection to our true self, our spirit, our soul.

There is no fear in our true self, our spiritual self. Religions profess that everyone is a child of God. They ask us to "love our neighbor as our self." God, Consciousness, Great Spirit, that one omniscient, omnipotent, and omnipresent force, is infused in all life. All creation shares this consciousness, spiritual energy, life force, or whatever name we give to that which is beyond names. We are all, therefore, in the spiritual sense, ONE.

This deep recognition of our spiritual kinship is shown in heroic moments. A person in a war zone transcends their ego's powerful self-preservation urge and dives on a grenade to save a life, while losing their own. It is shown when a person pushes someone out of danger and they themselves are struck by a wayward vehicle. It is shown less dramatically when two male athletes "lose themselves" and their strong culturally conditioned prohibition, and unite in an ecstatic embrace after a last-minute victory.

Fear is contractive energy that separates. It puts walls between people, and it is up to us to conquer the mind's fear, which create otherness. Ashvaghosha, in his book *The Awakening of Faith*, says it well: "When the mind is disturbed, the multiplicity of things is produced, but, when the mind is quieted, the multiplicity of things disappears."[90] A still, calm mind dissolves the notion of other.

The pace of the economic culture, with its manufactured desires, contributes to imbalanced primitive urges, creating stress and sloth. In this disturbed mental state, we lose track of humanity's common desire for justice, peace, and happiness. What is required is a shift from an outward ego-focused mind, enamored with the external enchantments of the economic culture, to a serene, more neutral mind trained to investigate the universe within. With a quieted mind, we can discover joy, peace, and fullness within—we can discover our spiritual self. In this peace, otherness recedes, and love and unity emerges. French philosopher Teilhard de Chardin captures the potential of this hopeful shift: "After we have mastered the winds, the waves, the tides and gravity, we shall harness the energies of love. Then for the second time in the history of the world, humankind will have discovered fire."

This is the real source of happiness young people have been hopelessly searching for in the barren wilderness and promises of the economic culture. Learning to still their minds and focus them inward

90.   From Tao of Physics by Fritjob Capra, Shambala Productions, 1975, 10.

increases the awareness of the love that is their very nature. This naturally leads to healthier choices and a fulfillment that allows for a deeper exploration of purpose, including how to use their talents and gifts to relieve the suffering of others.

The remainder of this book focuses on essential keys for increasing happiness and contentment. But before proceeding, this six-point summary reviews the suffering and painful consequences for young people of the implicit and explicit messages and perspectives promoted by and embedded within the economic culture's value system:

1. The message: You are not okay as you are. You need something outside yourself to be happy, which implies you are deficient. This blocks the awareness of a deeper and permanent source of contentment and joy within.

2. The message: Happiness is found in the external world. This creates almost an infinite array of desires, wants, overstimulation, and ultimately an epidemic of stress, boredom, lethargy, and depression.

3. The excessive desires created by the economic culture lead to over-consumption, causing imbalances in our physical, emotional, and mental health. Globally this leads to competition over resources, which can ignite wars, and is rapidly degrading the environment.

4. There is an emphasis on extreme individualism, competition, and hedonistic pursuits. This can lead to isolation, increased friction in relationships, poor social skills, and loneliness. Extreme individualism and egocentric pursuits decrease respect, compassion, and empathy for others, limiting the inclination to serve others.

5. The messages confuse and compromise young people's notions of who they are and what purposeful living is. This contributes to distress, malaise, depression, decreased motivation, and even suicide.

6. Messages of the economic culture lead to imbalances in our *FOUR PRIMITIVE URGES*. Imbalanced choices related to

the primitive urges of food, sex, sleep, and self-preservation are the source of all painful emotions and stress. These urges are interdependent; an imbalance in one affects the others. These imbalances deplete energy, increasing emotional reactivity and emotional pain. This causes a myriad of problems mentioned above. Handling the challenges of life then becomes more difficult and at times overwhelming and young people struggle to find fulfillment and reach their full potential.

The penetrating influence of corporate values, and their manipulation of our basic urges, have hurt us all. Youth now live in a "brave new world" where each year there are more decibels, more special effects, more new products, more hedonism, more pushing of limits, more fear and stress; and less happiness. This overstimulation distracts and attempts to obscure young people's growing awareness of the emptiness of it all. Yet, all hope is not lost, as one of our founding fathers, Thomas Paine, emphasized at another difficult time in our history: "We have the power to make the world over again."

Pain can have the effect of forcing us to look deeper into ourselves and examine what changes we need to make in order to decrease our suffering and create more joy in our lives. Pain can be a teacher and an ally in motivating us to make the changes our inner self beckons us toward. This beckoning comes from our "fifth" human urge—the longing for something transcendent. As this fifth urge intensifies, we often remain chained to deeply entrenched painful habit patterns and desires. How do we enliven that urge and escape those chains? Understanding how change takes place is critical if we are to satisfy this higher calling, and we explore the process of change in the next chapter. With that understanding, like the Phoenix bird that consumed itself in fire and then arises reborn and renewed from the ashes to start a new life, we will be better equipped to serve as a catalyst for a transformation that leads to a life of greater joy and meaning.

Chapter 15
The Essential Elements for Change

"Let one who would move the world, first move himself."

—SOCRATES

"In order to change an existing paradigm, you do not struggle to change the problematic model. You create a new model and make the old one obsolete. That in essence is the higher service to which we are all being called."

—BUCKMINSTER FULLER

Ralph Waldo Emerson said, "All life is an experiment. The more experiments you make the better." We engage in self-awareness experiments because we are stuck in habit patterns that bring imbalance and emotional pain, and we want to end our suffering. Our fifth human urge beckons us to experiment with ways to change and remove what blocks the awareness of our fullness, the awareness of our transcendent self. These experiments ultimately help us to satiate our constant cravings and balance disharmonies that are caused by our sense of inadequacy and incompleteness. Life is about change and growth. We work on changing and removing our blocks and grow toward the source from which our fifth urge flows.

Sometimes young people are serious about changing; but like all of us, they struggle to make or sustain change. Much of our work with youth as parents, educators, therapists, and other caring professions involves efforts to help them change their painful or destructive choices. Sometimes we are so entrenched in our effort, particularly when things are not going well, that we grow frustrated, which further obscures our ability to see what is blocking their progress. It is usually a bad sign if we find ourselves more concerned and working harder than the children, students, or clients we are trying to help.

What does the process of change consist of, beyond the particular behaviors we are trying to modify? If we understand the essential components of change, we will be more effective in facilitating or becoming a catalyst for change. We will be more successful in our roles as caregivers, educators, parents, or mentors. There are four principal elements in the process of change that can "nudge" probability, increasing the likelihood of successful transformation. These four essential ingredients for change are: cultivating a clear intention to change, increased self-awareness, unconditional self-acceptance, and a commitment to practice the new behavior.

1. WE NEED A CLEAR INTENTION TO CHANGE.

We have to want to change. Clear intention focuses the mind's attention, and whatever the mind attends to naturally grows and is strengthened. Seeing change as an adventure we have chosen is helpful in maintaining our intention. We often, however, have an ambiguous desire to change, which creates resistance and confusion that blocks lasting change: "I want to lose weight/Boy, do I love chocolate." "I want to be more assertive/I just hate conflict." This kind of internal ambiguity makes successful sustained change impossible. Competing desires paralyze effective action, because the mind is confused as to which direction to move. It is change that is wished for, but not willed. These conflicting desires are generated from a part of the mind that is indecisive, sometimes called sensory-motor mind or stimulus and response. There is no reflection or contemplation; the mind just makes a habitual automatic response to a particular stimulus. When the stimulus changes, our minds and choices change.

The stimulus can come from outside or inside, in the form of an external object or a stored memory. For example, the stimulus can be a piece of chocolate cake on a plate, or a thought of a double-fudge brownie. The desire triggered by the stimulus causes us to forget our "wish" to lose weight. We respond by eating the cake or making brownies. It is called *manas* mind in yoga psychology. The nature of manas mind is to be indecisive and easily influenced by desires. So, our firm clear resolve has to come from a deeper longing; from our conscience or our intuitive wisdom, from our fifth urge.

There is also often an unconscious resistance to change because the ego fears changing and letting go of its attachments. Ron, with his self-imposed rigid identity as a "bad ass," will frequently make self-destructive choices, imprisoned in actions that are congruent with his emotionally charged self-image. The ego's fear and uncertainty of becoming "someone else," and the pride of being a rebellious SOME-BODY, inhibits Ron's change.

Resistance to change because of fear often shows up in addictions. People have to face their pain, insecurities, hurts, or shame that are driving their addictions. People with obsessive-compulsive behaviors fear losing control and are often overwhelmed with anxiety when they do not give into their compulsive behaviors. Despite their significant suffering, the fear of not having control trumps the desire to change their painful habit patterns. They will have to gradually learn to face their anxiety, if they are to change.

A Clear Intention and Resolve—Agents of Change

So, we need to have a clear, unambiguous intention, and some willingness to experience emotional discomfort, if we are to enliven change within us. Our change intention is often gradually strengthened by the pain and exhaustion of our repeated suffering caused by clinging to old habits. Intention or change cannot be forced or coerced by teachers, case managers, parole officers, or parents; it has to come from within. As caregivers, we can sometimes coerce compliance and at times that may even be necessary, but compliance rarely leads to sustained change.

There is a phrase, "self-defeating kids," that describes young people who do the very things that complicate and in some cases "ruin" their lives. A student, for example, completes a paper essential for getting a passing grade that will ensure his graduation from high school, but he fails to turn it in. He privately shares that his father is overbearing and controlling. He confides with a smile that it will drive his dad, who is a doctor, crazy when he does not walk through the graduation line. This self-defeating behavior is a fight for control, and graduation is its casualty. So, trying to coerce real change is usually doomed to failure.

Self-defeating behavior isn't always this conscious. It occurs frequently in adolescents struggling for autonomy and control, and they usually unconsciously sabotage their own success. The graduation example illustrates that dad's expectations likely created a sense of coercion for his son; and even if it occasionally brought his son's compliance, in the long run it also bred resistance. For lasting change to take place, the intention has to be clear, not coerced, and consciously chosen. With clear intention we can "will" rather than "wish" change.

Will vs. Will Power

Many people confuse the idea of will with will power. Will power suggests having to be coercive with ourselves. "I need to change." "I should change." These phrases often suggest a kind of shame and internal judgment born of the ego's fears. It is a form of self-violence, because the ego feels our worth is diminished if we aren't successful with our change. This also will bring some form of unconscious resistance that impedes our change because the ego's very existence depends on maintaining control.

We need a clear intention to change, but we don't need will power to force a change driven by ego. We need a kind of will that is gentle and subtle, which is sometimes called passive volition. Volition means choice. Passive implies a quiet, relaxed, and unanxious choice. With passive volition, we make a clear resolve that we can and will make a specific change. We invite our deepest self, and providence, to support us. It is helpful to make this resolve when our mind is totally calm, "wrinkle free," and silent. The seeds of intention we sow grow more quickly and with deeper roots when they are sown in the fertile soil of silence. We then water our clear intention daily by repeating this quiet resolve.

Think of an example in your life when the harder you tried to accomplish something, the more you got stuck, and the more frustrated you became. You then "gave up," "surrendered," took a nap, "let go"; and suddenly things flowed. You attempted, for example, a difficult cord on a musical instrument, but couldn't get it right. You tossed the guitar on the couch and made a sandwich. Later, you unconsciously picked up the guitar and the difficult cord came forward effortlessly.

Athletes talk about getting in the zone, or playing out of their mind. They really are out of their minds, they are not thinking and analyzing, and their ego has stepped aside. This accounts for the joy and beauty of those moments. They are so absorbed in the moment that they lose the ego's anxious concern about performance and judgment, and their full potential flows unencumbered. The 1984 US Olympic swimming coach asked his athletes one day to swim at 90 percent. They recorded their best times. This is because trying hard had been interfering with their natural ability. The extra effort they were making created more inefficiency in their swimming motions.

In Zen traditions, this more relaxed engagement is sometimes called "effortless effort." It is our ego that tries to force performance or change. Even if it accomplishes its goal, we are often terribly stressed in the process. Quietly appealing through passive volition to a self that is already beckoning us toward growth is a natural, more efficient process for change. This process is reminiscent of a prayer-like attitude in petitioning our higher self.

This is the real meaning of discipline. In a culture of desire-driven impulsivity wherein we're all encouraged to do our own thing, discipline sounds pretty unappealing. *Webster's* defines discipline as a training that perfects the mental faculties or moral character; or develops self-control. That doesn't sound too bad. Discipline comes from the same root word as disciple—meaning a pupil, one who accepts or spreads the ideas of another. Our desire-ridden self, the ego, has thrown our primitive urges out of balance, causing painful negative emotions. However, when the ego becomes a pupil, a disciple that takes its instruction from one's intuition or conscience, we call that *self*-discipline and it helps perfect one's mental faculties and moral character.

Experiments with Passive Volition

I have a video of Jack Swartz, who was a fighter pilot who discovered while under attack that, when he let go of his fear of dying, he flew at his most skillful level. On the video, Jack asks the same self that he discovered while under attack to not allow any bleeding right before he sticks a knitting needle through his bicep. He said he never proceeded to puncture his arm until he received an internal "yes" to go forward. Then his punctured arm never bled. He did this demonstration to illustrate that we can have conscious control over processes we considered involuntary. He was able to regulate the flow of blood from a wound by humbly trusting this deeper wisdom.

I attended a conference at the invitation of my dentist, who was a member of the Minnesota Hypnotic Society. I deliberately sat in the front row, secretly hoping they would ask for a volunteer to be hypnotized. "Would anyone like to . . ."—I was already moving forward toward the stage to ensure I would be the subject. They had just shown, to a symposium of doctors and dentists, a video where a gall bladder was removed under hypnosis with no anesthesia.

The doctor led me through a hypnotic induction process. I felt relaxed but had no sense of any change in consciousness. He said he was going to stick a sterilized needle through my hand and that I could decide whether it bled out of the inlet or outlet hole, or neither, or both. He told me I would feel a sensation but no pain. I personally did not think I was hypnotized, but I quietly made an internal request that only the exit hole would bleed. That is exactly what happened. This kind of voluntary control can be accomplished without hypnosis; it requires a humble and quiet act of will. Humility is seen as a prerequisite for spiritual growth in most religions. Humility seems to be on life support these days due to the constant self-aggrandizing images of the icons celebrated in the media.

My faith grew in the passive volition process. Change, facilitated by a quiet intention, enlivens an intuitive wisdom that is beyond the conditioned thinking of the rational mind. This proved immensely helpful, when two years after the hypnosis demonstration, I accidently ran a chain saw through my thigh down to the bone. It allowed me to have surprising control over the degree of pain and even to some degree the blood flow, as the doctor cleaned and stitched my leg. Deepak

Chopra captures the essence of this process of egoless change that expresses itself through our intuitive wisdom: "The unconditioned self be a silent witness to that conditioning. That quiet awareness is nonjudgmental and has no agenda; yet because it enlivens the force of evolution within us, it will organize the process which frees the mind from its limitations automatically."

There is something within us that we can surrender to that facilitates our highest aspirations, our fifth urge, without the ego's judgment or coercion—though the ego might later be enlisted to carry out the actions that our intuition suggested. To summarize the first essential element of change: We need a clear intention and a quiet yet firm resolve that we have chosen in order to enliven the possibility of change.

2. INCREASED SELF-AWARENESS.

This is the second essential element for change. We can't change anything of which we are not aware. Our habits are, by definition, things we do automatically. So it is critical to make conscious our unconscious, automatic, robotic responses that are throwing us out of balance and causing us pain. We have to become mindful. This means we are aware and alert in each moment so we can make a choice rather than a habitual reaction. This gives us the power and control to reverse a habit, sometimes even a lifelong habit, more quickly than we might think.

One helpful practice to increase mindfulness is to begin noticing each time our mind has left the present moment, lost in a future fantasy or stuck in a past remembrance. I remember the first time I suggested this experiment to students. For one day they were to make a check on a sheet of typing paper, every time they caught their minds leaving the present moment. All of the students who tried this were literally stunned by the blackened sheets of paper they turned in. They said things like: "I am amazed by how rarely I live in the present moment; one second I'm here and the next moment my mind is gone."

This simple self-awareness practice, if continued for just ten days, begins to train the mind to more frequently stay in the now. We all live in the now, but when our mind has exited to the future or past, we don't experience this moment's fullness. We also don't live consciously with awareness. We live on automatic pilot a slave to our conditioned habits, never choosing freely or creatively.

Self-awareness around our four primitive urges can help us discern why we are feeling a drop in energy leading to emotional flatness or irritability. Did we eat right before sleeping, decreasing our energy and sacrificing our optimism, creativity, productivity, and enjoyment of the next day? Did we attach too much significance to a criticism, fueling our ego-preservation urge leading to defensiveness and feelings of victimization? By observing our choices surrounding these four urges and their energetic and emotional after-effects, we can identify and change the dysfunctional habits that are sapping our joy. So, a second requirement for any change is increased self-awareness.

3. UNCONDITIONAL SELF-ACCEPTANCE.

This is the third essential element for bringing about change. When we are trying to change, or serving as a catalyst for others' change, creating self-awareness experiments is important. It is important to maintain an attitude of self-acceptance during these experiments.

Judgment and Change

It is essential to forego judging because judgment impedes change. When we judge others, they feel our judgment and it triggers resistance in them. All of us want to be accepted even with our imbalanced habit patterns. When we judge ourselves, it actually intensifies the ego's identification with a limited notion of ourselves, and this further calcifies this identity in our psyche. This additional calcification makes change less likely. Psychologist Carl Rogers talks of the importance of giving ourselves "unconditional positive regard." All religions say we are children of God or made in God's image, and we can never lose this standing. We may not approve of a choice we made or a behavior we exhibited, and we are all responsible for our choices, but they are not us. These are conditioned responses born of our past identifications and coping habits and ignorance of our true nature—the unconditioned self.

Young people can tell when we haven't separated their worth from their behavior. Youth, particularly very insecure or wounded youth, have a hypersensitive antenna that registers any kind of rejection of them. Their childhood hurts fuel an unconscious scanning that monitors other people's voice tone, eye contact, and body language, seeking any hint of judgment. Can we dislike a young person's behavior, perhaps even hate what the person did, and still accept and even love the person? Can those of us trying to help young people leave their dysfunctional habits behind, monitor *ourselves* to notice, name, and let go of our negative emotional reactions to their outlandish behavior? As caregivers, we need to cultivate a kind of "compassionate neutrality" that allows us to love them and still address their inappropriate behavior.

Change starts with us. If we expect young people to modify and better control their emotions, we have to be willing to work on our own. There is great transformative power in love, but judging others rarely inspires their change. It is easy when working with wounded and difficult youth to notice their negative behaviors and quit seeing any positive attributes. It is like the story of the talking dog:

> A guy spots a sign outside a house that reads, Talking Dog for Sale. Intrigued, he walks in. "So what have you done with your life?" he asks the dog.
>
> "I've led a very full life," says the dog. "I lived in the Alps rescuing avalanche victims. Then I served my country in Iraq. And now I spend my days reading to the residents of a retirement home."
>
> The guy is flabbergasted. He asks the dog's owner, "Why on earth would you want to get rid of an incredible dog like that?"
>
> The owner says, "Because he's a liar! He never did any of that!"[91]

The owner had so identified with the lying aspect of his dog that he no longer saw the miracle before him. It's important to nourish what's positive in youth that can gradually lessen their identification with their "dark side." Encouraging young people to not judge themselves as they work on changing dysfunctional habits is important lest they, like

---

91. "America's Funniest Jokes" by Andy Simmons, Reader's Digest, June 2009, 108.

Ron, sabotage their own progress. Mother Teresa put it succinctly: "If you judge people, you have no time to love them."

A Results Orientation and Change

When working with youth, we don't control the results of whether, or when, change might occur. Focusing on results with superimposed timelines will bring more frustration and disappointment, impeding progress. Sometimes we work in an environment that demands signs of progress within a certain period of time. Insurance companies who fund therapy sessions have this orientation because they are trying to control costs. This is understandable but has nothing to do with empowering clients with their change.

We need to focus our attention on the process of change, being skillful and nonjudgmental in pursuing a plan for change. It is fine to have expectations and goals for youth, but whether they are realized is not within our control. If we are too invested in results in a prescribed period of time, we are likely to bring our stress into the process and, with it, hidden expectations. Stress adds nothing positive to the change process, and unconscious expectations usually trigger resistance. Our most important contribution is to model the elements of change in our own lives and in our interactions with students and clients. We plant seeds of awareness and acceptance. When they sprout as change is not ours to say. Our example of working with a clear intention, with self-awareness and acceptance, matters more than our words.

Experiments with the Process of Change

"Write down one habit or behavior that you would like to change. Keep it simple. What we are exploring in this experiment, if you decide to participate, is how change takes place; the critical elements in the process of change. Anyone willing to share what you would like to change?"

"I want to quit biting my nails—sometimes I bite them till my fingers bleed," said Michelle.

"This might seem weird but, I'd like to cut down on my swearing. I swear automatically without even thinking," Nick tentatively offered.

Some chose very challenging habits to break, like smoking.

"The experiment will last three weeks and you make a checkmark on a self-made calendar every time you exhibit the behavior you are trying to change. When you return to your old habit, remind yourself of your commitment to alter this habit. Make no judgment; however, accept you slipped up, and recommit yourself to stopping or reducing the behavior. You can graph your habit and write an overall assessment of your experience at the end of the twenty-one days," I said, summarizing the process.

"Hey, Mr. Nelson, you said you always try whatever you ask us to try; so what are **you** going to change?"

"I would like to quit judging my wife," I said to the inquiring student.

"Good luck," a muffled voice from the back chimed in.

"Yes, it should be interesting, and I even bought myself a counter to push each time I catch myself being judgmental," I said, while displaying my new toy. "It is more convenient than a calendar, and it's concealable as my intention is to not let my wife know. This is an experiment for changing myself."

The feedback in their summaries was so interesting; only two students in fifteen years did not make at least some progress. Those two students had both chosen major addictions that were getting the best of them. The rest made not only progress, but often reduced the behavior of choice by over 90 percent.

Nick, who wanted to cut down his swearing, said he was shocked by how often he swore. Seventy-six times the first day, eighty-four on the second, sixty-eight on the third, and a whopping ninety-five times on the fourth. He came to me after the fourth day and said, "This experiment is making me worse; I'm becoming a swearaholic!"

I told him he was just becoming more aware, and it only *seemed* he was regressing. I asked him about the fourth day when his swearing reached its crescendo.

He realized, upon reflection, that it had been an extremely stressful day. He had the pressure of two tests and some things going on at home. Nick committed to stay the course and in the last seven days of his graph, he had three "zero swear days" and the rest ranged between one and four. He was so pleased. He said he would catch himself at some moment of frustration, and now alert and his mind observing the moment, he was able to stop his reaction before it was expressed. He sometimes substituted words like "nuts," "darn," or "shoot" for his normal "four-letter words," and caught himself laughing.

The same happened with Michelle. She gradually got control of her fingernail biting. The increased nonjudgmental self-awareness allowed her to catch her hand moving toward her mouth, and she would say, "Ah, ah, ah, not so fast!" and redirect her hand.

These change experiments helped solidify an understanding of a process students could apply to any entrenched behavior. This process increases the likelihood of success and can be used throughout their entire life. I invite the reader to try this experiment with a habit of your choosing.

The more addictive behaviors, such as smoking, drinking, and drugs, often improved, but usually not as dramatically. Self-awareness, self-acceptance, and a committed firm unforced resolve are still the elements of change necessary to alter habitual behaviors. However, with more deeply entrenched addictive habits, self-awareness and acceptance will likely involve facing the insecurities and hurts driving those addictions. Self-awareness and acceptance will help young people realize that perhaps a change of friends, or facing their loneliness, will be required to successfully transform their addictive behaviors. The change process remains the same. Whether they are willing and courageous enough to act on their insights will determine the degree of their growth. Let me summarize the need for self-acceptance with a quote from St. Francis de Sales:

> Be patient with everyone, but above all be patient with yourself. I mean, do not be disheartened by your imperfections, but always rise up with fresh courage. How are we to be patient in dealing with our neighbor's faults if we are not patient with our own? He who is fretted by his own failings will not correct them. All profitable correction comes from a calm peaceful mind.

4. PRACTICE, PRACTICE, AND PRACTICE.

We need to commit to practicing our new replacement habits. When altering a habit we have been doing for a long time, particularly one charged with emotional energy, we must recognize and accept that it will take time to change. Sometimes through grace or deep conviction we quickly reverse course, but this is the exception. Change usually requires us to practice a new or opposite behavior or attitude until it gradually replaces the old habit, and it atrophies naturally. We have to literally "dig" a new groove in the mind through repetition. It helps if, throughout the process of replacing the old habit and fostering the new one through practice, we maintain a detached nonemotional attitude. This neutral attitude allows us to focus on the process and the feedback we receive, rather than superimposing expectations and the timelines of the ego, which is anxiously lost in concerns about results.

William James said, "Each of us literally chooses, by his way of attending to things, what sort of universe he appears to himself to inhabit." In regards to change, this implies consciously directing our attention to watering the seeds of our new habit. The more we practice, the quicker the new habit develops. The less attention and energy we direct to the old habit; the quicker it wilts. Whatever the mind focuses on grows. Attention and practice is the mind's fertilizer. Once we have a clear *intention* then we just have to direct our *attention* to it, over and over again. It is called practice. Eknath Eswaran captures in a humorous metaphor the value of meditation's neutral attention as a catalyst for changing negative emotional habit patterns:

> Life is a kind of play in which we are called upon to play our part with skill. But in meditation we are sometimes more like the audience, while our thoughts are the actors. If we could go backstage, we could see all the actors getting made up. Anger is there putting on his long fangs. Fear is rattling his chains. Jealousy is admiring herself in the mirror and smearing on green mascara.
>
> Now, these thought-actors are like actors and actresses everywhere: they thrive on a responsive audience. When Jealousy comes out on stage and we sit forward on our seats, all eyes; she really puts on a show. But on

the other hand, what happens if nobody comes to see the performance?

No actor likes to play to an empty house. If they're real professionals, they might give their best for a couple of nights, but after that they're bound to get a little slack. Jealousy doesn't bother with her makeup anymore; who's going to admire it? Anger throws away his fangs. Fear puts away his chains. Whom can they impress? Finally, the whole cast gives it up as a bad job and goes out for a midnight cup of chocolate.[92]

By practicing a neutral attitude toward intense painful emotions through mindfulness and meditation by not feeding the drama, our habits gradually weaken and the compulsive thoughts surrounding them decrease.

In regard to my experiment of not judging my wife, I had the same experience as my students. At first I couldn't believe how often I judged my wife, though most of it took place (thank God!) inside my skull. Some leaked out into the tone of my voice, rolled eyes, or a raised eyebrow. Over time, I gradually saw this judgmental impulse before it fully expressed itself. I tried to cultivate at that moment a deep love and acceptance of my wife. This was very satisfying, because I felt good about decreasing my judgments and it led to change that tangibly improved our relationship.

New habits have to be reinforced and practiced until they become our new norm. When I slipped back into my old habit pattern of judging, the remembrance of the experiment made it easier to recommit. I still have my counter, and it remains a symbol of noble intentions and increased self-awareness. Trying to decrease deeply conditioned habits and replace them with healthier habits, in order to sustain that change, requires practice over time.

We will need to practice all four elements of change in order to replace our current paradigm of the economic culture's notions of success. The ideas of success fashioned by the economic culture have penetrated our consciousness, but they have not delivered on their promise of happiness. We will need to consistently advance a new vision of success if we are to create a more meaningful future and satisfy our deeper longings.

---

92. "Life is a Kind of Play," Thought for the day by Eknarth Eswaran from the Blue Mountain Center of Meditation.

Experiment:

Change Negative Habits and Cultivate Positive Sentiments for the Mind

Every day, for a three- to twelve-month period, journal a minimum of three things for which you are grateful. These can be little or large things. The universe is constantly giving us blessings that we fail to acknowledge. For example our morning breakfast is a gift. People planted and nurtured the growth of the fruit and grains in our cereal. It was picked, washed, packaged, protected, and shipped many miles to arrive a short distance from our homes. The gas that allowed us to go purchase the cereal went through an elaborate process before it went into our car. All of this effort in order to provide us a meal.

Before unconsciously consuming the cereal (and other gifts received throughout the course of the day), cultivate an attitude of appreciation for the energetic source of each gift. Appreciate not only the gifts themselves, but the effort of all who gave their labor to bring them to you. Cultivate noticing and appreciating the kind and giving qualities of all people you are currently in relationship with, particularly your family.

Practice this "attitude of gratitude" over a period of several months, and it will be transformative. It can dramatically improve your sense of contentment. It alters our mindless robotic experience of life. By journaling your appreciation, this new positive orientation will penetrate your mind's way of looking at life. It will become your new habit; your new reality. You will begin seeing the world through a lens of appreciation that helps your mind stay in the present moment. You will change the mind's tendency to perceive life through a clouded, preoccupied lens that magnifies what is wrong, missing the gift that is life, because it is stuck anticipating negative fantasies.

Chapter 16
Redefining Success

"The achievement which society rewards is won at the cost of the diminution of personality."

—CARL JUNG

"Your success and happiness lies in you. Resolve to keep happy, and your joy and you shall form an invisible host against difficulties."

—HELEN KELLER

Evaluations of a person's status, worth, success, and certainly their power and influence are, in America, largely determined by how well you achieve the goals of the economic culture. If you drive a new Lexus vs. a twenty-year-old car that looks like a "rust bucket" people will tend to evaluate you differently. If you are a CEO of a major company vs. a custodian who vacuums the carpeting in that company, people relate to you differently. If you live in a large house in a wealthy suburb vs. renting a studio apartment in a rundown neighborhood, you are usually afforded more status, prestige, and privilege. People who experience great success in the economic culture are often related to as though they have greater worth. They are shown greater respect and deference.

Almost no one in our culture would think to question that the Lexus driver, the CEO, or "the big house guy" were more successful than the custodian, the "rust bucket" driver, or the "studio apartment guy."

How to Assess Success

The economic culture, because it has such a dominating influence in all areas of our lives, shapes the way we evaluate, judge, and relate to people. It conditions our thinking so we don't question, using an economic barometer for these kinds of assessments. We forget the distinction between what a person does or has, and their inherent worth as a human being. No wonder we're so anxious and stressed because, if we don't perform according to these external standards in some sense, we are considered "losers." The notion that success is determined by results, particularly economic results, is so imbedded in our psyche that it is rarely questioned. If we do our best and there are no tangible results, are we failures? If we do something well as judged by someone else's standard, are we necessarily a success? If the performance anxiety that accompanies our success makes us sick, unhappy, or hypercompetitive, leading to hostility toward others, even if our goal is achieved, is this really success?

Eckhart Tolle in *A New Earth* suggests another way to conceptualize success:

> The world will tell you that success is . . . winning, that finding recognition and/or prosperity are essential ingredients in any success. The conventional notion of success is concerned with the outcome . . . What the world doesn't tell you . . . is that you cannot "become" successful. You can only BE successful. Don't let a mad world tell you that success is anything other than a successful present moment. And, what is that? There is a sense of quality in what you do, even in the most simple action. Quality implies care and attention, which come with awareness. Quality requires your Presence.

Everyone needs to consider that there may be a different and more satisfying criterion for assessing success that isn't related to status, position, accumulation of objects, or performance in the market place.

Eckhart Tolle gives the example of a person who produces a product that sells well and makes money, but who was intensely stressed for two years before the product reached the market. Tolle argues that how one achieves a goal is actually more important than the goal. If a person was violent to his body and mind, by subjecting it to extreme stress for two years, this is not success. If his stress negatively impacted his relationships for those two years, again this sabotages real success. His toxic energy, and the damage he inflicted on himself and others, matters. Eckhart Tolle continues, "If the means does not contribute to human happiness, neither will the ends. The outcome is contaminated by the actions that led up to it and will create further unhappiness."[93] His point is that the quality of one's presence and interactions with others are the critical variables in determining a person's success.

Being kind, loving, relaxed, and present in the process called life is primary; destination and results are secondary. This is success: cultivating a compassionate, loving, relaxed, and fully absorbed mind open to each moment life presents. So, it is possible the "rust bucket" driver, the custodian, and the "studio apartment guy" could be the real successes, regardless of the economic culture's assessment. Was Bernie Madoff, the multimillionaire who launched the world's biggest Ponzi scheme stealing thousands of people's retirement hopes, a success?

If we made presence our quest, caring attention to each moment, this would be the end of performance anxiety and stress. Mother Theresa, when asked if she was a saint because of the many great things she had done, replied, "There are no 'great things' only small things done with great love." Being fully present to others is the way we express our love. Later she commented regarding her sainthood and simply said, "We are all called to be saints."

Training the Mind for Success

I mentioned earlier that all anxiety, including performance anxiety, is a thought with a future focus. The reality is that we are all the

---

93. A New Earth, Eckhart Tolle. Namaste Publishing, 2005, 270.

architects of our future which manifests through the quality of our awareness, directing our actions in the current moment. This moment-to-moment absorption and connection with being, with our spiritual self, requires a training of the mind. Again, the mind's nature is to move away from the present moment and into future fantasies or regrets or nostalgia from the past. William James speaks to the importance of training the mind: "The faculty of voluntarily bringing back a wandering attention is the very root of judgment, character, and will. No one is really in control of themselves if they do not have this. An education which would improve this faculty would be the education par excellence."

Education currently dedicates very little time to train young people's minds to stay relaxed and concentrated in the now. This, however, is the prime requirement for decreasing emotional pain, restlessness, stress, boredom, and helping to achieve true success. When we make progress in training our minds, we gain the power to direct its attention. The question then becomes, will we continue to direct it almost exclusively outward to the world of sense stimulation and hedonistic activity?

We live in an economic culture that entices our minds to focus almost exclusively outward. We have doubled our consumption per person over the past fifty years while decreasing our happiness.[94] Increasing numbers of youth are finding the goals and promises of the economic culture unsatisfying and stressful. The economic culture's notions of success have by definition assessed many people as failures. Even those judged as successes by their economic barometer often despair because they have found no real meaning and purpose for their lives. They know they can never escape the economic culture's evaluative treadmill, because they have to maintain their performance in order to continue to "earn" the economic culture's judgment of being a success.

I believe many people are ready and yearning to make a radical shift. They feel and know at some level that their hedonistic external addictions have not led to contentment or a lasting happiness. They are ready to turn more of their attention inward to the more satisfying world of self-awareness and self-discovery. In this discovery young

---

94.   Ibid.

people will realize their interdependence and deep connection with all life. This awareness will open their hearts, creating more harmonious relationships and incline them to direct more of their attention to relieving suffering. They will no longer be stuck in the tar pits of purposeless activity and mindless consumption.

It will be our youth who will energize this radical shift. The rest of us can serve as catalysts by joining them in our own inner journey, while supporting them in theirs. Discovering purpose, and its power to transform the painful and destructive malaise of our youth, will play an important role in halting the downward trends plaguing them and our society. There are already many encouraging signs in America and across the planet initiated or supported by young people to change the downward trends we are witnessing.

Craig Kielberg, at age sixteen, for example, launched "Free the Children," an effort to empower young people with the message that they can change the world. As a result of these efforts by youths, one million people now have access to clean water, and 270,000 others have received school and health kits. Three hundred and fifty thousand additional young people are touched by motivational speaking tours and leadership seminars each year, inspiring many to make their lives about positively changing the world. Craig's organization has joined with Oprah Winfrey's "O Ambassadors" to build sixty schools, and as a result over 55,000 students now have access to education.[95]

The "Rachel Challenge" is a program named after Rachel Scott who was the first student shot at the Columbine High School tragedy. The kindness and understanding she demonstrated toward others before her death inspired a national effort to bring acceptance and compassionate interactions in schools and also to the competitive corporate world. Jane Goodall has launched a youth-driven program called "Roots and Shoots." Young people are initiating efforts to monitor, protect, and restore environmental resources and participate in peace initiatives on behalf of all living creatures. These are just a few of the thousands of efforts, large and small, where youth are leading or participating in changing the downward trends that cause so much pain. A growing awareness of these efforts inspires more and more

---

95.   www.freethechildren.com.

youth to find their niche and to help positively transform the world. This is real success.

In the next chapter we explore in depth the remarkable transformative power of purpose as part of an emerging paradigm that will replace the confusing and destructive messages of the economic culture. We leave this chapter with a definition of success attributed to Ralph Waldo Emerson. His statement of success challenges the economic culture's perspective and puts true success within our reach:

To laugh often and much;

To win the respect of intelligent people and the affection of children;

To earn the appreciation of honest critics and endure the betrayal of false friends;

To appreciate beauty;

To find the best in others;

To leave the world a bit better, whether by a healthy child, a garden patch or a redeemed social condition;

To know even one life has breathed easier because you have lived; this is to have succeeded.

Chapter 17
The Promise of Purpose

"Those who learn to live in the now and have a purpose do not know sadness."

—SWAMI RAMA

"I went to the woods because I wished to live deliberately, and see if I could not learn what it had to teach, and not, when I came to die, discover that I had not lived."

—HENRY THOREAU

Economic activity is a necessary and important part of life. It provides a livelihood for our citizenry. Some of the productivity of the economic culture provides necessities and products that sustain life and enhance people's opportunities to express their talents. Much of the economic culture's productivity, however, is not essential, is unhealthy, and distracts and delays engaging in meaningful living. Tolstoy captured poignantly one problem with the modern economic system fashioned by the elites: "Love for humankind won't be served by amusing the well fed, while leaving the cold and hungry to die of want."

Objects and events are rarely satisfying ends in themselves. If seeking fame or fortune becomes an end in itself, there will be stress in the process of seeking, and ultimately disappointment even when successful. George Bernard Shaw shared this perspective with some humor: "There are two tragedies in life. One is not to get your heart's desire, and the other is to get it." Even when we achieve our heart's desire, it never satisfies us to the extent that we had hoped; it often stresses us to achieve it, and once it is acquired we worry about losing it. The attachments that trigger this kind of anxiety can be observed when you see an expensive car parked in the far reaches of a parking lot, angled to occupy two spaces so that no one will scratch or dent it.

Succeeding in the goals and enjoying the fruits of the economic culture has become an end in itself, creating stress but little lasting happiness. At the end of the day, we are never satisfied because one desire begets another. Emerson put this metaphorically: "Want is a growing giant whom the 'Coat of have' was never large enough to cover." And Jesus cautioned, "Watch out! Be on your guard against all kinds of greed; life does not consist in the abundance of his possessions" (Luke 12:15 NIV). Insatiable wanting intensified by advertising has led to youth's four primitive urges being painfully out of balance. In directing our attention outward to satisfy our cravings, we have become an attention deficit hyperactive disordered culture (ADHDC). This has contributed heavily to youth's boredom struggles, while confusing their understanding of the real source of self-esteem. This is the true alienation—to have lost the experience of our permanent, infinite self. Young people have almost completely and unconsciously identified with the mask of personality and the self-images promoted relentlessly by the media.

Those of us who work with youth can be catalysts to raise the questions Madison Avenue doesn't: Who am I? Where am I going? Why am I here? We can help strengthen youth's faint awareness that poor choices made regarding their four primitive urges become the sources of their emotional struggles. We can listen to the pressure they feel living in a culture that doesn't separate their worth from their performance. This leaves many youth hopelessly stressed and striving to gain acceptance through being SOMEBODY. To the ego, being "a bad ass" beats being a nobody.

Many youth are lost, left searching for something to enliven their existence through drugs, high-risk behaviors, or intense action videos and games. The goals and promises of the economic culture have left them empty. The values of the economic culture have usurped the values of charity and unselfishness and replaced them with greed and self-absorption. It has blown the horn of individuality too loud and forgotten the quieter, subtler tones of a collective harmony that holds a society together.

Greed itself is powered by insecurity, a haunting, often unconscious feeling that we are flawed and insufficient in some way. This internal inadequacy causes us to accumulate and cling to externals in a vain attempt to prove our value and importance. It is, however, impossible to heal our self-esteem scars through seeking status or things. Plato defined education as teaching our children to find pleasure in the right things, but the economic culture is educating children in all the wrong things.

Transforming Youth through Purpose

Lethargy and loneliness are the only consistent companions for increasing numbers of youth. Ravi Shankar once said that there are only four sources of energy: food, sleep, breath, and a happy mind. A happy mind is a relaxed, focused mind whose attention is directed toward uplifting thoughts, positive emotions, and the discovery of one's true self which provides an unending expansive energy. Having a clear and compelling sense of purpose can help youth focus and enliven their minds, bringing an end to their boredom and their energetic funk. Purpose, in some form, is the reason we get up in the morning. If we have a small purpose, we get up to avoid a dad yelling or the hassles of a truancy officer or to keep from getting fired, but we arise with no enthusiasm or zest. A noble purpose that young people have fashioned for themselves becomes a source of self-inspired energy. Purpose provides the motivation to stay engaged when challenges and obstacles present themselves. It is a powerful antidote to aimlessness that feeds depression and anxiety.

Dick Leider, author of *The Power of Purpose*, sites a US university study on suicide that I referenced in the first chapter that is illuminating. The study, remember, focused on sixty university students who survived their suicide attempts and were interviewed as to why they had tried to end their lives. Eighty-five percent of these students essentially said that life seemed meaningless and difficult. It is significant that 93 percent of these students reported having good family relationships, active social lives, and were performing well academically. Without having a sense of purpose, however, just doing things and having things wasn't sufficient to create happiness or provide enough satisfaction to stop their tragic choice.[96]

Research since this university study reveals over and over again that people with a self-chosen reason for living, a purpose, are not likely to even consider suicide. We know in times of national crisis, suicide rates drop. A crisis seems to help clarify what really matters. It also creates a collective unity that often spawns a purpose. It is harder for people to get as lost in their personal dramas when there is a real threat to the entire society.

Dick Leider interviewed elderly people asking them, essentially, if their life had mattered. The vast majority said they didn't think so. Many told stories revealing that their original ideas for a meaningful life had somehow been derailed. Events like war or the death of a father had intervened and turned their life in a different direction than they had intended. After years of studying purpose and counseling people to explore a deeper sense of purpose, Leider offered one conclusion through a metaphor. I will paraphrase that conclusion: Some people jump on a train and aren't even sure where the train is going—they are just along for the ride. Others know where they are going, stare out the window, and arrive having enjoyed some of the scenery. A few are luckier, as they are the engineers. They drive the train, know where the tracks lead, and have a broader vista to enjoy the trip. But, he concluded, "The really fortunate ones are the people who lay the tracks."

A purpose that we choose for ourselves, pursued with determination and passion, provides the energy and focus necessary for a life of deeper joy and meaning. This can end the listless, running on empty, zombie-like expressions that I have witnessed on the faces of so many of our youth. Purpose can curb much of their despair, but the false promises of the economic culture never will. The purposeless malaise where

---

96. The Power of Purpose, revised by Richard Leider.

they zestlessly squander their talents leads to a life half-lived, or worse, ends in suicide.

How to Find Our Purpose and Meaning

Victor Frankl, the psychologist who wrote *Man's Search for Meaning*, studied people who survived concentration camps. Many of these people, understandably, had trouble putting their lives back together after the war. They lived, but often in a state of depression and victim-ization, a prolonged "learned helplessness." Those who managed to rebuild their lives and were again able to experience happiness, were usually people who created meaning or purpose, even while they were prisoners in the camps. They had found a way to help others and make a difference in relieving, in some way, their fellow prisoners' suffering.

Victor Frankl, after observing escalating suicide and drug use in industrialized Western cultures, said:

> This happens in the midst of affluent societies and in the midst of welfare states! For too long we have been dreaming a dream from which we are now waking up: the dream that if you just improve the socioeco-nomic status of people, everything will be okay—people will be happy. The truth is that as the struggle for survival has subsided the question has emerged: survival for what? I pity the people who have the means to live and not the meaning.

So most of our youth have the means, but many lack the meaning. This purposelessness drives much of their drug use, increases boredom, feeds depression, and contributes to reckless, thrill-seeking, "extreme" behaviors to manufacture a sense of aliveness.

Students and clients over the years have asked me, "How do I figure out my purpose?" During childhood, others define for us what to do, because they provide approval and we do what's expected rather than what is meaningful. Young adults who raise this important question about purpose, and even those who don't, need some guidance as to how to answer it. Many of the life decisions we make are determined by the questions we ask or fail to ask. And the biggest question we need to ask and try to answer is "Who am I?" with its two corollaries: "Why am I here?" and "Where am I going?" Most youth aren't laying their own tracks. They have the "independence of the herd" thing going. Their choices are conditioned by the messages of the economic culture: happiness lies outside of you, and do what feels good to you. This external and selfish orientation explains why many don't question who they are or where they are going. They were born or pushed onto the economic culture's train, not realizing where they would end up.

Three Questions That Clarify Purpose

Here are three questions I found helpful in focusing young people's exploration of purpose that are an essential part of creating a meaningful and contented life:

1. **Who am I?** Encouraging and facilitating youth's exploration, reflection, and contemplation of this question is important. This is life's quintessential question that needs an answer. There is an experiment in Chapter 19 that started some of my students on a deeper exploration of this question. We investigate this question there.

2. **How might I serve others?** How can we align our talents, gifts, and interests away from egocentric pursuits and apply them to serving others? There is a wonderful experiential exercise at the end of this chapter that helps youth create a purpose statement. I say it's wonderful because all of the answers are generated by youth from their own contemplations.

Abraham Maslow, whose theory of human personality posited that each person is born with a "god-like quality within," studied extraordinary people. These people had accomplished a lot in the world, but more importantly had found a deep happiness and fulfillment doing it. He considered these people the psychologically and spiritually healthiest humans. The term he used for describing the process of applying one's gifts to their work in the world is self-actualization. Here is how Maslow described those who were truly laying their own tracks:

> Self-actualizing people are, without one single exception, involved in a cause outside their own skins, in something outside themselves. They are devoted, working at something, something which is very precious to them—some calling or vocation in the old sense, the priestly sense. They are working at something which fate has called them to somehow; and which they work at and which they love, so that the work-joy dichotomy in them disappears."[97]

Sometimes when people talk about the importance of serving others it can sound like an obligation. But, if you wed your passions and talents to positive work in the world, it is not an obligation, it is a joy. There is no should, only an "I shall," when one's actions are imbued with purposeful enthusiasm. Frederick Buechner, a theologian, said this regarding purpose: "Our calling is where our deepest gladness and the world's hunger meet."

3. **"What are the lessons I am meant to learn from the events and people in my daily life?"** Does the reoccurring suffering in my life that I often label as bad luck, or unfair, reveal my habit patterns and attachments that block my natural joy and hurt my relationships? Can I learn to utilize these events and relationships and even my suffering, to increase my self-awareness of things that I need to change, thereby bringing more harmony and purpose to my life?

Life as Teacher—Staying Open to Life's Lessons

Life is often compared to a classroom and we are students. Sometimes life is hard and, to all appearances, it also often seems unfair. I now believe everything that comes my way is for my growth, though initially I might not always respond that way. The most painful moments of my life, some of which I wouldn't wish on anybody, have also been my greatest teachers. For example, I had a girlfriend, whom I thought I might marry, cheat on me. It ripped open my heart. I recognized she

---

97. "On Motivation Part 1: The Self" by Michael R. Maude, president of Partners in Philanthropy.

bore the responsibility for her choice, but this event forced me to look in the mirror and see what role I had played in driving her away.

I had grown up in a family with four boys and had learned there, and from the larger culture, that being masculine meant not showing one's feelings. The night I discovered my girlfriend with another guy, I sobbed for hours. This was the first time I had cried in many years. This was the start of reawakening to my feelings and becoming a better partner in my future relationships. Recovering my lost emotional self didn't take too long, perhaps because I grew up with a mother who could go through three Kleenex boxes absorbing her tears, brought on by one television episode of *Little House on the Prairie*.

It's hard to get close to someone who doesn't share feelings, and my girlfriend had finally given up trying. I remember walking into a library a week or so after discovering her with another guy. I was still reeling from the loss. For some inexplicable reason my eyes were drawn to a very small book, barely visible among hundreds of others. I pulled it off the shelf. It was *The Art of Loving* by Eric Fromm, and the book became a catalyst for my transformation. The "coincidence" of the book jumping off the shelf at that moment didn't go unnoticed. The book, and the changes it inspired, was the first of many gifts that came out of my painful ruptured relationship. So this third question, about paying attention to what is happening in one's life, is important. Observing areas of friction, defensiveness, and emotional reactivity in relationships, as well as noticing the sources of our joy, is part of our purpose; to learn from the classroom of life.

Our relationships provide the main mirrors that reveal our insecurities, hurts, and fears. We can continue to project and blame others, or we can examine the role *we* are playing in creating reoccurring painful scenarios. Even if objectively someone is acting "nasty," "jerky," or "bitchy" (I use adjectives rather than nouns because nouns suggest unchangeable character flaws), I still have the power to not internalize someone's insults or rejection. Nouns with negative connotations, whether used in relationships or applied to ourselves through negative self-talk, make change more difficult. Scientist, inventor, and philosopher Buckminster Fuller said, "We are not nouns; we are all verbs in the process of becoming."

Taking responsibility for our emotions triggered in relationships, and deciding which thoughts to give energy to, keeps us from becoming a victim. This automatically ensures a brighter future. This perspective needs to be emphasized with youth who demand, against all odds, that the external environment, or someone in it, needs to change. Eleanor Roosevelt said, "No one has the power to make us feel inferior without our consent." If we live from this perspective, the exterior world has less power to negatively impact our moods.

It may seem paradoxical, but unless we take responsibility for our emotions, regardless of their triggers, we can never experience true freedom. This does not mean we should judge ourselves when we get emotional. As soon as we're able to step back and detach a bit, we can analyze what "button" was pushed. We need to recognize that button was present in us prior to someone pushing it, or we wouldn't have reacted. To use the language of insurance companies—we had a "preexisting condition." The hurts that lie behind our buttons require our kind attention, rather than blaming or hopelessly trying to manipulate the exterior world.

There are times to constructively address and try to change external irritants. Frequently, however, this is impossible. Regardless, we are still left with our historical hurts and fears, and our ego's over-identifications that drive our emotional reactions. We need to honestly and courageously take responsibility for healing or detaching from these internal triggers, for the sake of ours and others' happiness. Ane Pema Chodron, author of *When Things Fall Apart*, explains, "The only reason we don't open our hearts and minds to other people is that they trigger confusion in us that we don't feel brave enough or sane enough to deal with. To the degree that we look clearly and compassionately at ourselves, we feel confident and fearless about looking into someone else's eyes."

We do have the power to change the frustration and suffering in our relationships. But we have to become conscious of our thoughts and interpretations that create our reactive emotional patterns in order to change these frustrations. I am not suggesting we are the sole causes of problems in relationships. I am suggesting we are the only one who can change our reactions. Sometimes we do have to leave toxic relationships, and having the courage to leave may be the lesson we are meant to learn.

Consciously and Purposefully Embracing All of Life

So again, one important aspect of purposeful living is using our relationships and situations to inform us of necessary changes to increase ours and others' happiness. There is a sixteenth-century small book written by two Jesuit priests called *Trustful Surrender to Divine Providence*. One of the main themes of the book is: "God only sends the good." Good doesn't necessarily mean easy. The perspective of the book is that whatever challenges come our way in life are sent for our growth and increased self-awareness.

Paying attention and observing patterns in our reactions can spur change and growth. When we look at life through a pleasure/pain prism, as we have been conditioned to do, our interpretation of events will be judged as either "good" or "bad." If we experience pain they are bad. If we experience pleasure, they are good. In fact, our very definitions of what is good or bad is the result of us deciding how the world needs to be for us to feel okay. This sets us up to constantly resist how life is unfolding, creating tremendous stress for ourselves. Life's events often flow in ways and directions we have little power to anticipate or influence. When we embrace life with all its external and internal challenges and look at life through the prism of learning, then even difficult experiences can be helpful, and pleasurable ones can become obstacles for further growth. Shakespeare wrote in *Hamlet*, "Nothing is good or bad except the mind makes it so." Sometimes what seems bad, like the affair of my girlfriend, carries an embedded gift in the pain it came wrapped in. I know I am a better husband and a happier person because of this "bad" event.

It is often hard when we're in pain to see things with this more neutral and patient stance, which is understandable. It is hard to hear the message or grasp the entire lesson when we're in the midst of a crisis or intense pain. It may be weeks, months, even years before the lessons life and providence are trying to teach us are thoroughly understood. To grasp the deeper meaning and purpose of an event may require time. Time allows us to develop a more neutral perspective that aids our understanding. There is a story that illustrates how our initial judgments and assessments may be wrong or premature:

A farmer living in ancient times was considered the richest man in his village, as he had a horse to plow his fields. The rest of the villagers dug their fields by hand. Right before planting season, neighbors stopped by and commented on his good fortune. All he said was, "Maybe." The day before planting, his horse ran away and his neighbors came by to offer their condolences on his horrible luck. All he said was, "Maybe."

The next day his runaway horse returned, followed by four wild horses that he and his son quickly corralled. His neighbors ran over, saying he was the luckiest man in the entire region, and he would soon have great wealth due to his ability to plow and plant an enormous area. All he said was, "Maybe."

The next day his son was training one of the four wild horses. He was bucked off and broke his arm. His neighbors came over again to commiserate over his bad fortune and mentioned how hard it would be, with his son unavailable to complete the planting. He smiled and said only, "Maybe."

The next day, conscription officers came to the village to draft all able-bodied young men for a distant war, but, his son was now exempt because of his broken arm. His friends and neighbors came again, asserting how unbelievably lucky he was. He not only avoided losing his son to war, but his son would be able to help him with the fall harvest. All he said was, "We'll see, maybe."[98]

If you wait long enough, things change; change is the nature of life. If you fear those changes, try to force or are attached to a certain outcome, you will experience stress. This philosophy is embedded in the common vernacular in phrases like: "Go with the flow," and "It is what it is," or "Let go and let God." One of the major teachings of the ancient scripture *The Bhagavad Gita*, which translates as "The Song of the Lord," is to "not be attached to the fruits of your actions." When it comes to results, the fruits of our actions, if we claim them as *ours* as the ego would like, we create attachments that will cause our own suffering. Doing our duties and performing our actions as skillfully as we can, with no attachments to results, allow us to live purposefully, but without the stress created by seeking an outcome that is beyond our control.

There is a worthwhile experiment to counter our tendency to fight and oppose reality. Try welcoming with a deep acceptance each morning

---

98. Story told by Judith Hinze at the Meditation Center in the 1980s.

everything that comes your way that day. Act as though you actually requested it. Do this for a week. This is similar to the perspective offered in the book *Trustful Surrender to Divine Providence*: Whatever comes our way is good, if for no other reason than we can grow and learn from it. This acceptance of reality is a way to relax the ego's attachments and expectations. Letting go of the ego's idea of the way things should be and accepting the way things are ends stress. Often these are hard perspectives for youth in particular to accept, implement, and internalize. Yet, I have found it very beneficial to explore these ideas and suggest experiments so that young people can directly experience their transformative value. These experiments are useful regardless of a student's academic ability. Jacob was an engaging young man with a low average IQ.

I was facilitating a large stress management group for at-risk eighteen- to twenty-one-year-old students. We were checking in and asking the students how their week was and if they had any particular stressors in their lives that they would like to share. The students shared some tremendously difficult situations. Some were a week away from homelessness, and more than one student was dealing with a rage-filled drunken stepfather.

When we got to Jacob, he said, "I am so upset, I can't even talk about it."

The group encouraged him but he was steadfast. "It is too upsetting and quit asking me to share because I am not going to tell you!"

We let Jacob be, and proceeded with the rest of the group. After group, Jacob stuck around and asked if he could schedule an appointment with me. He wanted to "get this off my chest, but not in front of everybody—even though it's hopeless."

Jacob came in three days later, and I was braced to hear some horrifying story about abuse that I may be mandated to report. I asked him, "So, Jacob, can you share what is going on at home? I can tell it is really upsetting you."

He replied, "It's my mom; she's impossible to live with."

"What is she doing that is so upsetting?" I asked.

"She does it every day, and I don't know how much longer I can take it!" he said with great animation but still not answering my question.

"So tell me what she is doing that is so horrible?" I asked.

"Every morning I wake up and immediately I am upset by her and I feel like screaming," he said, again not answering my question.

"Well, I can tell it must be hard to share, but can you tell me exactly what she does?" I persisted.

"Yes, she wakes me up with her singing!"

I battled smiling as I had images of cattle prods zapping Jacob into consciousness each morning.

"She is always singing, and she sings horrible songs with her horrible voice—all day long!" he said with exasperation.

"How long has she been doing this?"

"For years!" he exclaimed.

"Do you think she is going to change or stop singing?" I asked.

"No, I have told her she has a rotten voice and asked her to stop. But she just makes it into a joke—but it's no joke, and it's driving me crazy!"

"I want to explain to you, Jacob, an experiment that might help you lower the stress you have been experiencing for years. First thing when you wake up, I want you to say to yourself, 'Oh good, my mom is singing and it makes me laugh because she is so off key!'

I was about to launch into why this might work but he enthusiastically blurted out, "Oh, I get it, if I want her to sing, then I won't get frustrated when she does sing—even if she is awful at it."

Jacob somehow immediately grasped that his frustration was less about mom's voice, and more about his thoughts about her singing. He felt it was unfair to have to listen to her because he had the idea that people with bad voices shouldn't sing. And, they certainly should not sing all day long. He recognized if he could fully accept his reality that his mom is a singer, he would not be as stressed. He knew he couldn't change his situation.

"So, Jacob, when your mom starts singing tomorrow, can you 'go with the flow' and convince your mind to be glad that she is singing off key?"

"Yup!" he said. "I know I can and it will be fun to try to enjoy her bad singing!" he said with a smile.

Jacob was successful and no longer stressed about his mom's singing. I saw him over the next two years at school, and he would smile and often say, "Mom's still singing!"

Jacob had truly embraced reality and changed the habit and perspectives that made him a victim. Jacob had discovered what a couple of thousand years ago in Greece Epictetus had articulated, "We are disturbed not by what happens to us, but by our thoughts about what happens."

Often as caregivers, we are essentially planting seeds. Jacob's seeds bore fruit immediately. Often these seeds will take time to sprout. Additional life lessons are required in order to continue to water the seeds of awareness and transformation that we planted earlier. At some unanticipated moment, those seeds that were seemingly dormant, sometimes for years, sprout unexpectedly.

Many of my students did a slightly different version of this acceptance-of-life experiment. I had offered extra credit to students for trying to remain happy over the course of one week, regardless of what life brought forward.

The following journal, from an eighteen-year-old male student, reflects insights echoed by many of his peers who also chose to participate in this experiment.

One day I was really getting bummed out when I remembered your suggestion and decided that I was going to have a great day, whether I liked it or not! Throughout the day I had to constantly remind myself, and I went on to have a great day. So, I decided to try it again the next day. The next day came, and I reminded myself when things I didn't like happened that I was going to have a great day anyway. And I had a terrific day . . . I continued for the entire week, and it was a great week.

So even though this wasn't part of your suggestion, I wondered what would happen if I did the opposite for a week. The same results happened but, this time it was the opposite. I kept telling myself over and over each day for a week, that this was going to be a lousy day. I noticed when things went wrong, and then dwelled on them. My days kept getting progressively worse, and my energy went down and I became more frustrated . . . by the end of the week, things pretty much sucked.

After seven days of each, I've decided that your attitude is all psychological. If you have a good day, it's a decision not a happening. And, if you have a bad day, that is a decision, also.

THE PROMISE OF PURPOSE

Experiential options such as this, if sincerely practiced, can nourish a greater acceptance of life's natural ebb and flow. You can probably remember experiences that at the time they occurred seemed "bad," but ended up having a silver lining. You can also probably remember things that at the time they happened seemed "good," but later deteriorated and brought pain. This is often the nature of life and the change inherent in it.

Conscience and Intuition: Guides for Discerning Life's Lessons

The messages sent during life's challenging moments, and what we are to learn from those messages, is for us alone to discern. The receiver system to help us understand these messages is our conscience, our intuition; our heartfelt deep sense of truth. Bombarding the senses with intense and constant stimulation and exposure to hundreds of thousands of ads that encourage self-absorption in the external world can drown out the still, quiet voice within. I mentioned that the worst thing we can do is to lose connection to our conscience. This is true because when we ignore our intuitive wisdom or conscience, we have effectively declared war on ourselves. Conflicting desires, noble and selfish, wage a usually unconscious but stressful battle within. We have been given free will, which allows us to ignore our conscience, our discriminative wisdom, and choose to pursue our baser desires and attachments.

When we choose to ignore our conscience, we receive at some point a gentle yet somewhat painful reminder indicating we have violated our higher self's best interest. It is said providence initially sends a *feather*, in the form of remorse or pain, to signal our poor choice. If we ignore our conscience long enough, providence eventually sends a *two-by-four*, so we won't miss the lesson. Psychopaths bury their feelings and with it their conscience. We, too, can severely muffle or scramble the signal from our conscience and intuition, thus obscuring our clarity about ethical choices and meaningful living. In the cacophony of noise in the economic culture, it is easy to lose track of our internal voice of conscience that is constantly there to guide us. We then tend to give in to the tempting, conditioned desires that invite our own suffering.

Let us look at a simple example. We are considering having a second piece of pie; our conscience or intuitive wisdom sends a reminder that we are already full. The wisdom that is aligned with our fifth primitive urge that always seeks balance, harmony, and joy sends an unambiguous message to say no to our desire. But, the desire-filled mind reminds us the last piece was so—ohh . . . good! It even provides us with a rationale: "It was a pretty small piece, so what the heck," and we give in to our cravings and wolf down the second piece. Most of us have been in this battle many times, in many different contexts. It is characterized in cartoons as the devil on one shoulder (desire) and an angel on the other (representing our conscience or intuition). The feather, in the case of the second piece of pie, is the coma-like depressed state overeating brings, and perhaps a little guilt as we had earlier vowed to lose weight. The two-by-four might not come until years later, as we continue our indulgent patterns and suffer a heart attack, causing us to finally change our diet.

When we ignore our conscience or intuition, there is no God to blame; but it has appropriately been called "a sin against wisdom." It is the wisdom we carry within us at all times. The question is, can we hear it through the din of the economic temptress with its conditioned desires and the static and stress it creates in our minds? A desire or fear-filled mind, secretly hoping for a certain outcome, often blends its selfish urge with the pure signal of conscience or intuition. This amalgamation makes it easier for us to rationalize away the hard but correct choice of conscience, and justify our ego's desires. Someone asked, "What is the difference between a monstrous human being, an average human being, and a saint?" The answer is: a monstrous human never consults his conscience, the average person occasionally follows his conscience, and a saint always follows his conscience.[99]

There are different levels of decision making—legal, ethical, and moral—but deciding according to the truth in our self, our conscience and intuition, is the highest authority for good decisions. This is what the Greeks were urging when they said, "To thy own self be true." St. Augustine interestingly offered, "Let me know myself, Lord, and I will

---

99. A Personal Philosophy of Life by Swami Rama, Himalayan Institute Hospital Trust, 2002, 59.

know thee." At all times we should act in harmony with our intuition, our deepest values, our inner judgment, our deepest inclinations, our purest feelings—this is our truth.

Honoring our conscience is the way to find true peace and end the war of conflicted impulses within us. Freud, too, said we were at war with ourselves, and named that unresolved war: neurosis. The conscience I am referring to here, however, is not the conscience of Freud, which he called the superego. That superego was largely an internalized version of parental and cultural values and norms. His notion of conscience was often connected to shame and feared cultural consequences. The conscience referenced here is wisdom. This intelligence comes from a source that instantaneously considers all pertinent variables in context, and brings forward the right decision or insight. Our conscience or intuition's guidance and wisdom is unfailingly perfect, because it is linked to our true self. It serves as our constant guide for an authentic life.

Two Forms of Intelligence

There are really two kinds of knowledge or intelligence that are quite distinct. One is information gathered and assessed with conclusions drawn through rational, analytic, and logical consideration. This kind of intelligence or knowledge is useful if properly utilized. Serving and supporting the wisdom of intuition is its proper function. Absent wisdom and conscience, the mind can use information to rationalize poor behavior and can be manipulative and cunning. It is said that we live in the age of information. This is true. We have more and more information that is accessible quickly. However, I have witnessed little correlation between a mind filled with information and happiness. Many of my clients were bright and well informed, but deeply and profoundly miserable. T.S. Elliot gets to the heart of the limitations of information and analytic intelligence:

The endless cycle of idea and action.
Endless invention, endless experiment.
Brings knowledge of motion, but not of stillness.

Knowledge of speech, but not of silence;
Knowledge of words, and ignorance of the Word.
All our knowledge brings us nearer to our ignorance.
All our ignorance brings us nearer to death.
But nearness to death no nearer to God.
Where is the life we have lost living?
Where is the knowledge we have lost in information?[100]

Don't mistake information for wisdom. Living in the age of information has not left a legacy of human happiness or decreased personal or societal violence. We have more and more information, for example, about hundreds of different species living in the rainforest. Yet the rainforest continues to shrink, and many of its species become extinct every day. Where is the wisdom in that?

So, the rational, logical, reductionist mind has its limits. Einstein said something very interesting: "I never came to my understanding of the universe through my rational mind." How then did he come to his unique and expansive understanding? He gives an illuminating answer: "The intuitive mind is sacred, and the rational mind should be its faithful servant." Einstein's quote perfectly highlights the appropriate role of the two different types of intelligence. Einstein speaks to the limits of information, and the limits of the rational mind in the creative process.

The good news is that all of us have this other more dynamic and creative intelligence, our intuitive intelligence. With intuitive intelligence knowledge does not come piecemeal, but as a holistic knowing—a gestalt. It is a knowing in its purest form, and when not alloyed with desire, is self-validating because it comes from the direct source of truth within us. Sometimes we experience this knowing as an "aha" moment, a flash of insight when suddenly the "light comes on." Intuition can be a great ally for youth to receive clear answers regarding their purpose. Intuition can help young people understand the lessons their relationships and life experiences are trying to teach them. These lessons are often revealed through the very struggles that are causing their suffering and frustrations.

---

100. Poems by T.S. Eliot, New York: A. A. Knopf, 1920.

Many frequently lose contact with this authentic internal guide. The stress of our lives and our tense, restless, and unfocused minds make receiving a clear signal from our conscience and intuition almost impossible. We have not trained our minds to become still so that we can more clearly hear this voice of creative insight and wisdom. We explore ways to help young people find more peace of mind and more fully access their intuition in the remaining three chapters.

Elderly Advice

Dick Leider asked the elderly, who felt their life had not mattered or they had not lived the life they had hoped, a follow-up question. What would they have done differently if they could live their lives over again? They had three main responses:

1. **Be more reflective.** We need time each day to allow the mind to become still and get off the "train of life." Without building time for contemplation into our day, the mind is essentially on automatic pilot, responding with old habit patterns. It is difficult to intuit how we are meant to purposefully and creatively express ourselves without quieting the mind for self-reflection. Leider states it this way: "Great is the need in our lives for deliberate reminders of the 'Why' of life." This requires reflective time.

2. **Be more courageous, take more risks, and worry less about others' reactions or approval.** Risk taking doesn't equate to risky behaviors. Extreme behavior is often born of boredom, depression, and the desire to experience a brief adrenaline-filled sense of aliveness. Real risk is honoring the guidance from within, even when it may bring others' judgments or misunderstanding.

3. **Be clear earlier about their purpose.**[101] Leider suggests that each life has a built-in reason for being. And the heart of this reason, according to Leider, is the caring for our fellow human

---

101. The Power of Purpose, revised by Richard Leider.

beings. This is a big part of one's purpose. Young people's sense of worth will increase when, guided by their own intuition, they choose to make their unique positive contribution to the world. Leider, after years of studying purpose and counseling clients, believes as I do, that purpose resides inside all human beings. He says this quite beautifully: "Purpose is the recognition of the presence of the sacred within us."

Sacred work that flows out of our passions and talents, true artistry, has largely been lost—sacrificed on the economic culture's altar of assembly-line production and consumption. This loss has enormous personal and societal costs, as psychologist Bill Plotkin, founder of Animus Valley Institute, articulates:

> The rarity of finding sacred work is at the root of our Western despair and sorrow. When not acknowledged and embraced, our grief is acted out through violence, against ourselves (e.g., addictions, suicide, masochism,), each other (e.g., sadism, racism, sexism, war, child abuse, ethnic cleansing), and the environment (e.g., toxic waste, resource depletion, species extinction, forest destruction, environmental degradation). Unacknowledged grief also manifests as depression, anxiety, and a growing sense of meaninglessness . . . . By consciously honoring our grief—the absence of vision and sacred work—we take our first steps toward soul discovery and personal fulfillment. We begin to return to our true nature.

When we are doing what we love, when we discover and honor our interior calling—our purpose—then our work is in harmony with life. When we do not, we experience internal disharmonies that sabotage our enthusiasm and contentment and we do violence, in one form or another, to ourselves and to the world around us.

Wedding Youth's Talents to Purpose

Purpose, because it is uniquely a person's calling, provides direction and hope for youth's malaise. It is the salve for the pain of the negative emotions that have grown out of the external pursuit of imbalanced urges. One could ask, "How does focusing on creating clarity of purpose help youth with depression, suicide, and self-injurious behaviors, including drug abuse and growing dropout rates? How would purpose help decrease dropout rates that are close to 50 percent in urban areas and also for students often labeled as emotionally and behaviorally disturbed?"[102]

The answer is: when youth's talents and their deep interests have an opportunity to be expressed positively through purposeful activity in the world, most of these problems just naturally atrophy. Research shows that people who are engaged in a passionate purpose of their own making rarely kill themselves. It is also likely they would be less depressed, rarely engage in self-injurious behaviors, develop fewer addictions, and not drop out.

When Saint Theresa was asked by her student if she loved the Lord with all her heart, all her soul, and all her mind as suggested in the Bible, she answered, "Yes I do." The student then asked if she hated the devil, she responded, "I don't have time." Youth utilizing their talents, engaged in their deepest interests tied to serving others, don't have time to get as lost in their personal stories and dramas. They also are no longer lost in the despair and disappointment wrought by pursuing the transient pleasures of the economic culture. That culture rarely calls forth the full expression of their talents and gifts, but purpose does. Knowing what we do well and enjoy doing is important, not only for career decisions, but for empowering our purpose. When we have a clear idea of our gifts and what moves us, we then experience the power of purpose that provides energy and aliveness.

Re-engaging Students through Purpose-Driven Curriculums

I suspect that dropout rates could be significantly reduced if the educational system that relies frequently on extrinsic rewards and punishments built education around intrinsic rewards while exploring questions of purpose. It is easy for parents and teachers who guide and

---

102. Ibid.

instruct children to project preconceived notions of what these children need to become. Our own expectations, often an expression of our unmet childhood needs, obscure seeing the child's unique gifts and passionate interests. Our first task as parents and teachers should be to quiet our own minds enough to witness and let go of our unconscious expectations. Then we are able to clearly see and nurture the interests and talents of each child. If we were to build school curriculums and parental attention around children's natural passions and gifts, education would flower. Einstein said, "Everybody is a genius. But, if you judge a fish by its ability to climb a tree, it will spend its whole life believing that it is stupid."

Utilizing children's interests and talents as their initial curriculum would ignite their passion for study and observation. Schools would still teach reading, writing, and arithmetic because these would become vehicles for sharing what these inspired children are learning, as they passionately pursue their interests. Children love to learn, and they love to share what they have learned. Most schools impose a curriculum that each student engages in at the same time. A bell rings and it's math time. Another rings and students are asked to immediately shift their interest to English, regardless of how engaged students were at those moments.

Intensity of interest is the leading variable that heightens memory and recall. Because everything in the universe is interconnected, youth's interest would fan out to many other areas of study. Determination is the leading factor behind genius, and determination and motivation are driven by passion and interest. So, our curriculums should reflect this. Gandhi said, "Education should maintain the child's capacity to maintain a state of awe." Maintaining this awe requires a more intrinsic curriculum for our youth. Intrinsic motivation is the desire to participate in an activity for its own sake. It is why babies learn to walk. There are four components of intrinsic motivation according to John Tauer, a professor of psychology:[103]

1. **The person must enjoy some degree of competence.** Rarely do people have an activity they love if they are terrible at it.

---

103. Connie Podesta presentation in 2001 where she cited John Taurer's Four Essential Qualities of Intrinsic Motivation.

This is why we should develop children's early curriculum built on students' strengths to help sustain motivation.

2. **The person needs to have some sense of autonomy, a degree of control over what they are doing.** Students' interests and gifts would initially suggest the curriculum.

3. **With intrinsic motivation students feel a sense of relatedness, being part of something greater than themselves.** Teachers and parents can help the students link their interests and talents to helping others.

4. **Students with intrinsic motivation have a sense that what they do is valued, important, and has meaning.** Teachers and parents' enthusiastic support for the gifts and interests children were meant to express will help these students realize their full potential in ways naturally meaningful to them.

Gandhi, again commenting on education, said, "I would develop in the child his hands, his brain, and his soul. The hands have almost atrophied and the soul has been altogether ignored." Gandhi's prescription suggests an intrinsic curriculum inspired by children's natural soul-inspired inclinations.

An educational system focused on external information and built on a business model that relies on extrinsic motivators, largely absent opportunities for self-discovery, will not satisfy purpose or the talents waiting to blossom in our youth. Motivating children through rewards or punishments, like grades or parental incentives, takes us in the wrong direction. The more we reward a child for an external accomplishment or a generous deed, the less likely they are to do it without a reward. Giving feedback and listening to children as they express and develop their natural passions is instructive. A bribe, however, is really just a pleasant threat. Education built on extrinsic rewards and evaluations based on how well one regurgitates external information, results in a disconnection from youth's inherent purpose. Boredom and disappointment will set in, along with the loss of children's natural love of learning. High dropout rates will be one bitter fruit of that disconnection.

A purpose- and interest-driven curriculum is a critical antidote to youth's malaise and would heighten intrinsic motivation. While I believe in this educational model, I recognize issues like poverty continue to restrict access to a quality education for so many of our youth. This fact precludes many incredibly gifted young people from reaching their full potential, and limits building a more cohesive and illumined future for our entire society. This needs to be changed. A child's access to opportunity should not be restricted by financial circumstances beyond their control.

We have to enliven the educational system to guarantee a better future for youth by wedding their talents and interests to service. The goals of the economic culture, consumption, and frivolous fun cannot satisfy deeper longings. I referenced earlier how more than one study has concluded that Denmark has the world's happiest citizenry. Denmark is sometimes called a post-consumer society, because shopping and consuming is not their top priority. The Danish do sometimes complain about high taxes, but this tax structure has created a minimal income disparity between rich and poor. This has led most people in Denmark to choose careers based on interest, not income. This is likely part of their increased happiness because their careers are wedded to their passions. Psychologist Abraham Maslow said it well:

> Even if all the needs are satisfied, we may still often (if not always) expect that a new discontent and restlessness will soon develop unless the individual is doing what he is fitted for. A musician must make music, an artist must paint, a writer must write, if he is to be ultimately at peace with himself. What a man can be, he must be. This need we call self-actualization.

Through reflection, introspection, and dedication, youth can discover and develop their unique self-actualizing purpose, through evolving answers to these three questions:

1. Who am I?

2. How can I serve others through linking my talents and passions to meeting humanity's needs?

3. How are my life's circumstances revealing lessons I need to learn and changes I need to make to create more balance, contentment, and clarity that will advance my purpose?

Exploring purpose with our youth holds great promise. "If education is not designed to give the child a philosophy of life, then all the information piled up in his brain is useless." This quote from an unknown author recognizes that information without a connection to purpose or a philosophy of life is sterile. If parents and teachers nurture children's first expressions of their interests, passion, and unique gifts, they will be honoring who those children were meant to become. They will also be inspiring their children's happiness while decreasing future dysfunctional behaviors. This will keep young people from getting lost in the economic culture's mirage of happiness through pursuing stuff and activities that can never satisfy them.

It's not that youth won't have things or do things, but these will be tied increasingly to meaning and purpose. Youth won't cling to external pursuits as ends in themselves, because their gifts have been nurtured and their purpose will have emerged through the educational process. They will be content with less because their sense of worth and contentment come from within. This will inspire a better future, not a future of deprivation, but a future of satisfying consciously chosen simplicity. Life will have a more measured pace, be more family friendly, and allow for spontaneous, creative, and fulfilling exploration of one's talents and purpose.

When we follow our bliss, guided by intuition, our life unfolds as intended. We experience synchronicities, so-called coincidences, that reveal the universe's support for our unfolding. When talents and purpose merge, the mind is naturally focused and content. This facilitates the mind's immersion into present moment, allowing even the pleasures of the senses to be more fully experienced. There will be no need to "freeze frame" these pleasurable moments, however, for they will be part of a dynamic life of purpose. Each moment will have its own fullness as the separation between work and play narrows. The next chapter explores the powerful tool of breath awareness that helps absorb the mind in every moment, leading to a natural quieting and harmonizing of the imbalances produced by stress.

Purpose-filled youth, who are expressing their reason for being, will inspire others toward a brighter future, for a sense of purpose develops character and leadership. Purpose always accompanies true greatness for it feeds courage and resolve. This greatness will not be born of ego, but is a natural and wonderful expression of a purpose-inspired life, where youth nurture the seeds for their own flowering. Robert K. Greenleaf said, "Purpose and laughter are twins that must not separate. Each is empty without the other." Living the life we came to fulfill will inspire more laughter and a lasting joy.

Exercise:
Creating a Purpose Statement

Twenty-five years ago at a leadership retreat, I was exposed to this purpose exercise. I have used it ever since with students and clients between the ages of fifteen and twenty-five. Most found it beneficial and clarifying. It results in a purpose statement unique to each individual:

1. Write down all of the things you are good at—your talents, your skills, your gifts. You can also include qualities of your personality that you consider strengths.

2. Circle the ones that give you joy, that you like to express, or love to do.

3. Now write a story, at least one page long, describing the world you would create, a world you would love to live in. Assume you have the power to make your vision of this world happen. What would be in that world? What would it look like? What would you and others do or act like? Enjoy yourself and be as creative as you desire.

4. Now create your purpose statement. Take the talents, skills, and strengths that give you joy, and express in one or two sentences how you would use these gifts to help nudge the world closer to your vision of the wonderful world you described in question three.

The above exercise can be done individually or as part of a group activity and discussion. It can be linked to career choices. Here are some additional questions that can initiate an exploration or deeper discussion of purpose:

1. Why did you get up this morning? This may initially initiate superficial comments like: "My mom made me," or "I would get kicked out of the house if I didn't" or "To avoid bed sores"—who knows? Eventually it shifts to things like: "To get

a high school diploma." You then can follow up with additional questions like: "Why do you want a diploma?" "To make more money." "What is the dream you have that you think money will provide?" Ultimately everyone is seeking happiness or joy, even though they may be looking in all the wrong places. These questions, and the discussion it invites, can enliven student interest around the topic of purposeful living and its benefits.

2. Do you think life has a purpose? What do you think it is? Does your life have meaning—what brings meaning to you?

3. Do you have anything that you would consider your duty? To whom do you have duties or responsibilities? Where does your sense of duty come from?

4. State three jobs you would want to do for a career, assuming you had the ability? This question can help students identify their interests and possibly their talents.

5. How old do you think you will live to be? Imagine you're that age. As you look back on your life, what would you like to be able to say is your legacy? How would you like to be remembered? Is there anything you're doing now that you wouldn't be proud of, or would consider changing, so that at the end of your life you would have fewer regrets?

Chapter 18

The Mind/Body/Breath Connection

*"Breath is the bridge between the body and mind. . . .
Who is giving you this breath? The Lord of life gives it to all.
Breath is the direct link with the Lord."*

—SWAMI RAMA

*"In all mystic philosophies, the breath holds the secret
to the highest bliss."*

—ALEXANDER LOWEN

Breath connects the body and mind. The physical and mental self function together. The breath connects the two as a vehicle for prana, chi, or the Korean equivalent *ki*, the energetic life force that permeates the universe. Breath is the conduit of this essential energy, somewhat like wires are the vehicle that carry the energy of electricity to light a home.

The fact that our breath is the connection between body and mind has profound implications. When we are stressed, many of us have found successful interventions that lower our stress levels at least to some degree. Exercising, listening to music, taking a nap, or walking in nature all work in varying degrees to decrease stress. Breath awareness, however, is the stress intervention par excellence. These other interventions may be helpful, but we can't always access them. We usually cannot bring most of them, for example, to our work place. Breath, on the other hand, is with us every instant unless we are dead, and then breath doesn't matter. In Genesis, God breathed into man, and he came alive. Breath is life. So, Giovanni Papini's declaration that "Breathing is the greatest pleasure in life" is literally true.

Breathing and Stress

The Greek word for breath is pneuma, meaning spirit or soul. Breath has unique stress-reduction potential because it quiets, harmonizes, and energizes both mind and body, and can be accessed anytime and anywhere. The restlessness of our minds can be tamed and focused through breath awareness. Even at a silence retreat, when we think we have withdrawn from the noise of the world, the noise of the mind hasn't gone anywhere. The constant chatter of the mind, which is our greatest source of stress, travels with us unabated.

We become acutely aware of this noise of the mind when we try to enter the silence of sleep and our mind has another idea. The mind can't quit obsessing about this or that. We sometimes try to force the mind into complying: "I've got to get some rest, I have to be up early!" We cannot strong arm the mind into becoming silent. We cannot force the mind to relax; we have to "let go" in order to fall asleep. If we wound up the mind all day, or are concerned and anxious about tomorrow, the mind won't easily settle down. Coercing the mind into sleep is like saying to someone, "I'll race you to sleep. On your mark, get set . . . go!" When we do wake up the banter of the mind is off and running again: "I think I will have a quick bowl of Cheerios . . . funny name, Cheerios . . . I wander if they got that from the British . . . boy, the British have bad teeth . . . I better brush when I finish this . . . boy, look at my teeth, they're dull and look at this face in the mirror, what the hell happened . . . a zit at my age? . . . And when did I get this old . . . I wonder if anyone will come to my funeral . . . I am kind of hoping for a big turnout . . . I lived a good life but I wish I had . . . "

So how do we let go of this exhausting continuous chatter of the mind where one association feeds on another? Breath awareness is a great ally. If we train the mind to flow with the stream of each inhalation and exhalation in our nostrils, we can capture our restless mind and quiet its incessant thinking. Polygraphs and biofeedback machines reveal that when a thought changes, it registers as a ripple in the diaphragm muscle, the muscle responsible for creating our inhalations and exhalations. This reveals the intimate connection between breath and mind. The parade of thoughts goes on all day in the mind and many are responsible for creating our stress and agitation. "We usually think of peace between nations as a gap between two wars. We can create our own personal peace by absorbing our minds fully into the flow of breath, extending the quiet or peace between two thoughts." [104] We can literally create a peaceful mind through breath awareness. And a peaceful mind is our greatest contribution to the world.

Breath and the Mind

A simple two-minute breathing exercise can demonstrate the breath's power to quiet the chatter of our minds. The following is an experiment I often do with students and clients not just for sleep problems, but to lower stress. You can try it. Read the following suggestions and then do them before you continue reading:

1. Watch your mind for a minute or two. Do nothing with your breath. Let your mind think about anything it wants, just as it normally does.

2. Now, sit relaxed and still, with your head, neck, and trunk of your body in a straight line so that your breathing process is not restricted. Feel the rise and fall of your breath in the stomach region. As you inhale, the stomach rises and expands, as you exhale it contracts. As you inhale, hear the sound *one* in your mind, not on your lips; and as you exhale hear the sound *two*. Let the breath flow effortlessly with no

---

104. A Personal Philosophy of Life by Swami Rama, Himalayan Institute Hospital Trust, 2002, 59.

jerks or pauses. Let your mind rest in the sound of *one* as you inhale and *two* as you exhale, and let it flow with the breath. Let the mind ride the wave of breath in the stomach region. Observe the gentle rise and fall of each inhalation and exhalation with eyes closed for the next two minutes or so.

Did your thoughts slow down? With practice, doing short breath awareness interventions a few times throughout the day can keep stress from building up and getting out of hand. The breath is sometimes compared to reigns that control a wild horse. Breath can quiet our high-strung mind and keep it from veering into undisciplined and unproductive terrain. Breath can direct, focus, and energize a lethargic mind and keep it from mindlessly grazing in the pastures of the senses.

Breath and the Body

Breath awareness not only quiets the mind, it also simultaneously quiets, heals, and strengthens the body. Heart and pulse rates drop. Blood flow to the heart improves. The immune system is strengthened. There is often relief of chronic pain. Cholesterol levels can drop and there is a reduced need for insulin due to improved regulation of glucose. Breath even provides some relief for many asthmatics.[105] These are just a few of the positive impacts for the body, brought about by relaxation through breath awareness.

Exercise, walking in nature, and a short nap can also positively impact stress and aid the body and mind, and all can be valuable. In fact, recent medical research is documenting aerobic activity's ability to positively impact depression if it's done vigorously several times a week. I always recommend a vigorous exercise regimen for depressed clients. Recent research shows in many cases it outperforms antidepressants because there is no habituation or side effects with exercise. There is still a place for antidepressants to jump start a person whose brain chemistry has gone dramatically out of balance, but it doesn't have to be our first or only intervention. The point is that we are not excluding

---

105. "Doctors Get Excited over Relaxation" by Daniel Goleman, New York Times, May 13, 1986.

other stress reduction options, but breath awareness is available to help keep body and mind in balance at every waking moment. It has been underutilized for quieting the stress of mind and body that leads to illness, anxiety disorders, depression, and even suicide. The quotes touting the power of breath at the beginning of this chapter are no exaggeration.

Breath and Emotions

There is another phenomenal attribute of breathing that is still underappreciated in Western schools of psychology. We have examined how painful negative emotions flow out of imbalances in our four primitive urges. When those urges are well regulated, we have balance, more energy, and we naturally experience positive emotions like peace, joy, and contentment. Breath is the barometer of our emotions. Through proper breathing, we can harmonize our negative emotions. Quieting painful emotions is essential if we are to access our positive emotions. When we regulate the primitive urges and practice breath awareness, we create a deep, integrated harmony.

Reflect on the connection between emotions and breath. What happens to our breath when we get angry? It becomes uneven and jagged. If someone snuck up in back of you right now as you're reading and screamed at the top of their lungs, what would happen to your breath? Fear stops the breath. We call it the startle response. Few people recognize, however, that every fear thought causes a small pause or jerk in the breath. Every stressful thought—"Oh my God, I'm going to be late to the airport!" creates a pause or jerk in the breath. Stress is fear and fear thoughts interrupt smooth breathing.

The pauses in breath induced by fear can cause the diaphragm muscle to freeze or restrict its movement which can create chronic stress. It is said that we have over 60,000 thoughts a day, and I don't know who counted but let's assume their estimate is close. How many of our thoughts are stressful thoughts, little and big worries, about this or that? The more stressful or fearful thoughts are, the more pauses and jerks in our breath. This increases our emotional imbalance.

There is evidence demonstrating that pauses in our breathing actually cause the death of our brain cells.[106] Some of this evidence comes from deep sea divers who hold their breath for long periods of time. We know a permanent pause in breathing leads to death; brain cells die rapidly and brain function ceases. It makes sense then that brain cells might die due to interruptions in breathing that restrict oxygen flow. We know sleep apnea, where the breath stops many times for relatively long periods while sleeping, is correlated with increased likelihood of heart attacks and strokes. So, decreasing the jerks and pauses in our breath is important, and smoothing out our breath during the day can even carry over into healthier breathing patterns while we are sleeping.

Many people, due to chronic stress, become chest breathers, losing their natural diaphragmatic breath. Chest or "thoracic" breathing causes the heart to work 65 percent harder, significantly increasing the likelihood of heart and other health problems. If we have enough stress-producing thoughts, which is more likely in a culture of fear, we can observe significant pauses and jerks in our breath. Over time this can lead to two chronic unhealthy breathing patterns. One problem, already mentioned, is that we become chest breathers and lose the natural diaphragmatic breathing we were born with as a baby. Diaphragmatic breathing is critical for health, and all relaxation techniques are built on its foundation. Deep exhalation draws the abdomen in, expelling carbon dioxide. Deep inhalation expands the lungs, creating more space for oxygen. Shallow or poor diaphragmatic breathing minimizes the lung movements leading to anxiety, lethargy, and other health issues.

The second unhealthy breathing pattern is called paradoxical breathing. Prolonged stress can actually cause a reversal in the natural breathing process. When we inhale, the stomach region should rise; but in paradoxical breathing, it falls. With the exhalation in paradoxical breathing, the stomach rises, when naturally it should fall. Both of these breathing patterns can keep us in a "fight or flight" mode. These two dysfunctional breathing patterns leave us perpetually stressed and emotionally imbalanced, regardless of what's occurring in the world

---

106. A Personal Philosophy of Life by Swami Rama, Himalayan Institute Hospital Trust, 2002, 36.

around us. So, smoothing out the pauses in our breathing and maintaining or reestablishing diaphragmatic breathing has many benefits for our health and our emotional balance.

Many at-risk students I worked with had very damaging and traumatic childhoods that threatened their security and safety needs. Their breathing patterns reflected their traumatic backgrounds. They were chest breathers who had almost no movement in their stomach and abdomen area. Many of them breathed between twenty and thirty-four breaths a minute, which is close to hyperventilating. Some breathed paradoxically and were constantly in "fight or flight" mode, hypervigilant to potential sources of agitation. Because breath is the barometer of emotions, their faulty breathing habits left them with very little emotional control. Their chest or paradoxical breathing patterns were analogous to creating emotional dry kindling, just waiting for a spark to set things off. It took very little provocation to set these students "ablaze." Our language reflects this emotional volatility in the phrase: "He is so thin skinned!" It is not the thickness of their skin, but rather the disturbed breathing patterns from their dysfunctional childhood that made their emotional reactivity almost inevitable.

Proper breathing creates a healthy balance in our autonomic nervous system (ANS). The ANS has two aspects, the sympathetic and parasympathetic systems. The sympathetic system revs up the autonomic nervous system, and the parasympathetic system quiets it down. Either system can become imbalanced. Anxiety-producing thoughts (and dietary choices like caffeine) rev up the sympathetic system. This is what we normally think of as stress. However, there is also something called the "possum" response. Here the parasympathetic system is over engaged due to exhaustion from negative and hopeless thoughts (and dietary choices like high-fat foods), and we physically, emotionally, and mentally shut down. If we continue our habit of negativity and/or poor diet choices, we will eventually become depressed.

These imbalances in the sympathetic and parasympathetic nervous systems are both expressions of stress. They are initiated by imbalances in the four primitive urges, particularly the stressful thoughts triggered by something our ego has judged as a potential threat to its worth. Breath awareness can play a major role in quieting these stress-producing thoughts and keeping our autonomic nervous system in balance.

Depressed people frequently have a characteristic breathing pattern. They breathe with a short inhalation, followed by a longer exhalation and a fairly long pause before inhaling again. This breathing pattern reflects the parasympathetic dominance. My point about the breathing rhythms of fear, anger, and depression is that each emotion has its own "fingerprint" in terms of breath pattern. The great news is we can use breathing to reverse the old stress-producing pattern, and create a new balanced pattern of breathing. In the process, we quiet our racing minds and decrease our negative and painful emotions. At the end of this chapter is a breathing exercise that can help in creating this healthy balance. It slowed breathing rates after just one fifteen-minute practice session, an average of seven breaths per minute in my stress management groups. Even the students were surprised, because this practice affected more than their breathing, it affected their mood. Almost all commented that they felt better.

The Ideal Breath

What are the characteristics of a breathing pattern that quiets negative emotions, allowing a greater expression of our positive emotions? The ideal breath is diaphragmatic, nasal as opposed to mouth breathing, even in volume, with no jerks or pauses. The inhalation and exhalation should be even in length and quiet, gradually becoming longer and deeper over time. This kind of breathing will bring a balance to the mind and body as well as harmonize negative emotions. It is sometimes helpful to imagine one's ideal breath as a circle, a sign wave, or an infinity sign. A long free-flowing pauseless breath brings a feeling of peace and a quiet joy. It often takes time and practice to reestablish the diaphragmatic breathing rhythm that all of us were born with.

Breath and Personality

"Please, don't leave, bus," I said to myself racing back into the school. It was Friday and I had almost forgotten my baseball glove in my desk. It was late May and fourth grade was almost over. The weather was nice and there was no way I was going to be without my glove for the weekend. I went racing down the hallway, and quickly looked back to make sure the bus was still there. I turned and ran full speed into a solid door. I had somehow managed to hit the narrow inch-and-a-half portion on the edge of the door with my already oversized nose. I heard my nose crunch, and blood exploded everywhere.

I was ushered to the nurse's office, still bleeding heavily. They held the bus while they tried stopping the bleeding. I overheard the nurse whisper to the teacher, "I think the nose is broken." I was given my own bus seat, so I could lie flat on my back. I held a towel to my nose with my right hand to limit the bleeding while wearing my baseball glove securely on my left hand.

I had shattered my nose, but money was limited and, despite a new bend in my nose, I was never sent to a doctor. My personality began to change that day because my breathing changed.

I became mostly a mouth breather and I suddenly felt like I needed to eat very fast in order to catch my next breath. Years later, I learned I had a severely deviated septum, with almost 90 percent of my left nostril blocked, allowing for little passage of air. The right nostril flowed freely. The flow of breath in a particular nostril relates to brain hemispheric function; right nostril flow increases left hemispheric dominance, and left nostril flow increases right hemispheric activity. The over-activation of my left hemisphere, due to constant right nostril dominance, caused me to struggle to shut off my analytical thinking. My mind raced with ideas, I became more hyper and developed insomnia. Normally, in healthy people, one's nostril dominance alternates every ninety to 120 minutes. This natural alternation brings balance to mind and body, and that balance ended for me the day I broke my nose.

There is a very beneficial and harmonizing breathing practice called "alternate nostril breathing," which gives one control over this alternating system. It is helpful to anyone who uses it systematically and holds particular promise for issues plaguing youth. Alternate nostril breathing has proven useful in calming emotional disturbance, in anger

management, in drug dependency, and in manic depression.[107] If practiced regularly, it creates a harmonic balance for body, emotions,
and mind.

I knew none of this when I broke my nose, but that event changed
my breathing patterns dramatically, and had many painful consequences. In addition to my increased restlessness, I started having
occasional panic attacks not long after my nose said hello to the door. I
was out of balance; my brothers thought I was weird, or weirder. I would
have been diagnosed with ADHD if I had been assessed. I remember
part of a poem that I wrote in school only weeks after my nose injury:
"I'm as skinny as a worm and I sure like to squirm. I sit in my desk all
day and goof around and play!" This poem reflected the changes my
"nose concussion" brought about in my behavior and personality, but
obviously did nothing to advance my poetic talents. I never made the
connection at the time between my broken nose and the altered
breathing pattern that likely triggered many of these changes.

Looking back, I could choose to label breaking my nose as a bad
thing. However, like the farmer with the runaway horse, "maybe" might
be the more appropriate response. My hyperactive mind, which I
mistakenly took as a sign of creativity and genius, ultimately led me to
yoga. Yoga, along with my early Christian roots, has guided and transformed my life. I started taking yoga classes around age twenty-four. I
felt like a really slow learner. It took me five months to stop being a
mouth breather and shift my chest breathing, fight or flight breathing,
back down to my diaphragm and stomach region. One reason it took so
long was because I was an athlete. I kept trying to relax, but it was the
"On your mark, get set . . . go!" approach to relaxation. I just didn't
know how to let go.

I'm really not sure why I persisted in yoga because I progressed so
slowly. The yoga I had chosen to study and practice wasn't just postures.
The postures were but a small part of an ancient tradition with a vast
spiritual philosophy and a deep psychological system to help understand
and relieve human suffering. That was a significant part of why I
persisted but the main reason I kept practicing was, though my progress

---

107. Chariots of Sadhana—Yoga of the Inner Teacher by Martin and Marion Jerry,
    Unlimited Publisher LLC, 2007, 81, 116.

was slow, there was progress. Yoga is a path of direct experience, and I experientially knew breathing was beginning to decrease my anxiety and quiet my racing mind. Being persistent changed my life.

Despite making progress with breathing techniques, I decided around age twenty-nine to have surgery to correct my deviated septum. I had not had panic attacks for years, but after surgery, when they put plugs in both nostrils to help the cartilage set, panic returned. My nasal breathing was blocked and I paced for two days, unable to sleep. Mouth breathing did nothing to quiet my mind, body, or my anxiety. When the plugs were removed, I experienced a penetrating transformation. Nasal dominance now alternated, and my breath flowed longer and more evenly in both nostrils. I became a much calmer and, I felt like, a more patient person. I was witnessing life with more stillness, acceptance, and joy for extended periods of time. This lasted for three weeks.

My doctor knew I played tennis and warned me to wait a month before playing again, so the cartilage would be solid and healed. I didn't heed his advice. After not quite three weeks, I was at the tennis net when my doubles partner hit what must have been the worst serve of his life. I heard it bounce in back of me. I turned to look, and the tennis ball hit me smack in the nose. It reduced the benefits of the surgery well over 50 percent. I was very disappointed and mad at myself for violating the doctor's orders. Looking back, however, I am again unable to conclude that this was a bad event. I was forced to pay even more attention to my breathing. This provided many subtle benefits including training my mind through breath awareness to stay more in the present moment and not as frequently anticipate the future or get as lost in the past.

Breath and Mindfulness

Perhaps the main benefit of breath awareness is that it increases mindfulness—our ability to stay calmly present and absorbed in the current moment. Mindfulness is often referred to as meditation in action. Our restless minds tend to get preoccupied with future fantasies or they drift into regrets of the past. This often brings with it anxiety, sadness, anger, or guilt. George Bernard Shaw said, "The philosopher is nature's pilot. And, there you have our difference: to be in hell is to drift; to be in heaven is to steer." We can significantly diminish the mind's tendency toward forward and backward drifting, which can lead to a hell of our own making. We can consciously pilot our mind into the beauty and fullness of Now through the continual awareness of our omnipresent breath.

When we increase our mindfulness through breath awareness, we enrich our lives in so many ways. We actually start living. Being on remote control, doing things with no zest or presence, is a kind of death. Many of my students exhibited this "dead men walking" almost zombie-like state. Breath awareness helps us come alive, and we experience everything more profoundly. Buddha, when asked if he was a god, simply said, "I am awake." The name Buddha means to awaken. Christ said, "Old things have passed away; behold, all things have become new" (2 Corinthians 5:17). Witnessing our breath throughout the day brings us into now; we awaken from our dross, and we see the world afresh.

Breath awareness brings a peace. This peace isn't the absence of problems, or the suspension of a clamoring world, or escape from relational difficulties. Peace is staying calm in the midst of these potential stressors. So, in addition to the physical, emotional, and mental health benefits of conscious breathing, breath awareness can be spiritually transforming through a growing mindfulness and openness.

There are many subtle breathing practices that bring balance to body, mind, and emotions. In yoga these practices are called pranayamas; prana being energy, and yama meaning the control and expansion of this energy. If practiced regularly, these practices sharpen our intuition; the discriminative wisdom that Einstein understood can help enlighten our decision making and enhance our creativity.

Benefits of Two to One Breathing

One breathing practice in particular helped many clients and students quiet their minds, harmonize emotions, improve sleep, and improve their diaphragmatic breathing. It is called two to one breathing (2:1). This practice involves exhaling for twice as long as you inhale.

272

Yogis claim that doing this every day, three times a day for fifteen minutes for one month will bring transformative benefits for body, emotions, and mind. So I tried it, and it did!

Two to one breathing is an excellent practice for those living in a polluted environment because the longer exhalation will reduce the effects of pollution. It is also well suited for our high-demand fast-paced culture that over-stimulates our sympathetic nervous system. People who do 2:1 breathing engage the parasympathetic nervous system that helps relieve sympathetic stress. Two to one breathing, therefore, will also aid falling asleep. It is also particularly helpful when we feel acute stress.

Experimenting with 2:1 Breathing

During my month-long experiment with 2:1 breathing three times a day, I missed a few times. Even so, at the end of the experiment, I never felt so harmonious and integrated. I decided to offer it as an extra credit option for my students after observing significant benefits for clients struggling with anxiety. Students were asked to journal each day, and write an overall summary at the end of their experiment. They were encouraged to do 2:1 breathing at least three times a day, but the minimal requirement was two times a day. I promised them something would improve during the month—their sleep, their eating habits, their emotional control, or their relationships. If not, I would buy them a dinner at a restaurant of their choice. This demonstrated a lot of faith in the breathing technique, as well as trust in the students' honesty, as adolescents are known for their avarice appetites.

I kept journals of students who gave me permission to use them if I ever wrote a book. I changed their names anyway, along with some other minor details, to further guarantee their privacy. It usually took students about a week to establish their 2:1 breathing with minimal effort. Here are two students' journals a week or more into their experiment. They are both very bright and thoughtful seventeen-year-olds, as you will see. We start with Scott:

Day 7: Today was a trying day at school, things didn't go the greatest, but of course, it was a Monday. I did my breathing after school to

273

relax. The breathing helped and overall, I have to say, I have noticed a little change in myself. I've been more peaceful, more alive than before I started this 2:1 practice. I am also falling asleep faster than usual.

Day 8: Today I was as alive as I've ever been. It's hard to explain but it's like getting a second wind after I've done the 2:1 breathing. I also have noticed I don't snap at people when they say things that would normally bug me. I was very skeptical that breathing could affect sleep, emotions, and relationships when you first explained 2:1 breathing and the potential benefits. But, I thought that either way I would get extra credit **and** you might have to buy me a steak dinner!

Day 12: Today I was stressed because of a big test in Trig. I calmed myself down with 2:1 breathing before the test. It was harder to concentrate with everyone talking, but I did it. My test seemed to go pretty smoothly. Where I work, everyone wants to punch the boss, and today the boss was being more of a jerk than normal. But I stayed calm and ignored him. I'm convinced, because of this breathing experiment, that I'm calmer than normal, and today proved it. Later at work I did 2:1 breathing on my break, and again it calmed my nerves, allowing me to deal with the stupid people we get in our store. I also noticed at the end of the day I didn't feel tired at all! I was really surprised. Usually I feel like I'm fighting sleep, completely exhausted when driving home.

Day 17: It was Sunday so I did my 2:1 breathing four times. I felt great all day. My girlfriend and I are getting along better. And, over the last two weeks, my sister and I are arguing much less. Today she was being extra irritating, but I just walked away rather than yell back. She later came down to my room and asked if anything was wrong. I said, "No nothing's wrong," in a somewhat joyous voice because I was proud I didn't react to her. She actually said in a nice way, something about me being different. Other people have been saying this to me, too; but the last one I expected it from was my sister!

Day 24: Today I felt alive because I got a great night's sleep. And, because it was Sunday, I did my breathing before getting out of bed, and I felt even more alive. I notice that I am catching myself breathing 2:1 when I am not even trying. Is this starting to change me? I think so. I am not so moody anymore and it's helping my relationships a lot. I guess you're not going to have to worry about the steak dinner!

Day 28: I was in a great mood today because I found out I'm getting a "B" in Trig. Everything went great. And I felt great.

My summary of the 2:1 experiment: I will start by saying something that may sound odd. Yesterday, I saw a flower for the first time. What I mean is that I noticed this flower in the garden, and for some reason I walked over and really looked at it. It was beautiful; the colors were brilliant. I also felt it and it felt a little sticky and like it had a very thin rubbery covering. It also had a wonderful smell. Not since I was a little kid have I done anything like this. This is part of the change of the breathing experiment. My mind's not only more relaxed and peaceful; it seems I'm enjoying and paying more attention to things going on around me. Usually my mind is preoccupied, thinking all the time. I also am definitely more tolerant with people at work, and with my sister at home. Strange as it might seem to someone else, this 2:1 breathing seems to be helping my relationships. I am also a little more outgoing with people. I don't know what that's about but, I'm enjoying it. My sleep is better and I have more energy. I had only one or two headaches during these thirty days, and I usually get a lot of headaches. My grades have improved and I think it's a combination of my improved sleep and better concentration. I've taught my girlfriend this, and she's starting to enjoy it. I would like to thank you for teaching me this; it's made a big difference. It's much better than a steak!

Not everyone's journal is as articulate and open as this, but many of the things Scott shared showed up in other students' journals. It was nice having permission to share these journals because they became a recruiting tool for my next year's students. It helped entice new students into giving this powerful "pranayama" or 2:1 breathing technique a try.

"Judy's" journal begins on the tenth day after her 2:1 breathing was flowing easily. I chose it because Judy had some unique challenges during her one-month experiment.

Day 10: "I am trying to do this three times a day, but with my busy schedule it's usually only two except for weekends. I am ten days into this, and I am finding it so interesting and so helpful. I can be very emotional at times, but this is having an impact on that. Sometimes when I'm really upset or down, I go into my bedroom, lie on my back, and start my 2 to 1 breathing. It has become more effortless, and within minutes my breath is flowing. When that happens, my emotions begin to change; it's hard to explain. They are still there, but they like recede. I'm not lost in them so much— I'm just breathing and somehow they feel like they're getting less dense. It's hard to explain but, when I get up I feel so much better.

Day 13: I shared with you that I had been sexually abused as a child. Sometimes clouds of depression wash over me, and I feel overwhelmed and hopeless, wondering if my pain will ever go away. Well, this evening was one of those times. So I went to my room, and locked my door. I didn't cry; I just felt hopeless and weary. I decided to do my second round of 2 to 1 breathing just to meet the requirement. And, I was amazed after less than ten minutes, the cloud thinned and I felt light and peaceful. How is this possible, Mr. Nelson? Nothing had changed except I felt so much better. I don't understand how breathing can do this?

Day 17: I finally started therapy six months ago, and I had a session with my therapist this afternoon. I decided toward the end of the session to tell her about the 2 to 1 breathing and how it has been helping me. I don't think she got it. She listened, but it didn't feel like she was that interested. It might be because it's hard for me to even understand how or why this helps, and I can't expect her to, either. She did say I seemed to have opened up more during our session today. I think she's right, I think I'm feeling less ashamed.

Day 22: I have noticed some other things that I haven't commented on since doing the breathing experiment. I am definitely sleeping better—sometimes when I do my third time, I do it as I am falling asleep. I am falling asleep faster and I have more energy the next morning. Also, I get along great with my mom, but sometimes my dad and I argue. I usually shut up and say nothing because I am afraid of him. I still do that the majority of the time, but now I just let what he says go in one ear and out the other. To use your word, I'm more neutral. It doesn't get under my skin. And once in a while, I will calmly say something like, I don't agree—I can tell he doesn't like it but he hasn't gone ballistic. I feel better when I don't yell, but can still have an opinion.

Day 27: Had a great day. My energy has been better since I started 2 to 1 breathing. Maybe it's my better sleep, but I also think I am less stressed and that helps my energy. I remember when you said "worry thoughts deplete energy," and I think you're right—because my thoughts have been more positive.

Overall Summary: I am going to continue my 2 to 1 breathing, it's become easy and it's something I look forward to doing, unless I am completely exhausted. I was in a pretty hard place when I started this practice, but I seem to have turned a corner. I was pretty depressed and I've always been emotional and at times very irritable. But, I've made real progress on that. My sleep is much better. I feel like I am making progress in therapy. And, I am enjoying my family more and starting to enjoy being with my friends again. There is probably a lot of reasons for that, but no one could convince me that 2 to 1 breathing wasn't a big part of these changes. I felt better every time I did it, and it seemed to not only lighten my mood, but it also gave me a more hopeful perspective on things. I learned a lot—I'm so glad I did this.

After I read Judy's journal, I wrote a note to respond to the questions asked in her journal. I explained how breathing can bring forward a witnessing presence, untouched by the hurts of the personality. This helps us disengage from feeding hurts that solidify us as victims. We may have been victimized, but we don't have to live as victims. Breath awareness brings forward a more neutral yet naturally compassionate presence that can help with the healing process.

These two journals, and dozens of others, give testimony to the power of breath awareness and pranayama practices. In fifteen years, I only had two students who said they didn't benefit much. I offered them their free meals, but they refused. I got the sense, perhaps unfairly, that they didn't accept my offer because they hadn't been consistent with their 2:1 practice. Regardless, I hope you will consider the breathing exercise suggested at the end of this chapter. Then you will be able to directly experience some of the benefits and perhaps teach others. I will not promise you a meal at your favorite restaurant, as I suspect you may have expensive tastes! Hopefully, like with Scott and Judy, the benefits will be their own rewards.

Because breath is the link between mind and body, and the barometer of our emotions, it can unify and harmonize all aspects of our personality. This allows the light of the soul to shine without the refracted occlusions of an imbalanced personality. Then the mind becomes a friend to help us realize our true nature, and understand why we are here and where we are going.

Experiment
Breathing

This practice is helpful for chest, rapid, and/or paradoxical breathers. It can help people suffering from ADHD, insomnia, or if you are extremely stressed. It works with children and elderly. I have experimented and some young people are unable to stay engaged for fifteen minutes while lying in crocodile doing just 2:1 breathing. By sequencing several different breathing practices during the fifteen minutes, it maintained interest and increased the number of students who were able to stay engaged. Therefore they were able to stay longer in the crocodile pose, which deepened their diaphragmatic breathing. Before leading someone through the following sequence, it is interesting to see how many times they breathe in one minute. This establishes a baseline. Inhalation and exhalation count as one breath.

1. Just observe and accept the movement of your breath for two minutes lying in crocodile.

2. Now begin to notice the average length of your inhalation and exhalation. Whatever it is, is fine. Match the inhalation and exhalations lengths without struggle—whether that's two seconds or four seconds. Do 1:1 breathing while mentally counting, for two to three minutes.

3. Gradually, while maintaining the count, allow the exhalation to gradually lengthen and deepen. Without struggling, allow the exhalation to become twice as long as the inhalation, or as close to that as you can do naturally. This is 2:1 breathing—exhalation twice as long as inhalation. Do this for three minutes.

4. Now let go of the count and let your mind relax while still allowing the exhalation to be approximately twice as long as the inhalation. Just observe this 2:1 breath, without the count, for two more minutes.

5. Finally, focus on the transition point where the inhalation merges into the exhalation, and the exhalation merges into inhalation. Be aware where the pause takes place and just allow that gap to gently close a bit. Do this for two to three minutes. Come to a sitting position.

After they complete the entire sequence, again determine how many times they breathe in the next minute. Have them share their numbers. Some people may not improve because they are trying too hard, as this is a new practice. The majority usually show progress, some very significantly. Ask them if they feel any different. Sometimes they say they are more tired because many carry tremendous fatigue. Others report feeling more refreshed or mellow. It is helpful to do this every day two to three times for a week. The more it is practiced, the more the dysfunctional breathing patterns change. With this change comes more emotional control, harmony, and an increased peace of mind.

Chapter 19

Are You Your Shoe?
A Case of Mistaken Identity

"He has placed eternity in their hearts."

—Ecclesiastes 3:11

"The self is never born, nor does it die,
nor after once having been, does it go into non-being.
The self is unborn, eternal and changeless. It is never
destroyed even when the body is destroyed."

—Bhagavad Gita

On the first day of my psychology class there is a question hidden behind a map. Students will soon be asked to write a page or two on this question. Once the question is revealed, there will be a few muffled groans, almost exclusively from males who will struggle to compose a paragraph or two, let alone a page. The map goes up, revealing the question: Who are you?

Even students who wrote longer essays filled them with information like: "I am five-feet-four, outgoing, love pizza, Pepsi, and music. . . ." Regardless of what they wrote, I learned a lot about how they viewed themselves, even if it was just a few sentences. With rare exceptions, they understandably described themselves through their interests, physical characteristics, and occasionally their personality traits. I informed them that we would be exploring this question in more depth throughout the semester, and we would see if their answer evolved. On occasion, one or two students, always male, made a beeline to their dean's office to register for a different elective.

Who am I? This is the quintessential question; the **real** "million-dollar question" we need to answer to fulfill life's purpose. Life also has a very important secondary purpose that helps to deeply enrich our lives, as we continue to engage the essential question of who we are at our core. Some students before graduation would tell me they were still trying to figure out their purpose, implying that they were looking for just the right job or vocation. Perhaps a better way to conceptualize purpose, beyond one's career, is to see our purpose as skillfully addressing all that comes our way each day. We briefly addressed one aspect of this secondary purpose when we discussed paying attention to life's lessons in Chapter 17. Our secondary purpose then is to cultivate mindfulness in all that we do, letting our intuition guide skillful actions. We need to give life our full attention because what life is presenting to us is often not a coincidence and it is there for our learning. And, it is only in our daily relationships and activities that mindfulness and intuition can express themselves.

It is beneficial, therefore, to infuse all of our duties, actions, and relationships with our love and full attention. Yoga itself is sometimes defined as skillfulness in action, so approaching our lives with love and attention would satisfy this definition. In yoga terms, this is how we burn karma or create positive karma. In Christian terminology, we would be doing God's work, serving God's will, or being God's instruments—serving as the hands and feet of God, if you will. There is a poem that hangs in my home written by Mother Teresa about giving our very best in the midst of the demands and activities of life:

People are often unreasonable and self-centered. Forgive them anyway.

If you are kind people may accuse you of ulterior motives. Be kind anyway.

If you are honest, people may cheat you. Be honest anyway.

If you find happiness, people may be jealous. Be happy anyway.

The good you do today may be forgotten tomorrow. Do good anyway.

Give the world the best you have, and it may never be enough. Give your best anyway.

For you see in the end, it is between you and God.

It never was between you and them anyway.

Regardless of a person's religious beliefs, approaching life with this attitude creates relationships with less friction and less stress, thereby increasing happiness. So, lovingly embracing life's duties and mindfully and skillfully executing one's actions is our secondary purpose that serves others and increases our enjoyment of life. It also supports our search for discovering the answer to life's primary question: "Who am I?" Beyond describing favorite activities and personality characteristics as students did the first day of class, how can we help youth more deeply engage this question?

Us Beyond the Mind—an Experiment

"Half of you, grab the readings off the table and go out to the resource center and complete the questions after you finish reading. You will be in the discussion group tomorrow. The other half stays here. I will need your help moving the desks into a circle for our discussion. Now that they've left, I have a few questions for the rest of you," I said to the remaining fifteen students. I always liked reducing the class size for discussions.

"This first question will sound weird, but there's a purpose behind my madness. Are you your shoes?" I asked because they were all wearing shoes.

In all the years I asked this question, every student had said no; that was true again today except for two girls who were friends almost simultaneously said, "Yes, I am my shoes."

I thought I might have to hospitalize them with some form of hysteria or delusion. But, instead I asked somewhat incredulously: "What do you mean you are your shoes? That makes no sense to me."

They both made the case they had taken a lot of time, and given a lot of thought, before choosing their particular shoes. The shoes were a reflection of their personality.

I reconsidered the hospitalization, after they eventually agreed that they weren't literally their shoes. Their initial response did, however, reveal a sense of self that had been warped by the economic culture.

"So we all agree we're not our shoes. Are you your hand?"

This time almost everyone said yes, and a few said, "Maybe—I'm not sure." I didn't pursue the maybes for the time being.

"What if you were cutting vegetables tonight and you lopped off your finger. Your parents rushed you to the hospital to reattach it, but, the graft would not take. You would be sad no doubt. If there was no hope to reattach your finger, and they offered you five hundred dollars to donate the finger to a research project studying cell regeneration, would you take it? You have no real use for the finger, so would you take the five hundred dollars?" I inquired.

They all said they would.

"Assume a year has passed. Your finger's been frozen and they begin to thaw and probe it. Do you think you would know they were poking your finger?"

Again, they said no.

"So are you your finger? Your finger's gone, but aren't your still here?"

Many students now agreed that they were not their finger, and a few more joined the maybe column.

"If you're not your finger, what if you accidently lopped off your whole hand? They couldn't reattach your hand, and you sell it to science once again. Then you are probably not your hand either. Am I right?" I asked.

"Right . . ." they murmured.

"So, if you lost both arms and legs and survived, perhaps you're not your body."

They all looked like they wondered where this was going.

Before they had time to think too much, I quickly asked, "Are you your mind?"

"Well, of course I'm my mind," said several students with the majority agreeing. There was, however, a noticeable hesitation in some students, and several of the former "maybe" students said no.

"Now I am going to ask you to close your eyes and do four

284

visualizations. I want to place a seed of doubt as to whether you are your mind. I want to raise the possibility; perhaps you **have** a mind but, you are **not** your mind. Just like you have a body and emotions, but they are not you. My theory is: whatever you say is yours isn't you. Just like the shoes: you have shoes, but they are not you; and perhaps it is the same regarding your mind," trying to make my point more understandable.

"Let's start with the first visualization. Imagine a time when you were really angry, perhaps you even exploded. Try to visualize where you were, who was there, and what happened, and relive it. I will give you a minute to intensify these images and feelings . . . Now, while re-experiencing the anger simultaneously, pay attention to what your mind feels like.

"Now, I want you to replace the anger with a smile. Visualize a smile being dropped in the center of the mind field and gently rippling across your expansive mind. Notice what that feels like.

"Visualization number three. I want you to visualize a cow. Do the best to make the cow as vivid as you can. . . . Now when I say 'begin' do not allow the image of the cow return. No matter what, keep the cow from reappearing. Keep your eyes closed and, if the cow returns, laugh lightly to let me know. For the entire twenty-five seconds, don't let the cow return—begin!"

Laughter broke out throughout the twenty-five seconds, particularly when I said "moo" toward the end.

"Finally, visualize a red rose in your mind's eye as clear and as red as you can . . . Now switch it to yellow . . . Now blue . . . Now black. Now visualize a bouquet of multicolored roses . . . Okay, you can open your eyes."

I then processed the four vignettes with them. "How did your mind feel if you were able to successfully recreate your anger?" I asked.

"Tight and tense," said one.

"Kind of dense and unhappy," said another.

"What happened when you introduced the smile?"

"It immediately erased the anger; my mind felt lighter," a student offered enthusiastically.

"It's interesting how quickly we can shift out of a negative emotion. This smile technique illustrates our ability to quickly change our moods, and we can do it consciously. I teach this smile technique to clients who sometimes feel overwhelmed by negative emotions. The ones who develop a habit of it tell me it's quite helpful," I explained.

"Now, what happened with the cow?" I asked.

"It only came back once, when you mooed," Tom said laughing.

"How were you able to keep it away?" I inquired.

"I just put my mind on something else," Tom replied.

"That's great, Tom. If we can direct our mind with concentration else-where, we can stop negative thinking and change our feelings. What did you focus on instead, Tom?" I asked.

"A skunk chasing me," Tom said, as others laughed.

"My obsessive-compulsive clients struggle the most with the cow. They try so hard to keep the cow away, they give energy to the cow and therefore, it keeps popping into their mind," I shared.

"I don't know if I'm obsessive, but that cow kept coming back," said Bobbie.

"How many of you could visualize the red rose, make it change colors and create a bouquet?" I asked.

Almost everyone raised their hand.

"That's great, but let's get to the major point of this visualization exper-iment. How many of you realized when you were looking at the images and feelings in your mind, there was something doing the looking? Someone is observing and directing the scenes in the mind," I offered.

"That's true," JoAnn said excitedly.

"That 'someone' is telling the rose to turn red and it happens instanta-neously, and it watches the anger create tension in the mind. Who or what is that? Who is observing the mind beyond the thoughts, images, and feelings in your mind? Who is giving the commands to visualize this and that? Hold your answers until tomorrow, because the class is almost over. We will discuss this in more depth tomorrow," I said as the bell rang.

This activity started a deeper investigation of the question "Who Am I?" People who are interested in working with youth to explore this question would benefit from going through each of these visualizations themselves. The four vignettes seemed to energize student interest in pursuing what at first glance seemed like a very esoteric question. The more abstract thinkers in my class were actually intrigued by the axiom—"Whatever I say is mine, isn't me."

Additional Questions

We have a personality made up of a body, emotions, and a mind; but these may shroud our real self. The question of who we are beyond the masks and the multiple identities of our personality is a question we are all meant to ask and ultimately answer through direct experience. Saint Francis of Assisi gave a short and interesting answer to this question: "What we are looking for is what is looking." Who or what is looking at the cow, the red rose, and observing the effects of the smile in the mind field? Michael Singer in *The Untethered Soul* agrees with St. Francis and offers more detail:

> I am the one who sees. . . . I look out, and I am aware of the events, thoughts, and emotions that pass before me. . . . If you go very deep, that is where you live. You live in the seat of consciousness. A true spiritual being lives there, without effort. . . . You effortlessly look outside and see all that you see, you will eventually sit far enough back inside to see all of your thoughts and emotions as well as outer form. All of these objects are in front of you. The thoughts are closer in and the emotions are a little further away, and form is way out there. Behind it all there you are. You go so deep that you realize that is where you've always been. At each stage of your life you have seen different thoughts, emotions, and objects pass before you. But you have always been the conscious receiver of all that was.[108]

The "cow experiment" is an enjoyable way for young people to begin engaging the question of who they are. Their direct experience left them knowing, just as Michael Singer suggested, that there is an awareness or consciousness beyond the mind, observing the mind. Earlier in this book, I quoted Eckhart Tolle from his book *The Power of Now*, which said that all fear is the ego's fear of death. The ego forgets its role and extends its identity into almost everything and feels threatened by challenges to its multiple identities. Tolle pointed out that we get in arguments, fights, and even wars because of the ego's

---

108. The Untethered Soul by Michael A. Singer, New Harbinger Publications, Inc., 2007, 28, 29.

over-identification and attachment to the ideas in our minds. Let me finish Tolle's quote about how to go beyond the combative fears of the ego, in the light of discovering that there may be an awareness that exists beyond our mind:

> Once you have disidentified from your mind, whether you are right or wrong makes no difference to your sense of self at all, so the forcefully compulsive and deeply unconscious need to be right, which is a form of violence, will no longer be there. You can state clearly and firmly how you feel or what you think, but there will be no aggression or defensiveness about it. Your sense of self is then derived from a deeper and truer place within yourself.
>
> What are you defending? An illusory identity, an image in your mind, a fictitious entity. By making this pattern conscious, by witnessing it, you disidentify from it. In the light of your own consciousness, the unconscious pattern will then quickly dissolve. This is the end of all arguments and power games, which are so corrosive to relationships. Power over others is weakness disguised as strength. True power is within, and is available to you now. . . . So anyone who is identified with their mind and, therefore, disconnected from their true power, their deeper self, rooted in being, will have fear as their constant companion.[109]

In the discussion that followed our experiment, students recognized that whatever was witnessing the qualities of their angry mind remained neutral. In each vignette, the observer was a neutral witness, yet it seemed to be involved in the command that turned the red rose to yellow or brought a smile to replace the constricted energy of anger. Yet even the commands were carried out with no loss of neutrality. "What do you think it would be like if you lived in this witnessing state all of the time?" I asked my students. "Would you be more or less creative? Would you be more or less stressed?"

They all came to a consensus they would be less stressed, and the vast majority came down on the side of increased creativity. "How can a person constantly stay aware of the neutral observer because I always get lost in my thoughts?" a student asked.

---

109. The Power of Now by Eckhart Tolle, Namaste Publishing Inc., 1997, 36.

"The mind naturally moves. It has been trained by the culture to look outward. By focusing the mind inward we can maintain better connection with this witnessing presence," I offered.

Many more questions and many more tentative answers were spawned by students. It was such a rich dialogue. I wasn't so much trying to provide answers as I was trying to facilitate a discussion by framing questions that led to introspection and *their* answers.

Inner Science

Beyond this very useful but introductory cow experiment, how do we and students continue to explore and hopefully answer with deep satisfaction the question, "Who am I?" The Dalai Lama hints at what is required:

> The unhappiness and suffering that we experience arise through our inability to control our own minds, and the happiness that we wish to achieve will only be achieved by learning to control our own minds. . . . You can use inner science to educate each individual to understand himself or herself, to control his or her negative emotions and disturbed notions, and to cultivate his or her highest potentials of love and wisdom.

This quote is extraordinary because it communicates so much that is helpful regarding the path to greater happiness and discovering our deeper self. Though I have been offering quotes from various religions, a person doesn't have to be religious in order to engage the question of who they are at the center of their being. Engaging and answering this question requires controlling and focusing our minds, which is difficult. John Milton said, "The mind . . . in itself can make a heaven of hell, and a hell of heaven." Milton is correct, and his quote suggests controlling our minds will not be an easy task. The Dalai Lama suggests that we will have to use "inner science" so we can understand ourselves and control our emotions and our thoughts. Inner science, he suggests, will help us experience our highest potential for love and wisdom; qualities of our real self.

What is inner science? Well, one thing it is not is using and losing the mind pursuing the external charms of the economic culture. Inner science requires introspection and contemplation. We need to examine, for example, which attachments and expectations led to our negative emotions, causing pain to me and others. Which of the four primitive urges did I fail to regulate, causing a sloth that is now blocking my wisdom and joy? What changes are required to chart a new course to conquer these imbalances? Introspection, contemplation, being a steward of our own thoughts, and self-awareness are the tools that can help provide answers to these questions. They are part of the "inner science."

In addition to introspection and contemplation, we will have to learn to control and direct our mind, which is capable of creating its own hell. How do we use the mind and train it so we can experience greater love, wisdom, and happiness? We have discussed the importance of breath in training the mind and reducing its inherent restlessness. Once we have made progress in training the mind to stay in the moment by linking it with our breath, we can begin to direct the mind away from its destructive thoughts and anxiety-producing obsessions.

Buddha said, "We are what we think. All that we are arises with our thoughts. With our thoughts we make the world." Proverbs 23:7 says, "As he thinketh in his heart, so is he." The thoughts we give concentrated attention to create our experience, painful or sublime. We know worrisome stress-producing thoughts deplete energy and beautiful, peaceful, and loving thoughts elevate our energy. Attention is the fertilizer that feeds our seedling thoughts, or in its absence, causes a thought to lose energy and wilt. The more repeated attention we give a particular thought, the more likely it will express itself in speech or action. Speech and action are the expressions of "fertilized" thoughts.

If someone wrongs us and we think, "She can't get away with that," it is more likely by replaying that thought that we will say or do something out of anger. We tend to make our worst most impulsive decisions out of our strong emotions. It is empowering to realize we have a choice to not energize thoughts of perceived grievances. Our words and our actions are the concrete expressions of thoughts that we have given our attention. The good news is we can give our attention to thoughts that uplift our spirits, grow compassion toward others, build hope for a better future, or incline us toward peace rather than hostility.

The guide that helps us to determine which thoughts to ignore and which to fertilize is our conscience or intuition. Our intuition can help us discriminate which thoughts to cultivate so we can avoid creating a hell of our own making. Our conscience directs our focus to helpful thoughts that bring a serene heavenly mind. When some negative emotion has grabbed us and we want to say something out of emotion, remember this piece of wisdom offered by Dr. Urshabudh Arya: "When you most want to speak, don't." Following this advice has saved me on more than one occasion. When experiencing intense emotions, we need to exercise a self-imposed timeout from any speech or action. During this timeout we work to quiet our mind rather than feed its thoughts about perceived injustices. The quieter our mind gets, the more we can access and listen to the still, quiet voice of conscience/intuition that flows directly from our higher self.

We also need to train our mind to become more laser-like. A still, focused mind directed inward is the means to help us experience our deepest self—amid the noise, distractions, and stresses of life. "If there thine eye be single, thy whole body shall be full of light" (Mathew 6:22) is the biblical expression suggesting the value of a concentrated mind. When the mind is pointed, fully focused, and directed inward, it will take us to our spiritual light, our soul.

Meditation for Mastering Our Mind

The training of the mind that allows us to infuse our positive inclinations with laser-like intentionality and concentration is called meditation. Meditation also allows a neutral witnessing of emotionally charged thoughts so that their destructive potential dissipates and their energy is assimilated and harmonized. Meditation is a part of every religious tradition. Meditation is the cornerstone of yoga, which isn't a religion, but where many people of varied belief systems have discovered meditation's unique value. Swami Rama said, "Meditation can give you something nothing else can; it introduces you to your self." There is a brief meditation process at the end of this chapter that you can experiment with, if you are interested, and gather your own data.

Yoga has become synonymous in the West with exercise and

stretching. Yoga, in its essence, is really a process for self-discovery and becoming aware of all aspects of our being. Yoga is all about direct experience. You practice and decide if your experience was beneficial. Yoga is self-validating, your experience itself informs. You don't have to have blind faith or even a belief system to meditate. Meditation provides its own data and experience, which then inspires and enlivens your faith, and validates your beliefs.

For those who do have a chosen religion, meditation will enhance their experience and understanding of that religion. Religion comes from Latin "religare," meaning to bind back or to bind together. Yoga means union, or to unite, and is related to the biblical word yoke.[110] What both meditation and religion are suggesting is that we can bind or yoke our individual self, the self of personality, with the transcendent self. A single drop, a soul, can merge with the ocean of God. "I and my father are one," Jesus proclaimed (John 10:30). Meditation is the means for that union. Meditation also unites or yokes the compassion of the heart with the wisdom of the mind.

Meditation will answer the question "Who am I?" Is there something in me that doesn't die, that is unconditioned, permanent, infinite, unborn? In meditation we are not tall or short, male or female, a mother or a daughter. Meditation is a state beyond all conditioned and limited identifications of self, and is beyond all polarities. Meditation answers the question of who we are through direct experience; it is the means to a great revelation. Meditation turns the mind inward and reveals that we are consciousness itself, a living spirit. However, because the mind is scattered and restless, its concentration needs to be sharpened. To concentrate the mind, it initially needs something to focus on that redirects its attention from externals and random dissipating thoughts. Sometimes this is a visual focus; sometimes it is a sound. When it is a sound, it is a prayer or a mantra.

The word mantra is related to the English words mind and mental. These are derived from the Latin word "mens" (mind) that comes from the Greek word "menos" (mind). All of these words derive from the

---

110. Superconscious Meditation by Dr. Urshabudh Arya, audio lecture at the Meditation Center, Minneapolis, MN, 1977.

Sanskrit verb root "man" which means "to meditate."[111] Man is the being who can meditate. Meditation comes from the Latin "medi," meaning middle; and tare, to stay.[112] To stay in the middle or to stay centered. One meaning of the word mantra is "protector of mind." Repetition of a mantra protects the mind from slipping into mindless banter, stressful thoughts, and external allurements. It helps us stay centered. Every thought carries a certain vibrational energy that ultimately creates our entire personality. Our personality is the sum total of all our thoughts.[113] Mantras are vibrational purifying thoughts that keep "garbage thoughts" from being added to the landfill of our unconscious, while simultaneously energizing and harmonizing the conscious and unconscious mind. Mantras essentially balance our self-preservation urge by weakening the ego's false identifications and attachments while simultaneously intensifying our fifth urge that leads us to our transcendent self.

The Bible urges people to "pray without ceasing" (1 Thessalonians 5:17). Mantra thoughts, with sufficient practice, maintain a constant positive vibrational energy in the mind throughout the day—truly praying without ceasing. "In the beginning was the Word, and the Word was with God, and the Word was God" (John 1:1). The whole universe is vibrational energy. Mantras are said to be sacred vibrational sounds that come out of the depths of silence or stillness, God if you will. When the universe was created, its vibrational energy was expressed in one of two ways: light or sound. "Let there be Light, and there was light," it says in Genesis 1:13. Mantras are the sound vibrational equivalents of light. The theory is that, by repeating and internalizing these sacred sounds, it brings one closer and closer to the spiritual source of those sounds. Whether or not you accept this perspective, there is an ever-expanding body of science documenting meditation's and mantra's efficacy in relieving emotional pain and suffering.

Meditation can bring about dynamic positive changes, including changes in the brain, that can be truly transformative in helping

111. Ibid.

112. Ibid.

113. Ibid.

struggling young people. Research shows that when we pray or meditate with an absorbed mind, the brain's alpha waves change to theta waves, shifting us from a state of arousal or stress to a state of deep relaxation. Anxious, bored, aimless, and stressed-out youth would all benefit from a meditation practice, but clearly not all will be interested. Those who are interested will benefit more from meditating if they first lay a strong foundation by better regulating their primitive urges and establishing balanced breathing. This will stabilize their emotions and increase their energy, allowing the full transformative benefits of meditation to express themselves.

Benefits of Meditation

Meditation consists basically of calming and focusing the mind through nonjudgmental awareness of each moment. Beyond the philosophy underlying meditation, it provides tremendous practical benefits for anyone who practices regularly. Meditation lowers blood pressure, heart rate, respiration, and very recent studies reveal it even influences healthy gene expression.[114] This suggests that we could potentially improve future generations' genetic health, if meditation was practiced by young adults prior to having children. Meditation helps insomnia, premenstrual syndrome, hot flashes, infertility, tension headaches, anxiety, anger, hostility, and mild to moderate depression. Meditation also holds great promise for youth by soothing painful emotions and lowering overall emotional volatility.

Meditation expands and strengthens positive new circuits in the brain, and weakens the circuits connected to negative habits through their disuse.[115] This is critical in changing painful or destructive habits. This ability to change the architecture of the brain is known as neuroplasticity. Studies have revealed dramatic increases in high-frequency gamma brain waves in meditation. This is done by creating a mental state where compassion permeates the entire mind field. Gamma waves

114. "Relaxation Revolution" by Brian Johnson, Experience Life, September 2011, 75, 76.

115. "Scans of Monks' Brains Show Meditation Alters Structure, Functioning" by Sharon Bagley, Science Journal, 2004.

seem to link widely spread brain circuits that underlie higher mental activity, like consciousness. Novice meditators show slight increases in gamma wave activity. Experienced meditators show an extremely large increase in gamma waves.[116] In essence, gamma waves seem to be correlated with improved concentration and awareness.

Other positive patterns in the brain are being revealed in research on meditation. People under stress or suffering from anxiety or depression usually exhibit over-activity of electrical impulses in the right frontal cortex. People who tend to be calm and happy typically show greater activity in the left frontal cortex. In one study, twenty-five people were taught meditation for eight weeks. They were matched against a control group that did no meditation. In just eight weeks there was a pronounced shift in frontal lobe activity from the right to the left frontal cortex in meditators. The nonmeditators had no shift.[117]

John Spayde, writing in the October 2010 *Experience Life* magazine, reports on neuroscientists Richard Davidson's and Matthieu Recard's research regarding this shift:

> High ratio of activity in the left prefrontal areas of the brain can mark either a fleeting positive mood or a more ingrained positive outlook . . .
>
> Veteran Buddhist meditators demonstrate initial heightened activity in this region, along with ability to recover from negative responses brought on by frightening images shown to them by researchers. This suggests that their long-term meditation practice has helped build brains that are able to not just enjoy but sustain a sense of positive well-being even in stressful moments.
>
> Neuroscientist Rick Hanson . . . has extensively studied the effect of meditation on the brain says, "Stimulating areas of the brain that handle positive emotions strengthens those neural networks, just as working muscles strengthens them." The reverse is also true, he explains, "If you routinely think about things that make you feel mad or wounded, you are sensitizing and strengthening the amygdala, which is primed to respond to negative experiences. So it will become more reactive, and you will get

116. Ibid.

117. "Meditation and the scientific method" by Judy Foreman. Star Tribune, Health Section, 2003.

more upset more easily in the future."[118]

These changes in the brain suggest the power of meditation to actually change the function, structure, and wiring of the brain. "What we do changes the architecture of our brains. It's called neuroplasticity and it's the underpinning of everything we now know about the brain," Jon continues, "Pursuits that require intense mental focus . . . 'switch on' the nucleus basalis, the control mechanism for neuroplasticity. This actively promotes synapse connections and leads to strong neural 'wiring.'"[119]

Meditation provides the intense mental focus mentioned that is required to switch on this rewiring process through mantra or repetitive prayer. Meditation can help youth by changing their brain and increasing their inclination to notice that their glass is half full, rather than half empty. Meditation can also help develop new neuropathways that would encourage new habits that create less hostility and less emotional reactivity. These changes would all translate into healthier relationships and greater happiness and contentment.

Happy and calm people also release less of the stress hormone cortisol. Cortisol is correlated with the body going into fight or flight mode. Over time, this stress hormone can actually shrink the hippocampus, which helps in regulating our stress. This can increase the likelihood of disease, memory problems, and even early onset Alzheimer's.[120] Brian Johnson quotes Herbert Benson Harvard MD, author of the best-selling book *Relaxation Revolution*, in September 2011 issue of *Experience Life*: "Any condition that is caused or exacerbated by stress can be helped with a well-designed mind-body approach. Furthermore, because all health conditions have some stress component, it is no overstatement to say that virtually every single health problem and disease can be improved with a mind-body approach."[121]

The mind-body approaches of mediation and relaxation Herbert

---

118. "Upgrade Your Brain" by John Spayde, Experience Life, October 2010, 54, 55, reports on neuroscientists Richard Davidson's and Matthieu Recard's research.

119. Ibid. Citing Barbara Strauch in The Secret Life of the Grown-up Brain.

120. Ibid.

121. "Relaxation Revolution" by Brian Johnson, Experience Life, September 2011, 76.

Benson encourages have far-reaching health benefits. It turns out that the dysfunctional breathing patterns of my at-risk stress management group were not only creating emotional kindling, but they likely also exposed these students to long-term health problems. People who meditate also usually have a significantly higher level of "killer cells," which reflects a stronger immune system essential to fighting disease.

Subjects studied at Massachusetts General Hospital who used a mantra in their meditation revealed a particular beneficial pattern of activity in their amygdala. The amygdala often reflexively triggers emotional reactions based on the brain's associations to past painful experiences. The meditators who used mantras exhibited vigilance and a focused attention, but without the characteristic emotional reactivity that normally characterizes activity in this part of the brain.[122] Experienced meditators have demonstrated excellent emotional control even in challenging situations. The Dalai Lama was once asked why he didn't show more outrage toward the Chinese Communist government that took over his country and slaughtered thousands of Tibetan monks, many of whom he knew personally. He said, "They took my country, do you want me to give them my mind also?"

Emotional control is an area of challenge for many adolescents and young adults. Meditation could provide tremendous benefits in this area. Meth addicts frequently damage their amygdala, making emotional regulation difficult, which often shows itself in their heightened paranoia and frequent mood swings. Meth use also severely depletes serotonin, often fueling an overwhelming depression when meth addicts attempt to give up their addiction, which greatly increases their likelihood of relapse. Very recent research suggests that meditation may increase serotonin and also GABA levels, a neurotransmitter associated with improved mood.[123] These are two potential benefits of meditation that could help many struggling with depression.

Paul Eckman, a psychology professor at the University of California, San Francisco, developed a method to measure facial expressions and the ability to decipher them. People, in general, respond poorly in decoding rapidly changing facial expressions that represent specific

---

122. Worried Sick, PBS Home Video, Scientific American Frontier.

123. "Do Yoga, Be Happy," AARP Magazine, You & Your Health section, 2010.

emotions. Several monks, who were meditators, were able to almost perfectly read fast-changing expressions.[124] Interestingly, this is one of the problems bullies have; they often misread facial expressions and respond aggressively to benign expressions. Experienced meditators have also demonstrated the ability to show no reaction to unanticipated extremely loud noises. Their minds had such concentration and control that they actually inhibited the startle response. This suggests an extremely high level of emotional control.

Young people inundated by the economic culture's seductive temptations, which create attachments damaging to their emotional balance, would benefit from a regular practice of meditation. Meditation decreases emotional reactivity and harmonizes negative emotions. Balanced primitive urges and meditation naturally bring forward our positive emotions of peace, joy, contentment, and love. These qualities are often sadly absent from many of our young people's lives.

Afterglow from the "Cow" Experiment

Minds can be trained to stay in the moment, as we suggested, by linking the mind with breath and focusing the mind on an image or sound vibration. This training, this inner science, is a way out of our and youth's suffering and unhappiness. We can use the mind to go beyond the mind. This is the path to Love, Truth, God, Consciousness, Self, Awareness, or whatever name you give to ultimate reality. Meditation provides the means to directly experience the reality that answers the questions: "Who am I?" "Why am I here?" and "Where am I going?" An ancient scripture, the *Katha Upanishad*, expresses it this way:

> The self-existent Lord pierced the senses to turn outward. Thus we look to the world without and see not the self within us. But when the sage withdraws from the world of change and seeks immortality, he looks within and beholds the deathless self. The immature run constantly after sense pleasures and fall into the widespread net of death. But the wise,

---

124. "Meditation and the Scientific Method" by Judy Foreman, Star Tribune, Health Section, 2003.

knowing the self as deathless, seek not the changeless in the world of change.[125]

We were never this philosophical or spiritual in my classroom discussions. Each person was left to their own understanding of whom they were and the best way to construct their life. The cow experiment had a more profound ripple for many youth, however, than those four simple visualizations might at first glance have suggested. I invite you to repeat some version of this experiment with your children, clients, or students to inspire a dialogue with them. The four vignettes were powerful because they inspired introspection, spawning questions for further investigation. Socrates illustrated how good teaching is principally about raising questions that inspire deep contemplation. Our role when working with youth is also largely to frame quality questions and encourage experiments that lead to increased contemplation and self-awareness.

For many students, the cow experiment was an interesting diversion before they got lost again in habits driven by the desires promoted by the economic culture. However, for some youth it started or rekindled a journey. Who is that observer looking at the rose, directing their change of colors, and witnessing the effects of a smile in the mind field? How can I invoke that presence to decrease my and others' suffering? Cultivating breath awareness and practicing meditation allows one to deepen the connection to this eternal witness, which eliminates the false identifications and attachments of the ego. Then, the self-preservation urge is no longer activated and distorted through me, mine, and "I"—the "little selves" of ego and personality. The self that we were desperately trying to preserve, we realize, is impermanent and impossible to preserve. Breath awareness helps us maintain mindfulness and allows the ego to play its proper role; it becomes an instrument, a servant, a disciple of our divine nature and will. The disidentification from our false self, and the identification with the real self, is the end of all fear and stress. We are left with a harmonious mind where intuition and conscience inform every moment. Confusion disappears and true creativity is born. We then are truly the architects of our lives.

---

125. Kathaupanishad.

Students sometimes stop in to see me, or I receive their emails at school. They often mention something in the psychology class that was transformative for them. Most often the change or growth they share in their emails was the result of a direct experience from an experiment that they chose to engage in. Their experiments led to a deeper self-awareness. Galileo said, "You cannot teach a person anything, you can only help them find it within." We cannot teach anyone else something we haven't practiced or experienced ourselves. Then, and only then, are we in a position to inspire others to find their answers within.

Experiment
Learning to Meditate

Until you have the opportunity to get some training in correct sitting and breathing, this simple procedure will introduce you to the benefits of meditation. This is adapted from a CD by Swami Veda Bharati who has worked on behalf of the United Nations, the World Council of Religions, and has taught mediation for nearly seventy years to diverse audiences and a variety of spiritual and religious traditions.[126] He has founded or guided close to a hundred meditation centers worldwide. He is the author of dozens of books and pamphlets including *Unifying Streams of Spirituality*. Meditation is one of those unifying streams. Follow the sequence in order. If questions arise you can visit www.themediationcenter.org.

1. Sit as straight as you can on an even, firm cushion(s) or on a chair.

2. Relax your forehead.

3. Relax your facial and physical musculature.

4. Bring your awareness to your breathing.

5. Breathe slowly, gently, smoothly, evenly, without jerk or sound in the breathing.

6. Now feel the touch and flow of the breath in the nostrils.

7. Let there be no pause between the breaths; as one breath is completed, begin to feel the next breath flowing and touching the nostrils.

---

126. Learn to Meditate—First Step Toward Peace, CD, with Swami Veda Bharati, AHYMSA Publishers.

8. After a few breaths, begin exhaling and inhaling with one of the following options:

  • Whichever name of God is your favorite according to your tradition or religion.
  • Or a sacred but short phrase or prayer from your scriptures or tradition.
  • Or use "one" as you inhale and "two" as you exhale, or the yoga Himalayan traditions—"so" with the in-breath and "ham" (pronounced hahm) with the out breath.

9. Let there be no break between breaths or between your chosen phrase or thought.

10. As soon as you become aware that you have lost the flow, and other thoughts have begun to arise, restart the same procedure.

11. Sit for as long as you wish.

12. Let the quietness of the mind continue after you arise.

Practicing meditation for a few minutes several times a day will allow you to notice subtle positive changes in yourself. Whatever you do repeatedly with the mind becomes the mind's habit.

Chapter 20

Final Thoughts on
Our Journey to Joy

"Do not search for Jesus in Far off Lands:
he is not there. He is in you.
Just keep the lamp burning and you will see him"

—MOTHER TERESA

"He is not elated by good fortune or depressed by bad.
His mind is established in God,
and he is free from delusion."

—BHAGAVAD GITA

It is possible to cultivate and create positive emotions through the choices we make. We express emotional immaturity and experience its attendant pain when we are seduced by the many desires created by the economic culture. It is important to understand the temptations and consequences of this culture, but not get overwhelmed by them. The shallowness and pain embedded in the economic culture can actually serve as a catalyst to inspire youth to pursue positive desires that can elevate their lives. There is potentially as much awareness and learning in suffering as in nonsuffering. Suffering can inspire youth to refocus their attention to thoughts and habits that create a greater joy.

We have studied the four primitive urges that are the key to our survival, which when imbalanced, cause all of our stress and emotional turmoil. When these urges are well regulated we experience balance, and we can more easily discern the suggestions of our conscience and intuition. These suggestions are informed by our spiritual self, through our fifth human urge, the positive desire for higher knowledge—for transcendence. This urge toward something admirable, pious, complete, uplifting, something noble, is in all of us. Like the four primitive urges, we are born with this fifth urge. An agnostic or atheist who can't worship Christ, Buddha, or Allah will honor and admire Lincoln, Gandhi, Mother Theresa, or their own father or mother.[127] This fifth urge is for something extraordinary, for something superior. The Latin word for super means something above, something greater or higher. If a person doesn't seek God, he or she might pick up a Superman comic book or attend a superhero movie.[128]

This fifth urge, if honored, can channel the energy gained from balancing our primitive urges into a means for discovering our spiritual self. Our still, quiet voice can then guide our choices so they are aligned with this transcendent desire. If we honor the desire for higher understanding and wisdom, our minds become one pointed; and it is easier to let go of our dependencies and our attachments. The desires of the senses seem less consequential and they begin to lose their hold on us as our fifth human urge comes alive.

Engaging the Path of Life

There are two narrow lanes we walk, one foot in each lane running parallel on the path of life. One path is riddled with obstacles—our attachments, expectations, and fears—that cause us to trip and falter.

---

127. Yoga Psychology of Life, audio tape by Dr. Urshabudh Arya at the Meditation Center in Minneapolis, MN. 1976.

128. Ibid.

We stumble because we have identified with our brokenness and cling to material things and desires that slow our journey. We forget we are already "a special heaven whole and unbroken," and we cling to impermanent transient satisfactions of our desire-filled mind. This keeps one foot stuck in a tarpit-like eddy where the harder our ego struggles to maintain itself, the more it restricts our movement toward spiritual progress.

Abraham Maslow said, "All learning is subtraction." Yoga psychology supports this perspective, urging us to let go of all conditioned notions of self, and the selfish desires that they spawn. We have thousands of conditioned ideas about who we are and who we are not. We were called a certain name from birth, and now we think that name is us. When someone mispronounces our name, we can become annoyed, or even hurt and embarrassed. Our names and similar notions of self are things we have been taught; they are conditioned. Who are we beyond those conditioned notions, habits, and roles? This is what Maslow means by all learning is subtraction, we have to subtract or disidentify from these conditioned notions of self, so our real self can be revealed. This speeds our journey on the pathway to joy.

Replacing Destructive Thoughts and Habit Patterns

Initially we change any destructive conditioning through what Western psychology calls cognitive behavioral therapy. This involves replacing negative thoughts, and the habits they spawn, with hope-producing thoughts and habits. Yoga psychology also stresses the need to cultivate positive, beneficial, and uplifting thoughts and choices. This is essential to transform our personalities and character. We will also have to be willing to face our fears, hurts, and insecurities. It is not our fault that these painful feelings exist, and it is important to remember that we are not less pure because of them, because ultimately they are not us. Emotions come and go just as thoughts come and go, but the true self remains. When we expand our consciousness through selfless action, speech, and thoughts, we bring harmony and peace to our personality and transform our egos' fears and attachments. This expanded consciousness allows us to go beyond the limits of mind and experience our spiritual self.

Anais Nin said that we don't see the world the way it is, we see the world the way we are. It is like the story of a person who awakens lethargic, and dreading work. He spills on his shirt at breakfast, slips on a patch of ice in his driveway, and has to jump his car battery because he left the lights on overnight. It is unlikely his mind will allow him to enjoy his ride to work. In his stressed-out state, it seems every "idiot" has taken to the road with him. It is as though they all have walkie-talkies to communicate with so they can coordinate their actions. "Don't signal! Hesitate at the green light! Cut in front of that blue car! Slam on your brakes!" This coordinated effort is all seemingly designed to tick him off and make him miserable.[129]

He awakes another morning with energy and in a good mood, takes in the beautiful sunrise, and mindfully enjoys the birds singing while breathing in the fresh spring air. He heads to work in a wonderful mood and all the "idiots" apparently took the day off. Even if one idiot escapes onto the freeway and fails to signal or hesitates at a green light, he scarcely notices and is unperturbed. He colors the world dark and ominous or colorful and bright, depending on the palate of his mind. A simple quote from Picasso, suggesting the value of a flexible state of mind, makes me smile: "When I haven't any red, I use blue." It is good news that we can influence how we color our days.

Balancing our four primitive urges is an essential step that influences and increases our energy and helps us experience the positive emotions that lets most of the "idiots" on the path of life sleep in. We find ourselves more accepting of others as we focus our increased positive energy on becoming the architects of our own lives. We refuse to live as victims because a few lost souls bumped into us on the path to joy. Our increased energy from balanced choices and trained minds is now directed to helping some of these lost "others," while we smell the roses on the path of self-discovery.

---

129. Paraphrase of story told by Dr. Arya at a lecture in the 1970s at the Meditation Center in Minneapolis, MN.

Training Our Inclinations

There is a Greek word, *eupsychia*; a rough translation is "good mindedness." Eupsychia is fostered by cultivating a habit in the mind of looking for "what is there here to enjoy." This changes the way we experience our lives. We live in a time of complaints, entitlements, perceived victimization, and excessive litigation. Yet, many more positive than negative events are occurring each day. If we cultivate a habit of appreciation rather than looking for the complaint box, we will create more of a heaven and less of a hell. If you saw a tiny black ink spot on a perfectly white shirt, does your mind forget the white and get lost in the black dot?

When we change our negative inclinations and attitudes and cultivate more positive ways of looking and being, we experience more joy. Recent research reveals there are plenty of reasons to cultivate a more positive perspective. In an article in the *Los Angeles Times*, "Find the Good," Terrence Monmaney summarizes some of that research:

> Dozens of recent studies show that optimists do better than pessimists in work, school, and sports, suffer less depression, achieve more goals, respond better to stress, wage more effective battles against disease and, yes live longer. . . . Optimists have long been portrayed as foolishly oblivious to problems. But numerous studies show that optimists . . . confront trouble head on . . . Women recently diagnosed with cancer were more likely to acknowledge the seriousness of the disease. They experienced less stress and took more active steps to cope with it. . . . "Pessimism was associated with denial and a giving up response." Optimism was associated with positively reframing the situation. They are studying the origins of optimism and pessimism with an eye toward reducing what some have called the "epidemic" of depression among the young. Among students . . . who said they had never been depressed, seventeen percent of the pessimists and one percent of the optimists became clinically depressed within the next three years—the first clinical evidence that pessimism appears to increase vulnerability to depression.[130]

---

130. "Find the Good" by Terrence Monmaney, Los Angeles Times.

So optimists don't bury their head in the sand, but many pessimists do and they are unable to engage the reality that life puts before them. Optimists chose to "reframe" challenging situations while still addressing them constructively. A positive perspective decreases the stress, hopelessness, and helplessness that keeps us from sustained engagement in a challenge, thus bringing about more positive outcomes.

Another study reported in Martin Seligman's book *The Optimistic Child*, referenced in the same *Los Angeles Times* article, sights a program for fifth and sixth graders. They attempted to arm children with optimism to inoculate them against the growing wave of depression they were witnessing in children. They did this through a variety of messages including a cartoon character "Gloomy Greg," who is cut from a baseball team and reacts by thinking, "I have no athletic ability." Over twelve sessions, they pointed out to the students, who had the similar tendency to hold sweeping negative thoughts as Gloomy Greg, that there were alternative interpretations for difficult events. These students explored more flexible possibilities if they were to get cut from a team. These alternative explanations kept hope alive for future at bats and baseball opportunities, such as them dedicating more time to practicing. In a test of 118 at-risk children who participated in this program that cultivated this more hopeful mental approach, they found it reduced their susceptibility to depression by 50 percent over a two-and-a-half-year period.[131]

This study illustrates that optimism can be taught. It's never too early to teach and help children become stewards of their own thoughts. Christ said, "As he thinketh in his heart so is he" (Proverbs 23:7). Buddha said, "With our minds, we make the world." So the path of joy requires us to change our habitual tendencies to think in distorted, shaming, or self-destructive ways. The International Optimist Club was founded in the early 1900s, and has a junior version that influences thousands of young people in America and across the planet. They recite the following creed at the beginning of every meeting:

---

131. Ibid.

The Optimists Creed

Promise yourself

To be so strong that nothing can disturb your peace of mind.

To talk health, happiness, and prosperity to every person you meet.

To make all your friends feel that there is something worthwhile in them.

To look at the sunny side of everything, and make your optimism come true.

To think only of the best, to work only for the best, and to expect only the best.

To be just as enthusiastic about the success of others as you are about your own.

To forget the mistakes of the past and press on to the greater achievements of the future.

To wear a cheerful expression at all times and give a smile to every living creature you meet.

To give so much time to improving yourself that you have no time to criticize others.

To be too large for worry, too noble for anger, too strong for fear, and too happy to permit the presence of trouble.

To think well of yourself and to proclaim this fact to the world, not in loud word, but in great deeds.

To live in the faith that the whole world is on your side, so long as you are true to the best that is in you.

This creed, with its positive and empowering perspective, would be worth repeating every morning until it permeates our minds and infuses itself into every moment. Research now shows that negative thinking habits actually dig negative neural pathways in the brain. We literally get stuck in the canals of mental habits that we dredged, making change more difficult. When we choose to think and repeat beneficial thoughts, we are deepening positive neural grooves that create more balance and joy, while simultaneously shrinking negative neural pathways in the brain that delivered our misery. We create both neural and psychological changes by noticing what is good and cultivating a feeling of appreciation for all that we receive.

When things go "bad," it is okay to acknowledge that "right now things are hard," because this statement is not distorting reality. We do not have to be Pollyannaish. However, by letting go of the bad label we can more easily open to the question: "What can I learn here?" The alternative is to feed our "black wolf" with complaints and negativity, magnetizing our minds to attach to what is wrong and missing all that is positive around us. This leaves the "white wolf" emaciated, struggling to feed the longings of the soul. We forget that our positive desires also need nourishment, the nourishment of our attention. We have the power to literally train our minds to be happier by where we place our attention.

Despite all my concerns about the messages of the economic culture that mislead and damage youth, this does not equate to powerlessness. With all the pain it causes, it doesn't eliminate the possibility of a joyful life. One thing that helps me maintain some positivity is realizing that my concerns and interpretations are influenced by a compressed time-frame—my lifetime. We cannot say with certainty what the downward trends we've examined will bring forth in the long term. We all need to cultivate the perspective of the farmer who recognized that life is change, rather than attach ourselves to permanent notions of good or bad. He found freedom, and a mind more aligned with reality, through the word "maybe," which facilitated detachment from negatively labeling life's momentary changes.

Perhaps the very imbalances that the economic culture helped to create will spur many youth on an inward journey with an even faster trajectory to joy. Hitting one's head against a wall gets old. Eventually we wake up from the dream that external acquisitions or selfish hedonistic pursuits will lead to happiness. I saw evidence of this in my classroom. I continue to be inspired as I witness more people simplifying their lives. They are beginning to look more inward than outward for meaning and joy. Mother Teresa said, "Let me live simply so others may simply live." Perhaps this credo, that has already inspired a simple, profound, and purposeful life for many, will become the dominant cultural norm.

A path to joy requires removing the psychological obstacles that block the joy that we are. This is hard work that requires us to take responsibility for our attitudes and our life. We are literally, as Emerson suggested, "standing in the way of our own sunshine." The first lane of the path to joy requires us to remove these inner obstacles that are blocking the sunshine within. This brings forward our joy and creates a purposeful life that positively impacts others and contributes to changing the society as a whole.

The second parallel lane on the path to joy, which we are simultaneously walking, is the lane of meditation and mindfulness. This lane provides the training for our mind to become more one-pointed in its concentration. Then our attention can stay in the now. We no longer get lost in the dreams and fantasies of thoughts that keep us imprisoned in the past, or anxiously anticipating a future that hasn't happened. The more our attention stays in the now, the more we experience the joy and miracle of life within and without.

The now is more than what things are happening in any particular moment. It is also the space or stillness in which those events happen. A concentrated mind developed through meditation provides the means to find our still spacious center, our eternal witness, our spiritual home, our soul. This spiritual self is said to have three qualities: existence, wisdom, and bliss. It is unborn and does not die, it is expansively intelligent, and it is joy filled. It is comforting to remember this is our birthright. These qualities are our very nature and they are indestructible. It is who we are and why we are here. We are here to experience the full awareness of our true self. Swami Veda reminds us that: "Freedom is the awareness of that fullness within. From that Fullness, that creative power, anything can be created."

Positive Desires—Service, Love, Joy, and Peace

There is another positive desire along with the fifth desire to experience our true self, and that is the desire for other's welfare. It is a desire born out of a deep recognition of our spiritual kinship to all of humanity. We are all God's children, souls in the ocean of God. This desire for others' welfare is unlike any other desire because unselfishness leads to freedom, unlike the pain that follows our attachment to selfish desires.[132] Service to others is a path away from the self-absorption and the pain of the ego's desires. It benefits the people who are served and also the

---

132. Emotion to Enlightenment by Swami Rama and Swami Ajaya. Himalayan International Institute of Yoga Science and Philosophy, 1976, 141.

ones doing the service.[133]

There is either contractive or expansive energy in life. We expand our consciousness through selfless action, speech, and thoughts. We contract our consciousness and vision through selfish actions, speech, and thoughts. When we help others we are cultivating the highest positive emotion—love. Love inspires humanity even when things are falling apart. Love is an emotion and a path to expanded consciousness or awareness that can be practiced by anyone at any time.[134] It is the simplest path, but often our love is not pure because it is alloyed with our ego's fears and desires.

It is said love makes no demands. Another way of understanding this idea is that love requires detachment; detachment from *my* wants, desires, and expectations. True love is when I want nothing from you. I want only your happiness. Eknath Eswaran sheds some light on how challenging this can be:

> All of us begin the quest for love with a great deal of attachment. That is human nature. But, with the help of meditation . . . we can diminish selfish elements day by day by putting the welfare of others first and our own personal predilections last. But practicing detachment in personal relationships does not come easily. . . . A spiritually detached person, who to me means a very loving person, will never allow relationships to degenerate to stimulus and response. The test is simple: Even if you are angry with me, can I stay calm and loving with you and help you overcome your anger? If you persist in disliking me, can I continue to like you? . . . . This problem of disliking people . . . is really a problem of disliking images we have formed of them. . . . For in almost all human relationships, we see others not as they are but as we are. To a suspicious person everyone seems suspect; . . . to a loving person, everybody is worthy of love . . . and every occasion is an opportunity to practice love. It is not that people aren't difficult when you are detached . . . but the choice of response is in your hands.[135]

---

133. Ibid.

134. Ibid.

135. "The Joy of Detachment" by Sri Eknath Easwaran, Yoga Journal, September/ October 1993.

Practicing detachment from our expectations is challenging. Eric Fromm said, "We can't fall in love we can only stand in love." Love is a state of being. When we're standing firmly in that place of love within us, we can set limits on someone's rude or hostile behavior. But, we do this limit setting for their sake, not out of our emotional reactivity. I have moments like this, but I often fail to meet Eswaran's standard; I get stuck in stimulus and response. But it is a standard I continue to aspire to without judging myself when I fail. Loving people without expectations is also a standard aligned with my conscience. Love is a noble and creative emotion because when we are "standing in love" we see options as to how to respond compassionately to difficult situations.

Another positive emotion experienced by all creatures, and what is called "the firstborn of love," is joy.[136] Joy helps replenish us and brings harmony to ourselves and our relationships. The inspiration and harmony experienced when we are joyous flows easily into peace. Peace is a state of deep contentment. Peace is not a passive state; it is a state of "fullness." In that fullness we lose all our neediness and our attachments to outside things naturally abate. We no longer try to fill ourselves with food, sex, or external acquisitions in the hope that something external will fill some insatiable void in our personality. Our four primitive urges naturally find their balance. This kind of fullness, born of a peaceful mind, is the promise of meditation. In meditation we experience union with our spiritual self. Our physical, emotional, and mental selves and our heart, mind, and soul all function as a unified whole.

Making a Difference

The message of this book champions a positive desire we all share, the desire to help youth. In my classroom, I had an inspirational quote on the board that highlighted the topic for that day. The last day of school the quote was usually from Saint Exupery: "Perhaps love is me gently leading you back to yourself." On that last school day, a student

---

136. Emotion to Enlightenment by Swami Rama and Swami Ajaya. Himalayan International Institute of Yoga Science and Philosophy, 1976, 143.

waited until every other student had left the classroom. She walked up to me and said, "This class did what St. Exupery said; it helped me to understand and like myself, perhaps even love myself, because I truly believe deep within me, I'm fine."

I have offered a comprehensive paradigm that explains the roots of our youth's suffering and a path to transcend their emotional pain. This paradigm, I hope, will relieve confusion and hopelessness, and much of the self-blame many youth carry for the "choices" they made that caused their pain and discontentment. Much of their quagmire and occasional "crazy" behavior is really a reflection of a world gone mad with selfishness and greed. They are still left with the responsibility of recreating their lives, making better decisions around their primitive urges, as well as a making a commitment to purposeful living. Without discipline or self-regulation of one's desires relative to our primitive urges, there is little progress in expanding our joy. This, however, is the gentle discipline of passive volition. I have shared youth's own experiments where they chose discipline over desire. These experiments empowered them with practical tools of self-awareness, which transformed many of their emotionally painful and destructive habits. The positive feedback from those experiments is now imprinted in their minds. This will serve as a seed of remembrance to guide them back to balance when desire gains the upper hand.

Sometimes those of us who work with young people, as parents, therapists, social workers, teachers, and other care providers, wonder if our efforts matter. The trends of our times sometimes feel overwhelming. Do we make a difference? Here are two final stories that address this question. The first comes from Dr. Arya, who told this story when my hair was still brown, and I was in my twenties:

> Once upon a time, a king of an arid country decided to have a reservoir dug that would be large enough to provide water and irrigation for much of the surrounding desert. It took years to dig and when it was finished, his wife, excited about the benefits the reservoir would bring to her people, wanted a special christening. She asked her husband to have the reservoir initially filled with milk! The king, deferring to his wife's eccentricity, issued an edict that everyone in the kingdom had to bring a pail of

milk and dump it in the reservoir on a particular date. One person who made his living selling milk, protested to his neighbors: "I won't give into this—I refuse to travel that far to give up a portion of my livelihood." Friends reminded him of the King's temper; the man could lose his freedom and maybe his life. He reluctantly gave up his protest.

The day of the commemoration turned out to be a scorcher—the hottest day of a hot summer. Therefore, people chose to travel during the cooler night, which would also allow them to be at the morning's inaugural event. The milkman noticed the thin sliver of moon that left the night black, and he got an idea. "I will fill my pail with water and pour it into the reservoir before daybreak—no one will notice and I will thwart the King and his wife!" He arrived at the reservoir in the dark of night gleefully pouring his water—laughing to himself with every splash.

The next morning, the King rode his horse out to inspect the reservoir and arrived just as the sun was breaking the horizon. He looked down to see the reservoir was filled—filled entirely with water!

Everyone had the same idea, and was sure that their individual pail of water would not make a difference and would not be noticed. After all, each of us is only one of over six billion people on the planet and whether we recycle, decrease our conspicuous consumption, or work on decreasing our anger and increasing our kindness, how much effect are we going to have on the planet? All of us, youth and those who serve them really do matter. We all have been given gifts and talents in various degrees—we all carry pails of different sizes. We all can contribute something positive to the wellbeing of our society and the world—to the reservoir. We can make a difference by offering our pails of milk. We can all share our talents, kindness, wisdom, and love, and contribute to a better world. The second story speaks for itself:

One day a man was walking along the beach when he noticed a boy picking something up and gently throwing it into the ocean. Approaching the boy, he asked, "What are you doing?"

The youth replied, "Throwing starfish back into the ocean. The surf is up and the tide is going out. If I don't throw them back, they'll die."

"Son," the man said, "don't you realize there are miles and miles of beach and hundreds of starfish? You can't make a difference!"

After listening politely, the boy bent down, picked up another starfish, and threw it back into the surf. Then smiling at the man, he said, "I made a difference for that one."[137]

We are all called to make a difference by leading a purposeful life. We cannot guarantee an outcome from our efforts, but our efforts matter. Every forgiveness silently granted to someone who slights us, every encouragement given to a despairing soul, every smile poured into a frowning child, matters. Gandhi said, "The victory is not in the result; victory is in making a full effort." My hope is the pail that is this book serves to add something of value to the reservoir.

---

137. The Starfish Story, original story by Loren Eisley.

About the Author

Jim Nelson graduated magna cum laude in psychology from the University of Minnesota, having served as Honors Student Council president. He has two master's degrees and worked for fifteen years as a licensed psychologist at the Family Life Mental Health Center. He served on the Anoka County Mental Health Advisory Board as an advocate for the mentally ill, taught high school psychology for over twenty years in the Anoka-Hennepin School District, and spent the last twelve years as a clinical psychologist for the district. He was the recipient of Medtronic's Outstanding Teacher Award and a member of the Who's Who of American Teachers. He served five terms on a local city council, championing environmental issues. As a member of the Board of Directors of the Meditation Center in Minneapolis for over twenty-five years, he served as chairman and board president. He has taught meditation for more than thirty years and is vice-president of AHYMS, an association of meditation centers throughout North and South America.

Recently retired from teaching and private practice, Jim remains active in his business, Nelson's Interactive Seminars, traveling and speaking nationally and internationally. He is a dynamic speaker on a variety of topics, including "The Art of Joyful Living," "The Power of Forgiveness," "The Sources of Emotional Pain," and "On Becoming Your Own Psychologist."

Jim lives just north of Minneapolis with his wife Candice and their dog Desi.